RUNNING THROUGH WALLS

How to Order:

Quantity discounts are available from the publisher, Prima Publishing & Communications, P.O. Box 1260LT, Rocklin, CA 95677; telephone (916) 624-5718. On your letterhead include information concerning the intended use of the books and the number of books you wish to purchase.

U.S. Bookstores and Libraries: Please submit all orders to St. Martin's Press, 175 Fifth Avenue, New York, N.Y. 10010; telephone (212) 674-5151.

RUNNING THROUGH WALLS

DAVID LIEDERMAN
Founder of DAVID'S COOKIES
With Alex Taylor III

Prima Publishing & Communications
P.O. Box 1260 LT
Rocklin, CA 95677
(916) 624-5718

126524

Cover photograph by Craig Cain, C.C. Cain Photography

Prima Publishing & Communications
Rocklin, CA

Library of Congress Cataloging-in-Publication Data

Liederman, David.
    Running through walls: a street-smart entrepreneur's guide to business success / by David Liederman, Alex Taylor.
        p.   cm.
    Reprint. Originally published: Chicago: Contemporary Books,   c 1989.
    ISBN 1-55958-052-6
    1. New business enterprises.   2. Entrepreneurship.
I. Taylor, Alex.   II.   Title.
HD62.5.L545   1990
658.4'21--dc20   90-8704
                                                  CIP

90 91 92 93 RRD 10 9 8 7 6 5 4 3 2 1

For my family—mother Adele, father Donald, brother Bill, daughters Katherine and Elizabeth, niece Chloe, sister Ann, and especially my wife Susan—all of whom, to varying degrees, put up with me all the years I have lived through the highs and lows of being an entrepreneur.

CONTENTS

RUNNING THROUGH WALLS

INTRODUCTION

The other day I got a call from a thirty-five-year-old woman who wanted to start her own business. I don't ordinarily give advice to strangers over the phone, but she knew my stepmother so I agreed to talk to her.

She had her product already picked out. She wanted to go into the upscale, all-natural, gourmet baby food business.

The first thing I asked her was: "Have you ever made the product?" The answer was no.

"Do you have a manufacturer who can make the product for you?" No.

"Do you know what kind of packaging you want?" No.

"Do you have any potential accounts?" No.

"Do you know how to sell this product to an end user?" No.

"How much money do you have to lose?" None.

I didn't ask her all those questions to show her that I was smarter than she was. I was trying to find out if she was ready to go into business for herself.

Surprise. She wasn't. There are truly hundreds of things she doesn't know about baby food that she would have to learn.

I told this woman that since she knows my stepmother, I would do her a favor. I would help her do some basic testing to see if her concept was sound. Assuming she could make her strained peas, and assuming she could get them packaged—not perfectly, just so they were sufficiently presentable to be shown to a grocery store manager—I would help her out. I would take her to see the best-known and most successful specialty food store owners in New York City—Zabar's, Balducci's, and Dean and Delucca's—to see if they would carry her line.

She said she would get back to me.

I didn't set out to discourage her. I think everyone should think about starting their own business. I did and it has been great.

But it was hard work.

In the course of a year, I get between 75 and 150 calls from people who want my advice about going into business for themselves. Here's what I tell them: being an entrepreneur has never been easy—not when I started in 1976 and especially not now.

That said, there is nothing mysterious about becoming a business success. It takes hard thinking, hard work, and the ability to put up with—and rise above—endless amounts of adversity.

SHOULD YOU BUY THIS BOOK?

This book is for two kinds of people: one, the people who have already decided to go into business for themselves and two, the people who think they want to but are not sure. One way or the other, I should be able to give you some useful advice.

I also want to try to convince some of you *not* to go into business. Before you quit your job and mortgage your house to fulfill your lifelong dream of running a one-hour photo developing center, you should find out what the real world is like. If it is not for you, you should find out up front.

WHO AM I?

I've started several businesses on my own. One, David's Cookies, has been a fabulous success and made me a household name in the United States and in a dozen countries around the world. David's Cookies has been going for nine years. In that time, we have grown from one tiny store making chocolate chip cookies on Second Avenue in New York City into outlets in dozens of states and overseas. I've diversified. I sell ice cream with chunks—not crumbs—of my cookies in it. I sell quality French bread, brownies, and pizza. I make my own ice cream and cookie dough in my 10,000-square-foot bakery and dairy, and I keep the supplies in a 10,000-square-foot warehouse.

My cookie business is now the foundation for an even bigger business: a company that imports, manufactures, and distributes very particular kinds of products that I call David's Specialty Foods. I think that in three to five years, David's Specialty Foods will be a very valuable company.

I also own and run a very popular French bistro-type restaurant on Manhattan's East Side called Chez Louis that has a city-wide reputation for wholesome, healthy food served in generous portions. Food critics, including Gael Greene, are wild about my restaurant. If things work out and I can figure out a way to do it, you may soon be dining in Chez Louis restaurants in other cities around the country.

Not bad for a guy who basically considered himself a misfit and didn't get serious about business until he was twenty-six years old.

I'M NOT PERFECT

Don't get the impression that everything in my life has been a bed of roses. It hasn't.

At times, I've worked 20 hours a day: from five in the morning until one o'clock the next morning.

The Mafia once wanted to be my business partner.

I've opened stores that lost money from day one and then went downhill after that.

Partners who I've trusted have abandoned me—and worse.

I've had running battles with landlords and suppliers, not to mention the city of New York.

So in addition to telling you what *to* do, I can tell you what *not* to do. From personal experience.

WHAT I CAN TEACH YOU

Anybody can do what I did. It isn't easy, but a man or woman with brains and determination can do it. First, you start with an idea. I'll tell you how to develop one. Then the idea has to be tested. You start small, by asking your spouse, friend, or mother, and then you gradually expand the circle. It doesn't have to cost a lot of money.

THEN IT GETS HARDER

Once you are convinced your product has merit, you start producing it. You make a few prototypes, inexpensively, and take them around to the people you want to buy them.

After you think you can find distribution outlets, it is time to start thinking about money. I'll tell you where to get it. You should be looking for enough money to get a lease on some factory or retail space. Your next job will be to figure out where you are going to locate and how much you are going to pay to be there. This is the second most important decision you will make—after deciding to go into business in the first place.

I have lots of ideas about how you can find customers, how to pitch your product to appeal to them, and how to garner publicity so that you get your name in the newspaper or your face on television. I've got some tips on how to hire people and how to keep them honest. Once your business is up and running, I have suggestions about expansion strategies.

Finally, I can advise you how to get out. Starting a business is a bigger decision than getting married. You can walk away from a bad marriage, but you can't walk away from your business. After it is going, you have to attend to it every day until you decide to either fold it or sell it. I've never read a book that tells you what to do after you've decided you've had enough.

WHAT I WILL *NOT* TEACH YOU

The first thing most books tell you is how to write a business plan. Not me. I don't believe in business plans. These days, anybody with a personal computer and a software package like Lotus 1-2-3 can develop reams and reams of numbers and charts that look highly professional—and make great wrapping paper for yesterday's fish. The computer-generated numbers are meaningless. They bear no relation to reality.

To make a business work, you have to get off your rear end and start promoting and selling your product. Not only will a business plan not do that for you, it doesn't tell you how to do it. Too many people think a business plan is a substitute for doing it themselves.

In the computer industry there is a famous story that has acquired almost legendary status. Around 1980, IBM was shopping for the operating system software it needed to run the IBM personal computer. IBM didn't have time to write the software itself and needed to buy the programs from somebody else. So some IBM executives went to visit software companies. Being IBM'ers, they were highly security conscious and didn't call ahead. At the first company they visited, the chairman was out taking flying lessons. So the IBM guys went away. The second company they visited was Microsoft; this time the president, Bill Gates, was in. The rest, as they say, is history. Bill Gates's operating system software is now on every IBM personal computer and every single other computer that works like an IBM. The last time

I looked, Gates was worth $1 billion. And he isn't even thirty-five yet.

Not going flying when there are deals to be done is one of the lessons you cannot learn from a business plan.

MY RULES FOR SUCCESS

It is only human nature to get carried away with your terrific idea and forget how tough it is out there. Take the baby-food woman. Even if she can cook and the food tastes great, and she can get it on the shelf of every supermarket in the country and get it written up in *Gourmet* magazine, she is still going to have problems. Why? Because she hasn't found anybody to make the baby food or deliver it to all those supermarkets.

A lot of people think that just because they have a wonderful product, the world will beat a path to their door. Not so. Lots of people with wonderful products never make a dime. The world is full of good ideas. The hard part is the nitty-gritty, day-to-day stuff: the basic aggravation you endure getting your gourmet baby food—or any other product or service—into the marketplace where somebody can buy it and you can make a profit.

I've developed some rules to live by—David's rules. They help remind me what business is all about. By the time you are finished with this book, you will have heard me repeat them so often that you will know them by heart.

1. Business is adversity.
2. Keep running through walls.
3. Follow your instincts.
4. Don't be afraid to take out the garbage.
5. If you don't love what you're doing, stop.
6. Keep your twitch factor.

BUSINESS IS ADVERSITY

To be successful in business, I am convinced you have to be endlessly aggressive. Every day is a struggle. If people fail, it is usually because they weren't aggressive enough.

KEEP RUNNING THROUGH WALLS

How do you cope? You have to keep surmounting insurmountable obstacles. Here's an example. Recently, the city of New York was threatening to repossess a building I own because I hadn't paid the boiler/elevator tax. But this is a one-story building, so it doesn't have an elevator, and it doesn't have a boiler, either. My lawyer had to spend six hours standing in line at a city office to get a building inspector to admit that he had been to my building a year earlier and that in fact it had neither a boiler nor an elevator. It turns out the city had the address wrong; it was the building *next* to mine that hadn't paid the tax. It took me one year and about $10,000 in legal fees to get it straightened out, not to mention endless aggravation. I got a letter apologizing for the "inconvenience" I had been caused.

Now it is a lot more difficult to do business in New York City than anywhere else I can think of. But that is the kind of nonsense, bureaucratic and otherwise, you have to put up with.

FOLLOW YOUR INSTINCTS

You can't hire an expert to tell you whether your idea for a business is viable. I could generate a whole new career for myself if I wanted to go into the consulting game. But I am incredibly skeptical of consultants. I find the typical consultant is somebody who is very well educated, is very smart, went to the right schools and got the right degree, and analyzes businesses that he doesn't have the vaguest idea of how to run.

If somebody wants to go out and start his own business, he would be better off buying this book than hiring some twenty-six-year-old who makes $100,000 a year at McKinsey & Company. He would learn more, and he would save a lot of money. You don't need to hire an investment banker either; they need the work. They don't know as much as you might think, given the fancy fees they get paid. Last year, some investment bankers came to look into the finances of my company because I wanted to sell some stock. I quickly discovered that they didn't know the difference between a cookie and a sausage hero sandwich.

The other night I was at a party and a guy wearing a yellow tie and fancy suspenders came up to me. He was an investment banker who specialized in electronics. For some reason his firm had asked him to investigate a food deal— the leveraged buy-out of a small bakery worth maybe $15 million—and he was assigned to find out if it was worth doing.

He didn't even know the right questions to ask. One of the biggest expense items in the food business is rent. But he didn't know what the escalation factors in the rents were or how the rents would affect the bottom line or the bakery's long-term growth prospects. In short, he did not understand the food business.

I can't tell you "What They Don't Teach You at Harvard Business School." I didn't go to Harvard Business School— or any business school, for that matter. Yet I think I'm as smart or smarter than most M.B.A.s. I may not have book smarts, but I have street smarts. I can teach you from real life, which is a whole lot more important. If you read Chrysler Chairman Lee Iacocca's book, the main thing that pops out at you in terms of anything you can identify with is his fight to get a good parking space at Ford World Headquarters. That isn't what I'd call really practical business advice.

DO NOT BE AFRAID TO TAKE OUT THE GARBAGE

The most successful entrepreneurs are those who, at least initially, are involved in every aspect of their business and every aspect of their business is important to them. No job is too big, too small—or too dirty.

YOU HAVE TO LOVE
WHAT YOU ARE DOING

You are going to be working so hard and for so many long hours that if you are not infatuated with what you are doing, you are going to hate it. Better find out early whether it is pain or passion.

THE TWITCH FACTOR

I saved the best for last. Every day I wake up twitching. My mind is turning over with ideas, problems, people to see, things to do. I can never relax; I'm always thinking about the business. I can be worrying about anything from a shortage of cookie dough—that always seems to happen at Christmas—to arranging a multimillion-dollar loan from some Japanese bankers. But I think I need that constant buzzing to stay ahead of the game. It helps me keep my edge.

I HAVE BEEN TWITCHING FOR YEARS

I'm not your average business person. In fact, I have always been a revolutionary. I make trouble if I don't like things. If I couldn't be employed in the right situation, I didn't want to be employed.

When I got out of law school in 1976, I took a $15,000-a-year job at a Park Avenue law firm. That was OK, but I had hoped to do better after three years of graduate school. And because I didn't go to Harvard or Stanford, the "right" law schools, I ended up in the low end of the litigation department. I could see right away that I didn't like the practice of law. So after three months, I quit. I figured right away I wasn't employable in a normal nine-to-five job. So I decided I had to start my own business.

SOME OF MY BIASES

If you want to be a consultant, or sell real estate, or write software, this book is not for you. I believe in businesses that make or sell something that you can touch.

Of course, what you make does not have to be cookies—or even food. As you know, I'm in the food business. In fact, I'm not just in it, I'm *obsessed* with it. Food has been a preoccupation of mine for as long as I can remember.

In most important ways, what works in the food business will work in any kind of business. Waffles or widgets, you still have to develop a product, get it made, and sell it to the public. You have to answer the same kinds of questions, breach the same kinds of barriers, solve the same kinds of problems. The food business has been great to me. If you too are interested in food, you should go into it. But don't stop reading here if your goal in life is to sell $100 cork-screws or open your own jiffy-lube franchise. The same kind of lessons apply. If you can sell cookies, you can sell anything—and vice versa.

DO IT NOW

There is never a best time to start a business, but there is never a worst time, either.

When I started David's Cookies in 1979, New York City was in the pits. Business was lousy everywhere. Real estate, which is a good proxy for the city's business activity, was terrible. Rents were 25 percent of what they are now. I made those terrible conditions work for me. Contractors built my first restaurant on credit because they were so desperate for jobs. Suppliers sold me equipment on credit for the same reason.

I think anybody who is aggressive and has a good idea can get into business for himself and keep a business going no matter what the economic climate is. If you want to do it badly enough, you will find a way.

The opportunities are endless. In the food business, the secret is to come up with products that are impeccable in terms of their pedigree. They have quality ingredients. You have to figure out very good basic recipes and be prepared

to charge a premium—you can't make it any other way—
and do a lot of things repetitively. That's what the success of
David's Cookies is all about. The same thing is true of $100
corkscrews. You can't cheat the public. You have to give
them a good product. Value for money is the way to build a
business.

WHY COOKIES ARE HERE TO STAY, AND I AM, TOO

There has been an enormous desire on the part of the press
over the past five years to bury the cookie. But a reaction has
already set in. As Phyllis Richman wrote in the *Washington
Post* in 1987: "If you check the past year, you find it littered
with discarded fads that wore out their welcome: blackened
redfish is passé, squid ink pasta fell short of the hit parade
and nobody talks much about sushi any more. But chocolate
chip cookies are still in high gear. In fact they may be
edging out the hamburger as the All-American Food."

If you read this book, you are going to have a much
clearer idea of what's involved in starting a business and a
much clearer understanding of how to do it. I'm absolutely
convinced that if you apply my principles to any business,
you will be a success.

1
DO YOU HAVE WHAT IT TAKES TO START YOUR OWN BUSINESS?

The best reason for starting your own business is independence. You want to do it yourself.

Forget getting rich. It is OK to want to be rich, but there are easier ways to do it than starting your own business: speculating on the stock market, going to Atlantic City, playing the lottery. Of course, none of those are guaranteed to pay off, but then working for yourself isn't either.

Forget getting famous, too. Fame is nothing. There are very few people in my mind who are enduringly famous.

Two of my closest friends are Michael Tucker and Jill Eikenberry. We were introduced about seven or eight years ago. They are very interested in food; in fact, Michael is my only close male friend who cooks well for an amateur. For years, Jill and Michael were journeymen actors in New York City. Now they are stars on "LA Law"—he's the short, charismatic guy, and she's the tall, gorgeous blonde. They are married on the show and in real life. And they are famous. They say it isn't that great. For any serious actor, a hit TV series is a real good-news, bad-news situation. You make more money and your visibility increases. But you work awful hours, the artistic satisfaction is low, and you worry about being typecast.

Fame can truly be fleeting. Jill and Michael often have dinner with Henry Winkler and his wife. When Henry Winkler was doing "Happy Days," he literally couldn't go to the supermarket. He'd get mobbed. Not anymore. The other day, Winkler's wife, Stacy, called Michael—they were having dinner that night—and asked him to stop off at the supermarket on the way over. Michael told her, "Well, to be honest, it is a little uncomfortable for me to go to the supermarket these days. In fact, I get mobbed." Stacy said, "Fine, I'll send Henry."

You can get your ego tied up in being famous, and you can come out of being famous pretty fast. Look what happened to John Travolta. From *Saturday Night Fever* to nothing.

I believe the food business is better than show business. You can stay well known in the food business for a long time because people's fantasies are fueled by food. Among the most intimate things people do is feed themselves. If people are living through your products, you are always on their minds. Who can forget Betty Crocker (cake mixes), Orville Redenbacher (popcorn), or Bartles and Jaymes (wine coolers)?

But you can't have your ego tied up in your business. You are basically trying to do two things when you are in business: stay alive and make a living. I love having my name on my business. But I have to be careful. If I got crazy about closing down a David's Cookies store because it had my name on it, you could check me into a padded cell tomorrow.

WATCH YOUR MOTIVES

Close to 99 percent of the people who want to go into business for themselves are just hardworking stiffs like the rest of us. The only difference is that they want a change in their situation.

If you're like most of them, you really want to quit your current job. You're tired of what I call the tyranny of bosses. The thing that pops into your head is, "I don't want to have that jerk push me around any more."

Or maybe you've just been fired. According to James Challenger, a Chicago executive recruiter quoted in the *Wall Street Journal*, 16 percent of fired executives were starting new businesses in 1988, double the number of a year earlier. Many were bitter from the dismissal and didn't want to get hurt again.

Be careful. That kind of attitude can lead you astray. According to Challenger, managers often fail as entrepreneurs because they don't anticipate how demanding the hours will be, the new stress, and the pressure of raising money. Once you start working on your own, you'll find out how difficult it is to do everything yourself and not have the support of an existing business around you. You may even wish you had your old boss back.

A SHORT PSYCHOLOGICAL TEST

The very first question you should ask yourself is: can I wake up sane on Saturday morning without having received a paycheck on Friday afternoon? If you think you can, go on to question two. If you can't, stay in your current job. You couldn't take the mental strain and aggravation of being your own boss.

The second question you should ask yourself is: assuming I don't get a paycheck Friday afternoon and my business isn't making enough money, how am I going to pay the rent? There are a lot of things about running a business that resemble skating on thin ice. You have to be comfortable with brinkmanship. If you are used to writing checks on the float in anticipation of getting money in your account or even buying a pair of theater tickets before you have a date, you have an idea about the kind of attitude I'm talking about. You have to be willing to take risks and have a good understanding of the consequences if you fail.

The third question—which worked for me better than anything—is: am I an entrepreneur at heart? I have a long-standing feeling about myself that I am basically unemployable. I can't picture myself working for someone else. Just the thought of it makes me itchy. The idea that a boss can come in and say to me "you're gone" gives me the shakes. I have to be in charge. That's a good attitude to have.

Finally, ask yourself: will it bug me to work on Christmas?

I don't think about long hours. I have to get through seven days every week. Some Mondays I don't do anything, and some Sundays I work all day. I don't differentiate between going to work in the morning and going home in the evening. Some days I don't go in until 11 A.M., and I don't leave the restaurant until after midnight. I don't feel I have to be home every night to tickle the baby, though I'm aware that I have to see my kids sometime. This notion of holidays, days off, is foreign to me. There are 365 days in the year, and I have to get through them.

When people ask me how many hours a week I work, I tell them I am on 168 hours a week. Do I work 168 hours a week? No. I like vacations too. But I have to be constantly aware of my business, and that's the pressure you have to be prepared to deal with when you open your own business.

OK, YOU PASSED THAT TEST. WHAT ELSE DO YOU HAVE TO KNOW ABOUT YOURSELF?

If a psychiatrist were to examine the sharpest entrepreneurs, in my opinion, he would find that most of them are anal compulsive—fixated on details. If you don't believe you have an organized mind, you probably shouldn't go into business. People who organize their closets, like their papers stacked neatly on their desks, get their laundry done on time—those are the kind of people I'm talking about.

Details drive most successful operations. If you are not into the small picture as well as the big one, you probably shouldn't go into business.

THE TWITCH FACTOR

Living with that twitch factor is the trade-off you make for not working for somebody else. If you think you can get a business up and running and then coast, you're wrong. Employees can go home at five o'clock and forget about work; entrepreneurs never can forget about work.

You get used to living with a very unfinished quality of life. A business is always in flux. Basically, you know that everything is never going to be tied up in a neat package with little bows.

MONEY DOES NOT MATTER

I'd love to be really rich. But the only way to get rich is to sell your business and get out. When you are in business, you have many more pressing concerns than getting rich. You are putting out fires, coping with lawsuits, dealing with employees. You are not thinking about how many more pennies you can put in your piggy bank.

Besides, if you are going to wait around until lightning strikes, you are not going to like what you are doing. Making the products and selling them is the fun part. It is a cliché, but money really *is* just a way of keeping score.

I can honestly say I don't know anybody who went into business to get rich. Because you are unemployable—yes. Because you want to buy yourself a job—yes. Because you want to make something grow—yes. To get rich—NO.

SUCCESS AND FAILURE

You usually hear that most small businesses fail within a year or two. That's true. If you think about it, it makes sense. The reason most businesses fail is that they are undercapitalized, the people didn't know what they were doing, or the concept wasn't any good. All of those things will knock you out quickly.

A 1988 study by two researchers from the Small Business Administration and Babson College in Massachusetts discovered that three out of five new businesses failed during the first six years. The results of the study were reported in the *Wall Street Journal.*

The researchers followed new businesses over an eight-year period. They found the failure rate was lower for companies that grew in employment during their early years. It makes sense that if you grow, you are probably doing something right and aren't as likely to fail. Companies that hired even one additional employee during the first six years had a failure rate of one in three. If they added five or more people, their chances of failure dropped to only one in four.

DO *NOT* THINK BIG

When you go into business, you have to be prepared to take out the garbage. When you start, you will be doing it all anyway, and later on, when you have people doing it for you, you are going to want to know what they are doing. The moment you lose sight of that, the moment that you think you are a big idea guy and too good for the little stuff is the moment that your business starts to fail.

QUIRKS

You won't find many entrepreneurs in Atlantic City or Las Vegas. That is because most of us hate to gamble. Note I didn't say "take risks," because taking risks means you have some control over the outcome. When you gamble, you don't. When I gamble I'm constantly second-guessing myself. If I win, I should have bet more. If I lose, I was a schmuck for losing. That is a classic the-glass-is-half-empty phenomenon.

When I was eighteen years old, I went to Las Vegas. I read a book about craps, and I stood there for fourteen hours and won $6. I thought, "This is ridiculous." The same thing happened at blackjack. I learned how to count cards, and I stood there for six hours and won $12. I said to myself, "This is even sillier."

DO YOU NEED AN M.B.A.?

Absolutely not.

I think business school teaches you about arithmetic equations and nothing about paying the rent. I would almost go so far as to say that if you are going into an entrepreneurial business, business school is a detriment. It confuses you about the differences between calculating cash flow and developing market strategies, and actually running a business. In the old days, you had to think about projecting what your income and expenses would be over the course of a year. Now you can figure it out in three hours using a personal computer and a spread sheet. That does not require using any business skills that I know of.

Of the people I know who are entrepreneurs, very few went to business school. Business schools are like professional cooking schools. They mold you to work for corporate America. Do not say to yourself, "I want to go into business for myself, so first I'm going to Harvard to get an M.B.A."

SOME PEOPLE HAVE IT IN THEIR BLOOD

I know a woman named Stacy Rosenberg who got her first entrepreneurial idea when she was fifteen. Eight years ago, she came in to sell me advertising for my cookie store. At that point, I wasn't even thinking about advertising; I was just trying to survive. She was starting a neighborhood newspaper called the *City Kiddie Scoop*. Her theory was that there are a lot of kids going to private schools in New York with a lot of disposable income who want to know where to buy stuff. It was such a preposterous situation. Here was this fifteen-year-old kid with this crazy idea, but I actually took an ad; it was the first one I ever placed for my cookie business. She ran *City Kiddie Scoop* for a little while, and she made a little money. Then she went to the Wharton Business School where she came up with another idea. Going to football games in Philadelphia, she noticed that spectators were keeping warm by using socks for mittens. So she dreamed up Penn Sox, decorated with the University of Pennsylvania logo, that people could wear either on their feet or their hands. And she made a little money selling those.

After she graduated from Wharton, she went to work for Estée Lauder, the cosmetics company. She lasted in that corporate environment for nine months. Now she is running her own consulting business.

I think Stacy is the kind of person who will wind up running her own show no matter what. In every case, the things that she sold were aimed at what she determined was a niche or a gap in the market.

Another woman I know named Barbra Isenberg runs the North American Bear Company out of her town house in Greenwich Village. She makes a Humphrey Bogart bear, a Marilyn Monroe bear, and all these other great bears. She's smart, and she's a good bear designer. So what if she doesn't have any business experience? She's making a living because she's intelligent, she's amusing, and she has good ideas. Everybody loves bears. She gives hers a profitable twist by combining well-known characters with a bear motif.

All of this is not to say that you don't need some basic business sense. You have to know how to keep track of expenses so you know where the money is going. You have to know how to keep a set of books—or hire someone to do it for you. You have to have goals. And you have to know something about people—the ones you hire and the ones you sell to. But do you have to know about strategic marketing or LIFO or FIFO accounting? No.

DON'T EXPECT TO BE LOVED

Business is adversity. Every day is a fight. I don't know any entrepreneur who doesn't basically believe that every day is a problem-solving nightmare. It is a fact of life.

A lot of people come to me with business ideas. When I ask them what they hope to achieve, too many reply, "Make me an offer." They are not the types of goal-oriented people I am looking for. Think about it. They want to be loved and have it spoon-fed. That can't happen if they are in business for themselves. They have to have goals.

Outside of the legal profession, I've never been offered a job. I think it would be great one day to have somebody call me and say, "David, come in. I want to talk with you; you're doing a great job, and we're going to give you a promotion, a new title, a raise, a Buick instead of a Chevrolet, and all the rest of that stuff." But at the same time, it doesn't bother me too much that that hasn't happened.

I've always created my own opportunities. I get satisfaction from that, but I don't get a pat on the head from my boss. You cannot go into your own business and expect to be loved. If you need to be loved and you need that peer gratification and approval, do something else.

TOUGHEN UP

An entrepreneur can't have thin skin, either. You can't be upset over being constantly turned down, rejected, or being told your idea is worthless. You have to keep coming off the mat. Perseverance is better than being a genius inventor in terms of making your business fly. If you go out to sell your idea and you get discouraged by being turned down the first time, then you shouldn't be in business.

There are some unbelievably difficult people out there.

One fellow who is the buyer for a big chain store is famous for being impossible. I went to see him one day. He kept me waiting for an hour and a half. When I finally got in his office, he didn't shake my hand, he just looked me in the eye and said, "I'm going to bend you over this desk obscenity, obscenity, obscenity." Things went downhill from there. Some people have to go through that four or five times a day. But you can't take it personally. You have to keep going back.

YOU CANNOT WORRY ABOUT BEING SHY

Ultimately, you have to be your own promoter. Nobody else can do it as effectively—not to mention as cheaply—as you can. Especially if your business has your name on it, like mine does.

In public Larry Tisch, head of CBS, appears very shy. But he sure manages to get things done. After all, he took over CBS with less than 25 percent of the stock. I have never seen him in action, but I assume that behind the scenes, he is not shy at all. He pushes and pushes and pushes until he gets what he wants. You have to be that way too.

DEMOGRAPHICS DON'T COUNT

Age doesn't make any difference in starting a business. There is a lot to be said for youth, because young people have endless energy and optimism and they don't know what they are going to run into out there. But there is as much to be said for those who have been kicked around and have a lot of life experience, as long as they can divorce themselves from the bad breaks they have accumulated in their life.

NEITHER DOES SEX

I have always believed that, by and large, women are more

creative than men. To me, at least, they seem to be more self-confident about what they are doing. More and more women are going into business for themselves. They are following in the tradition of Mary Kay of Mary Kay Cosmetics, Liz Claiborne the designer, and Julee Rosso and Sheila Lukins, who wrote the *Silver Palate Cookbook*. They have to be careful, though. Some women (and some men, too) confuse going into business for themselves, which may just be setting themselves up as consultants or sole practitioners, with actually starting a business that manufactures something and creates jobs.

TIMING

Don't wait to think about starting your own business until you get fired or laid off. That's the natural inclination, but it is all wrong. It is better if you have a job while you make a conscious decision about whether you want to be an entrepreneur. That way, there is no gun to your head and you can take time to make the important decisions you have to make.

If you don't like your position in the company and don't think you are being promoted fast enough, that's one of the signs that you are ready to go out on your own. From a timing standpoint, this is something that tells you that it is time to go. You should take a look at your boss and see if you aspire to have his job, do what he does, and make what he makes. If you are insanely jealous about his position in the company, that is a good sign that you are ready to go into business for yourself. But it takes more than jealousy. Never forget the additional responsibility you will be taking on—as well as the twitch factor.

SATISFACTION

The good thing about starting your own business is that if it works, you feel pretty good about yourself. Then once it is up and running, you start to get bored, and you want to do another one. I don't know any successful entrepreneur who is not looking for the next opportunity. That is basically one of the qualities that got him going in the first place (the twitch factor again). When do you get off the train? I keep telling my wife, Susan, I can't take the aggravations of business any longer, but the same kind of thought processes that got me into this business make me wary about quitting. The problem is finding a basic satisfaction level. If you get too satisfied, you have problems.

It is basic human nature to be rabbitlike, to want to grow. Why do I want to open more restaurants? I hate the hassles of the restaurant business. Do I need the respect of my peers? No. But I like the challenge.

Someday, if I think I am doing well and the Pillsburys of this world come around and give me a check for $100 million and the check actually clears, then maybe I'll think that I will get out. In the meantime, if I am fighting with everybody I need to move the business forward, then it isn't a main concern. A lot of people have gotten high enough up so that they can cash in their chips, but then what are they going to do? It's the game, the chase, that keeps them interested.

WIND UP

So there it is. You have to be a little crazy, like I was, to start your own business. You have to be ready to work hard, be involved in your business around the clock, be ready to run through walls, and develop the twitch factor. Do not ever forget that business is a struggle.

2
THE SECRET OF
MY SUCCESS

The secret of my success was that I made a lot of mistakes—and learned something from them. No matter how smart you are, no business ever gets off the ground the way it is supposed to. There are any number of things that can go wrong, and lots of them do. All you can try to do is create a mind-set where you realize that you are going to face a crisis every six seconds and learn how to deal with them.

Most important of all, don't get discouraged. Some of the biggest successes got off to the slowest starts.

My first six weeks in the cookie business in 1979 were a total disaster. I was making the cookies out of a twenty-quart mixer in the back of a store, everybody was wary of the cookies because they didn't taste like other cookies they were familiar with, and I was rapidly going broke. It was an open question whether I was going to be able to pay the next month's rent.

OPENING TOO SOON

One of the mistakes I made—and I am not alone in this—

was opening too soon. I didn't take that extra couple of days to rehearse the employees and role-play about what happens when the customer comes in and wants this or that, where the cash register is, and how do you turn on the air conditioner. You are in a hurry—no surprise, you want to make some money. So what you wind up doing is working out the kinks on the customers. That's not a good idea. You can alleviate a lot of problems by being charming, explaining to the customers you haven't been in business before, and being cute, and sometimes they will care. But some will get the feeling that you are running an incompetent operation. There is so much choice in a big city that they don't have to come back to your store if they feel that way.

DOING BUSINESS WITH THE MOB

After the cookie store was open for ten days, this Italian gentleman with no neck walked in, accompanied by two other Italian gentlemen, both of whom seemed to be over 6'9". He introduced himself and told me he was the "made man" in the neighborhood. He had a cookie store around the corner, and he had the exclusive franchise. I hadn't gotten permission from the person who controlled the neighborhood to open this cookie store, so I was violating his franchise. Even worse, since I had a better location, I was putting his cookie store out of business, so I had better move fast. He told me I had twenty-four hours to close up.

I didn't move fast enough. Forty-eight hours later, an enormous rock came flying through my very expensive plate glass window. It was clear that it wasn't my mother who threw that rock.

I soon found out through the grapevine that this Italian gentleman wanted to have another meeting. This time, he told me, "Youse don't have to close your cookie store but youse got to buy me out." He wanted $160,000 to close his store. Madness. It wasn't worth that much, and I didn't have any money. What was I going to do?

I decided I had no choice. It was either make peace with

this guy or go out of business. After protracted negotiations, I agreed to pay him $60,000 for his store. I didn't have any money of course, so I agreed to pay him in installments—$5,000 a month. Fortunately, the money started coming in very soon after that.

FAME AND SUCCESS

On July 25, 1979, Florence Fabricant of the *New York Times* wrote an article entitled "The Search for the Best Chocolate-Chip Cookie in New York." Lucky for me, she liked mine much better than anyone else's. The rest, as they say, is history. That very morning, there was a line of eager customers outside the front door when I opened up, and the line stayed there for months.

Florence subsequently became my friend, and, much later, I asked her how she had found my store in my out-of-the-way location and, more important, how she decided she liked the cookies best. As it turned out, the chocolate chip cookie assignment was one that she didn't want to do and was ready to treat as a throwaway. She went around Manhattan buying cookies indiscriminately and then took them home to taste. But before she ever got a chance, her kids started going through them. They told her that David's cookies were much better than the other ones, and she confirmed their opinion.

Thank God that Florence's kids paid attention to those cookies.

HOW BEING SUCCESSFUL
NEARLY KILLED ME

Overnight I became so successful that it nearly did me in. I didn't have nearly the capacity I needed to meet demand.

I had one twenty-quart mixer for cookie dough, and each batch took me fifteen minutes. I figured I could make 160 pounds of dough an hour times eight hours a day. That equals about 1,300 pounds of cookies times the selling price, which was then $5 a pound—a potential gross of

$8,000 a day. I figured, this is great, who the hell is going to sell that many cookies in a day, all I need is a twenty-quart mixer.

But I didn't figure on the confusion factor. I was making five different flavors of cookies. Since I didn't have five different mixing bowls, I wasted a lot of time washing bowls. There was no place to crack the eggs, so there were eggshells and egg whites all over the place. I had two guys walking around who were coated in butter and chocolate and looked terrible. Nothing worked the way it was supposed to on paper.

LOGISTICS

We had a major production problem. We'd make batter all night, and we'd still run out of batter halfway through the day. The way we dealt with it was simple. When we ran out of cookies after lunch, I would put up a sign on the door that said, "Out of cookie dough, come back in three hours." I did that for almost a month.

Then we moved down to the basement, and I bought an eighty-quart mixer. That alleviated the shortage. Number one, I had room to move around; number two, we got the mixing process out of the cookie store, where it was a world-class mess.

PROFESSIONALISM

I also didn't know as much about cooking as I thought when we started out. One thing I learned is that it takes time for the vanilla flavoring to seep into the dough. We were using this very expensive vanilla in the batter, and it wasn't tasting like anything. We discovered it takes three to four days for the vanilla flavor to permeate the eggs and the chocolate.

CHOCOLATE

The other big bottleneck we had was chocolate. We were

buying Lindt chocolate in thirteen-ounce bars. I was convinced at the time that it was the best chocolate in the world, but it wasn't available in bulk, only in these thirteen-ounce bars. I use a lot of chocolate in my cookies. In the beginning another guy and I would spend four or five hours a day unwrapping the chocolate bars to get them ready to go into the batter. Then the cookies took off, and I had four guys down there I was paying serious money to unwrap chocolate bars.

One day I got some exceptionally bad news. The chocolate importer called me up and said a shipment of thirteen-ounce bars hadn't come in; all he could send me were 3½ ounce bars. So I had to unwrap three times as many bars. I was going to go out of business doing this unwrapping rather than compromise my principles by using what I thought was inferior chocolate that I could buy in bulk. I tried dealing with Lindt from New York, but that didn't work. So I was forced to get on a plane and go to Switzerland to try to figure this out. Lindt wasn't really interested in helping me because I was still a relatively small customer. But I figured out the problem right away. When I walked through the Lindt plant, I saw the machine that wraps the labels on the bars. I told them they should keep running the bars through the machine but leave off the wrappers for my orders. *Voilà,* naked chocolate. A breakthrough!

THE PIT

During the early days, I had my office in a pit. It was a basement with no windows that you entered by walking down a flight of stairs. Originally, the floor was dirt. I had a concrete slab poured over the dirt floor. One day, I came in and found six inches of water on the floor. It had seeped through the foundation. So for the next two years, I had a submersible pump that I kept right outside the door. Every time it rained, I would do down with my pump and pump out the office.

It was the landlord's responsibility to fix up the pit, but he wasn't about to do it. He was eighty-eight years old, and he didn't want to hear about my problems. I couldn't afford to fix it, because it would have involved digging down below the footings and waterproofing them. It could have cost lots of money. I didn't have time to deal with it either. So it was easier for me to pump out the water every time it rained. After a while, the floods began to get worse. The foundation was cracking. The ceiling was only 6½ feet high, and we were already a foot off the ground. So finally we wrote the landlord and said we were leaving. The space was still vacant three years later.

SELLING LIKE HOTCAKES

That first Thanksgiving, we had a line of people around the block waiting to buy my cookies. People at the beginning of the line would take a number and then sell their place to people at the end of the line for ten or twenty dollars. It was an absolute madhouse. That one Second Avenue store was so popular I often think I should have stopped there and never expanded. But if I hadn't, I never could have supported a wife and two kids the way I do now.

There were times where we could literally not mix the cookie dough fast enough. We were selling hot, dripping cookies, though they really taste better after they have cooled for thirty minutes. We would tell customers the cookies just came out of the oven, and they would say, "I don't care if they stick together, just put them in a bag and I'll pay you double." People would take the cookies outside and discover their one pound of David's cookies had fused together into a horrible mess. This happened hundreds of times because I didn't know how to tell the customers "We're not going to sell you these cookies until they cool."

Finally, we just put a big sign up that said "We will not sell cookies that haven't cooled for thirty minutes under any condition." Even if somebody said, "I like to burn my tongue," we wouldn't sell to them. For the first couple of weeks there was a lot of yelling and screaming about "How can you dare not sell us those cookies?" until people began to buy into the system.

WHAT I LEARNED ABOUT HUMAN NATURE

When nobody had heard of David's cookies, people would come in and lecture us about how we charged too much, the cookies were ugly, the store looked like a men's room. They were enraged that there was a minimum order of a quarter pound of cookies, even though we gave them samples. We were doing everything wrong. Then when the *Times* article came out, the same people were like little mice: "Gimmee, gimmee, gimmee." We had become fashionable so everything we did was right.

EVEN THE RESTAURANT WORKED OUT

At the same time I opened my first cookie store in 1979, I also opened a nouvelle cuisine restaurant called Manhattan Market. I didn't want to do both at once, but the landlord had this big space to fill that he wouldn't subdivide. So I took the whole thing and put a cookie store in one side and a restaurant in the other side.

Since I couldn't run two businesses at once, I got Susan, my wife, to manage the restaurant. She had absolutely no experience, but she learned on the fly and it worked out fine. I also got lucky early in finding help. For instance, I found a friend of my brother's who had just graduated from cooking school. He had no experience, but I put him to work as a chef and he worked out.

That's not to say there wasn't plenty of craziness. One day I was visiting a friend at the hospital. It was the first meal I had missed at the restaurant since it opened three months earlier. Of course, I got a call at the hospital that Mimi Sheraton, the restaurant critic of the *Times*, had just entered the restaurant and was sitting down for dinner. Naturally, she wasn't there to pass the time of day but to gather material for a review. Nobody was supposed to know what she looked like, but I knew and had warned the staff to keep an eye out for her. It is no exaggeration to say that she was capable at the time of making or breaking my restaurant.

So I ran out of the hospital, grabbed a cab back to the restaurant, sneaked in the back door and changed into my chef's whites. We had the waiter offer her a one-of-a-kind special that wasn't on the menu—roast poussin (baby chicken) with foie gras. I knew she couldn't resist ordering it. She didn't, and I cooked it up. Mimi Sheraton, who usually shares whatever she is having with the other three people at the table, ate the whole thing. She stripped the bones.

Our ruse succeeded. She liked the restaurant. But when the review came out, she praised our food and didn't even mention the roast poussin.

CONCLUSION

I learned the retail business the way a lot of people learn— by doing, which is not the right way. You should really have a little experience. In fact, a lot of people I see that have successful businesses are people who have put in a number of years working for large companies who really understand a certain discipline or area of expertise. They capitalize on what they have learned by making that into a niche business and going out on their own. So this is another case of do what I say, not what I did.

3
INVENTING YOUR OWN HULA HOOP

The classic entrepreneur is the guy who develops and sells his own product: Henry Ford, Apple's Steve Jobs, McDonald's Ray Kroc. You get more satisfaction because you are doing your own thing. You get to express your creativity. You get a chance for a greater financial reward. And you get to work your tail off around the clock.

You should be willing to take a risk, have a deep-felt interest in what you are trying to sell, know more about making that product than anybody else, understand that your expertise gives you an edge over everyone else, and be prepared to run through walls to get the thing to market. And it is important to remember that you can't make yourself interested in something. If you don't love what you are going to do, you should forget about it.

NOTHING SUCCEEDS LIKE CONVICTION

To develop a really successful new business, you have to

believe in what you are doing more than anything else. Henry Ford wanted to get into the automobile manufacturing business so badly that he started two car companies— and saw them fail—before he got Ford Motor Company going.

You also have to know what you are doing. In my case, I really believe I know the food business. Before I went into cookies, I knew how to cook, I knew what good food tastes like, and I understood consumer likes and dislikes because I had been doing some unofficial testing among my friends. I felt pretty secure that the products I was attempting to sell were good.

The ability to make a business go involves a whole series of personality characteristics that we will discuss in depth later. But just like I really believe in my cookies, I think conviction and a passion for what you're doing are really crucial for anyone going into business. Remember, business is adversity. Every day is a battle. If you don't have a fire going underneath you, you'll be able to think up lots of reasons to quit.

YOU DO NOT HAVE TO PRACTICE ELSEWHERE

Some people say you should go to work for somebody else in a business like the one you want to start. But although experience is *usually* a good thing, it isn't *always* a good thing. Chances are, you'll have some bad habits to forget and some good habits to learn. None of our most successful franchisees had any experience in running other similar businesses.

Companies that are in the food business and try to run a David's Cookies store are the ones that get into trouble because they think they know how to do it better. One supermarket chain that was selling David's cookies couldn't figure out why the cookies smelled like fish. The reason was that the same guy who ran the fish counter was also scooping the cookie dough. They thought they were saving money by having one person do two jobs, but all they did was kill the cookie business.

People who come with a certain innocence about the business are often successful. Gary Comer, who started Lands' End, was an advertising man who had no experience selling clothing. Of course, people like him don't stay innocent for long.

YOU HAVE TO KNOW SOMETHING ABOUT WHAT YOU ARE GOING TO DO

Your business idea should be in an area you know something about. I think it is more or less an established fact that people who want to go into business have an idea in an area that they are either interested in as a hobby or where they are working. I think people tend to get more excited about their hobby than their job, simply because they don't have to do their hobby and they have to do their job.

A lot of times, though, people see things in their work environment that look promising. My mother used to work for the New York Chamber of Commerce and tried to get small-business people together who have similar problems. She saw an opportunity to go into something called Travel Connections. She is going to organize trips that revolve around some kind of educational opportunity where people can meet each other. If somebody is interested in photographing white gorillas, they can go do that; or if they want to hear lectures by prominent poets, they can do that. It is a true niche idea, and I thing it is going to be successful if she decides to go ahead.

DO YOU HAVE AN IDEA FOR A PRODUCT?

People are getting crazier and crazier about the businesses they think are going to fly. The hot thing now is all-natural, pure baby food. There must be fifty people going into the baby-food business. But if that is really a business,

Gerber and Heinz are going to wipe them out so fast they won't know what hit them. The big companies can make all-natural baby food much better than anyone just starting up can, and they already have the production, distribution, and marketing capabilities in place.

The fresh-baked cookie business is different. Nabisco and Pillsbury aren't in that business, and they would have a hard time getting started. Selling cookies out of a grocery store is a lot different from selling them out of a bakery. Now that I have a brand name, I can be even more competitive.

Just to keep things interesting, I'm getting into a new business where I *am* competing with Pillsbury. I'm selling fresh cookie dough out of supermarket refrigerator cases right next to the nationally advertised Dough Boy. I don't have nearly the muscle that Pillsbury does to make sure that I get into the right supermarkets in the right cities. But I'm tough. Plus, my cookie dough is better than Pillsbury's. The ingredients are better, and I sell it for more money. So don't count me out. As I write this, my dough is selling well.

INNOVATE, DO NOT INVENT

The basic question you should ask when you start your own business is: do I want to reinvent the wheel or just add another spoke? I've done both, and I can attest to the fact that adding another spoke is a much better way to go.

A key point is to distinguish an *inventive* product from an *innovative* one. Several years ago I started a company called Saucier that made a base for fine sauces. It was complicated and esoteric and didn't work right away.

I had this theory about how Americans could make three-star sauces at home in three to seven minutes using these sauce bases that took me twenty-four hours to make. I learned real fast that I had a good product, no real competition, and 100 percent market share. The only problem was that Americans didn't know what the stuff was. I beat my head against the wall to get people to understand that it took me twenty-four hours to get this sauce base into a little cup, and that's why it was so expensive.

After becoming very frustrated, I finally realized that I could not educate the public to what this product was all about without a lot of money that I didn't have. So I went to a product that I felt Americans understood—chocolate chip cookies. But I didn't come out with a me-too chocolate chip cookie—I twisted it a little bit.

Voilà, David's Cookies. They are made with real butter and chunks of real chocolate, not flavored bits, and baked right before your eyes. I sell them for twice what store-bought cookies cost—up to $7.50 a pound—and I'm making a living. It isn't great—things could always be better—but it isn't bad either.

The most successful businesses, long-term, are when you pay a nickel for a product and sell it for six cents. Like Hawaiian Tropic suntan lotion. Some guy whipped it up on the beach in Hawaii with cocoa butter and coconut oil or something. People liked the name and the idea of using the same gunk on their bodies that surfers do, so it became a big success.

SIMPLICITY

The best ideas are the simplest. For example, people in this country have an overwhelming demand for the instant gratification of their needs and desires. Everything has to be done yesterday. Domino's Pizza, which now has something like 3,500 outlets nationwide, is based on a very simple idea: delivering hot pizza in under thirty minutes. For that reason alone, and forget the fact that the pizza is mediocre, it is successful.

In New York City, where you could argue that every day four million people get up to feed the other four million people, the environment is very food-oriented. Yet the only ethnic group that has figured out how to *deliver* food is the Chinese. A lot of other people have tried and failed. A typical Chinese restaurant will do 70 percent to 80 percent of its business in food consumed off the premises.

There is a rule in the magazine publishing business that if you want to start a successful new magazine, you better be able to define the idea behind it in one sentence. If you can't, you do not know what you are talking about. The same is true in other businesses—you can define the successful operations in a very few words. The reason McDonald's worked initially is that it was clean, cheap, and fast. The reason that Kentucky Fried Chicken worked initially is that the recipe and the cooking process were radically different from anybody else's process. By the time other people, like Chicken Delight, caught up with the process, it was too late.

THE CREATIVE PROCESS

A little while ago, I was looking at an idea for prepackaged, fresh health food. I had decided that it was time for somebody to make serious money selling nutritious foods, based on the fact that nutrition is important and it's a way to lose weight. The technology of nutrition has all been written. Everybody knows now that carrots are good for you, coffee is bad for you, and so on.

So how did I go about coming up with this idea? I defined the area I wanted to be in—prepared health food. Then I took it to the second step by realizing that it had to be fresh food because you can't sell frozen greens and vegetables as health food. People won't buy them because they won't be as good as fresh.

Then I looked at the competition. General Foods has something called Culinova that is fresh and shelf stable, which means you can keep it in the refrigerator for up to ten days. Maybe a problem, maybe not, if I can do it better.

Finally, I asked myself what I bring to this party. The answer: I have the experience to set up a manufacturing facility to prepare the food and package it. I believe I have the taste buds to make my food as good as anybody else's. The container technology is buyable, so all I have to do is hire a packaging consultant. So I say to myself, great, now I can go out and raise the money. But then I thought, what is wrong with this idea? Unlike Saucier, I don't have to tell the American public what the stuff is, and unlike the cookies, it won't be immediately inundated with competition. Plus, I have the publicity talents to make it sell. So where is the hole?

The hole is that given the kind of budget I have, I can't begin to get the shelf space in the supermarkets that I need to sell my product. Getting space in supermarkets these days involves paying slotting fees to the operators. Shelf space is valuable, and they don't give it away, especially for unproven products. Even if I get my stuff out there and it is good and people like it, the Pillsburys of this world will come along and bury it. They will buy up all the shelf space before I can get it.

So I decided to forget about prepackaged, fresh health food. That's what I do: keep taking my ideas apart and trying to figure out what the bad news is. Unfortunately, ninety-nine times out of 100, there will be bad news. So you start over again.

ANALYZING YOUR IDEAS

If you look at all the angles, the upside potential, and the downside risks, and you really think it through, I believe you can figure out if your business is going to work before you start. I knew in my gut that if my cookies tasted good, somebody was going to buy them. It still took me a year and a half to put David's Cookies together and answer all the questions: What should the cookies look like? What should the cookies be called? What should the store look like? What kind of oven should I have? Where's the niche? What's the price? Who is the competition?

Opening the store was anticlimactic. The deal was done before the store was opened.

If you can't get that kind of peace of mind about your

product before you open the door, you're in trouble. I applied the exact same logic to my restaurant, Chez Louis. We had this place called Manhattan Market where we served nouvelle cuisine food. The restaurant did extremely well in its day. Then one day I looked at the food on the plate and said, "I don't want to eat this kind of food now." The customers were becoming jaded. The whole nouvelle cuisine concept was becoming dated.

What kind of food did I want to eat? Big portions, full-flavored, brown food. I said to myself, "Schmuck, I can't believe nobody else wants to eat this kind of food." So I decided to open a restaurant with big portions and lots of meat and potatoes.

So what were the holes? It wasn't diet food, so the beautiful people weren't going to eat it because they want to stay at 102 pounds. But the more I thought about it, Chez Louis's food was a returning trend, even though the Sunday night the first week we were open we served only four dinners. I knew Chez Louis would be a success because it was the kind of food I and other people like to eat. It has been.

BE RUTHLESS IN EVALUATING YOUR IDEAS

The other day, I met a carpenter who had developed an idea for a leaf proof gutter. Every home owner has a problem with soggy leaves that catch in the rain gutter and then have to be cleaned out. He showed me something that seemed pretty ingenious: a gutter with a curved top on it that would catch rainwater but would not get clogged with leaves. This guy had done all kinds of studies about how much water it could handle. For example, he discovered that because his gutter didn't get any leaves, it didn't have to hold eight pounds a foot of weight the way normal gutters do. A company that makes rolled steel had come to him and said it wanted an exclusive agreement to make and market this gutter. Sears was prepared to give him an enormous order to start with. So this guy clearly had a good idea. The only trouble was he hadn't thought it through. I asked this guy what he wanted from the deal with the manufacturer, and he said "Five percent." But he didn't know five percent of what. I told him to go in there and start negotiating with them about what they think the market is and what profit they think they can make on his type of gutter. Then he should ask for a guaranteed amount of money.

The moral is: once you come up with a good, simple idea—and this is a good one; I'd want one of these gutters on my house—you have to shape it. You have to take your rosy scenario apart. Within three minutes, he had presented to me an idea that could make him a multimillionaire. By the time I took it apart, he was so discouraged that the cigar almost fell out his mouth.

KEEP RUNNING THROUGH WALLS

Which brings up another point. Never quit.

Pizza Hut failed on Long Island twelve years ago, and now it is trying to come back in again. I wish them well. David's Cookies has never tried to go back to an area where we got thrown out, but we will in the future. You just try again. That's something that applies to all kinds of business ideas. Just because it didn't work the first time doesn't mean it won't work the second or the third time.

This is something I learned from the English retail chain Marks & Spencer. It is a billion-dollar company, and it doesn't do any marketing studies at all. Its whole approach to selling food and clothes is that it will put the product on the shelf in a good location right at the front door and give it five tries. If it doesn't make it after five prominent displays, the product gets permanently discontinued.

When I was in England trying to get Marks & Spencer to carry my private label cookie dough—David's dough sold with their label—they were trying to sell all-natural cereals. They had tried four other ways of merchandising them, and each one had failed. On the fifth try, they succeeded. What I found out is that their success rate is sixty percent, and the cost of introducing those products is minuscule compared to what Nabisco or Procter & Gamble or some other giant food company will spend test marketing a new snack food. The downside, of course, is Marks & Spencer will alienate customers by displaying a lot of goods that disappear and will never be seen again.

HOW LONG DOES IT TAKE?

As long as it takes. As long as you can afford to hold out and still eat and pay the rent, you're going to push this thing you've invented or created. A person who quits his job, goes out and starts a business, gives it a couple of months, doesn't make it, and goes running back to get another job shouldn't have been in business for himself in the first place.

In this respect, individuals have an advantage over big corporations. For business reasons, large companies cannot stay with new products that don't succeed right off. About 99 percent of Nabisco's or P&G's product ideas fail, which always amazes me. You have seemingly the smartest marketing, advertising, and production people in the United States coming up with this garbage, and one out of 100 product sticks. The message is that you should not be discouraged if you come out with something that doesn't work. If you believe it will work in the long run, you should keep trying.

BE REALISTIC

Henry Luce, the founder of Time Inc., waited for more than a decade for *Sports Illustrated* magazine to make a profit. Now it is a big success, selling three million copies a week, so Luce bet right. But most of us aren't as smart as Henry Luce, nor do we have his deep pockets. So you have to be realistic. Keep going as long as your instinct tells you that you have a good idea. But when baby needs a new pair of shoes and the bill collector is banging on the front door, it may be time to try something else.

BOTTOM LINE

Good ideas are not all that hard to find. Innovate, don't invent. Go with what you know. Believe deeply in what you are doing. Analyze your idea, but not to death. Don't quit prematurely. Henry Ford wasn't a success overnight, and neither was I. I don't believe in luck. People make their own luck.

4
INVENTING YOUR OWN EDIBLE HULA HOOP

To put Tolstoy in the consulting business for a minute, all successful businesses are alike. They produce something that people want to buy, they do it at a reasonable price that is competitive and still a profit, and they manage to keep from getting caught up in all the crazy stuff that can bring down a business.

Most of my working life has been spent in the food business. The food business is like any other business in that it contains lessons for the budding entrepreneur. Food also happens to be an easy thing to start a business with. All you have to do is to be able to make it and ensure it tastes good. The nice thing about food is that it is universal—everybody has to eat. So there are loads of opportunities.

KNOW WHAT YOU ARE DOING

You really need expertise in the area where you want to go into business. I get hysterical with these letters from people who *think* they want to go into the business. You don't *think* you want to go into the business. You either love it or you don't, and if you don't, you are going to fail. I think that is true of any situation.

GO FOR THE BEST

In the food business, the reality is that the only place you can make money is in very upscale food products. You are not going to compete with Kellogg in making the next cornflakes. You can't make enough to get the price down to Kellogg's, even if you don't advertise on television. You probably aren't going to change America's eating habits either, so don't try to introduce chocolate-covered halvah in Kansas City.

What you should try to do is give the world a better version of something that is already out there. I've seen it done in any number of areas: brownies, cheesecake, potato chips, pretzels, hot dogs, chocolate, coffee, beer, you name it. You should get into products that people are buying, then you look for a niche at the top of the market for people to buy a similar product with a twist, something that makes it a little bit more special.

A CASE IN POINT: HÄAGEN-DAZS

Reuben Mattus invented Häagen-Dazs ice cream almost twenty years ago. He came up with an idea to use more butterfat and less air to make ice cream taste richer and creamier. At that time, you could buy basically generic store ice cream—Breyers, Sealtest, Carvel—for as little as fifty-nine cents a half gallon. Mattus's plan was to sell this super-rich stuff by the pint. You couldn't buy more than that because it was four times as expensive as anything else in the supermarket. He was charging seventy-five cents per container for it.

Supercreamy ice cream was a good idea—but for the first thirteen years, Mattus had a hard time giving Häagen-Dazs away. In the early seventies, he was doing only a couple of million dollars a year in sales. Anybody else who had been in this business for thirteen years at that level would probably have quit. But he believed that his product was better than anybody else's, so he kept on plugging. His problem was that in those days, if you wanted to sell your wares in a supermarket freezer, you had to pay for the freezer, and he couldn't afford it. After 1973 or so, people began to wise up, and Häagen-Dazs started to catch on.

Mattus had developed one of the first mass-market specialty-food products in the United States. Usually, if you walk down a supermarket aisle, the competitors are all within a few cents of each other. Heinz catsup costs about the same as Hunt's catsup, and so on. Mattus made a breakthrough by saying, "Listen consumer, you are going to pay through the nose for my ice cream because it is so much better than the other ice creams in that freezer."

QUALITY COUNTS

There is a real lesson to be learned in that. Mattus was one of the pioneers in educating the whole population about what we now call upscale food. In those days, when people talked about "gourmet food," what they meant was chocolate-covered ants, stuff like that. People did not have a sense about what quality food was—they thought it was all this esoteric garbage. What's crazy about this is if you had talked to the food pioneers—the guys who started Campbell Soup or Pillsbury years ago—they were trying to produce better quality food than the other guy in terms of fresh ingredients and better processes. Somehow, that all got forgotten until the 1980s.

Today the consumer is more sophisticated. In the past few years, customers have begun reading labels. They can distinguish between quality and high-priced junk. If you came to the United States as a visitor from outer space and were dropped in front of a TV, you would discover that every food commercial stresses quality: "It's good for you; it's the best of its class." Years ago that wasn't true. I think the food business is going to continue to move in that direction.

So if you are going to come out with a product—especially if you don't have much money, as seems likely—go with quality. That's one area where you can make a difference and stand a chance of competing with the giants.

LOOK FOR EASE OF ENTRY

There are food businesses you can put a fresh twist on, say, with machinery. Fresh chocolate truffles—fancy candies, really—are a business I think is about to happen. How do you make that into a business? The machine that makes the truffles is proprietary, and you can build mystique around the fact that the truffles are made fresh at stores and not coming in by plane from Switzerland. Made-fresh-on-the-premises was the whole schtick behind fresh popcorn stores, though they are fading now.

One of the easiest food businesses for an entrepreneur to get into now is potato chips. There are handmade potato chip companies popping up from Florida to Maine. All you need is a bunch of potatoes, a knife, and some oil and salt. There are Hamptons potato chips and Cape Cod potato chips. The problem is, once you come up with the perfect potato chip, how are you going to get shelf space in supermarkets? Shelf space is worth more than gold, and it costs almost as much to buy.

GOING MAINSTREAM VS. EXOTIC

In deciding what kind of product to make, you will face a dilemma: Do you create a me-too product that people can understand but where you run the risk of being undercut by a commodity producer? Or do you do a unique product where you have to go through a long and expensive educational process to get customers?

It is part of my basic philosophy that if you are not a fantastic creative genius—and there are not a lot of Thomas

Edisons around—you should take a hard look at what's around you and twist it a little. I am convinced that it is better to have something that is somewhat familiar than something that is totally radical, where you have to educate people about the concept.

The current craze is barbecue sauce. Everybody is coming out with barbecue sauce. Most of them are just packaging and labels. Some bulk producer winds up making the sauce, and they all taste pretty much alike. Yet there are lots of people trying to become the next Heinz catsup of barbecue sauce, and I think it is a long way off.

My other theory here is that there is usually a market for a low-tech product with a high-tech image, such as specially fried potato chips or dry-roasted peanuts. In fact, a new brand of peanuts just came on the market that is attempting to differentiate itself from Planters, the market leader, by advertising that it contains no MSG (monosodium glutamate), the artificial flavor enhancer. You can think of your own examples. Maybe you can find a bestseller.

FIGHTING MARKETPLACE APATHY

Then you have to figure: Does this product taste better than all the other ones? And if it does, will anybody care?

In the case of potato chips, some people really care about quality. In the case of milk, they don't. For a while I was selling a special kind of cultured, high butterfat milk. The press loved it, but nobody bought it. Milk is milk, I guess.

I absolutely believe that David's Cookies gummy bears— they are kind of like Juju Fruits candy but they aren't as sticky and they taste better—are superior to anybody else's on the market. They aren't coated with carnauba wax—the stuff you get put on your car at a car wash for an extra buck—and they have real flavors with no artificial garbage. But at this point, even though the gummy bears are doing pretty well, they aren't setting the world on fire. Nobody really cares. They don't have the same kind of sex appeal that David's cookies have. People get sexually and mentally involved with those cookies, in a manner of speaking.

YOU DO NOT HAVE TO BE FIRST

We were the last ones in with cookies. Debbi Fields was thirty months ahead, Great American chocolate chip cookie was four years ahead, Famous Amos was five years ahead of us. But in every case, I felt that the cookies they were offering left room for the cookie that I wanted to offer.

I put out a product that by its appearance and ingredients was not mainstream. I used real imported chocolate, real butter, and lots of both. There were no chocolate chunk cookies available at all; everybody used chips. Moreover, there was no cookie on the market that used imported chocolate. Our cookie was special, unique. True, it was also ugly; the chocolate ran throughout the cookie.

When I started out, there were a lot of chocolate chip cookie stores in New York. There were six or seven Absolutely the Best Chocolate Chip Cookies in New York City, and a couple of places called Cookie Works. Most of them were buying dough from the same place in New Jersey. And, quite frankly, they weren't selling good cookies; they were made with margarine, not butter. They seemed fresh, but they were made from frozen dough.

I built a better mousetrap, but until Florence Fabricant of the *New York Times* had a contest to judge the best chocolate chip cookie, I was going broke. My cookies quickly developed notoriety because they were obscenely rich and delicious. If you can arrange to be notorious, you will have no difficulty getting people to notice you.

SELL IT YOURSELF

Once you have come up with your idea, don't bother trying to sell it to Pillsbury or General Foods or some other giant. They will send you back a confidentiality agreement that basically says: 1) we did not solicit this idea from you; 2) we probably thought of it anyway; 3) if we do go ahead with it, you agree to waive any rights that you think you have but really don't.

These big companies have hundreds of people dreaming up ideas every day. There is very little they haven't heard of before. What you see out there on the market represents only about 1 percent of the ideas they generate. So don't bother with them.

BIG GUYS MAKE MISTAKES, TOO

In a giant corporation like General Foods, they spend lots of money on research and development. Basically, they are trying to do two things: to come up with line extensions of existing products, like Diet Coke from Coca-Cola, or to create totally new products, like Pringles potato chips. On a yearly basis, they will actually devise hundreds, if not thousands, of names or ideas for food products. They look at market studies to see which products are growing and try to figure out where they have synergism with their existing strengths.

All that time, money, and expertise does not stop them from making huge mistakes. A couple of years ago, as I recall, a large food company came up with a caramel-covered apple product called Wrapples. It consisted of a package of caramel sheets that you could wrap around an apple and some sticks that you drove into the apple to hold it. What they failed to understand was that this product, in addition to having some fairly mediocre caramel, also had six weapons in it. Kids started stabbing each other with the sticks. Wrapples was taken off the market in a big hurry.

Soft and chewy cookies flopped for another reason. They were a huge new product in 1986: all the big guys had one. They all spent an enormous amount for advertising. But as soon as they stopped the ads, the sales went right in the toilet.

The soft and chewy cookies cost about 40 percent more than traditional dry, crumbly cookies. And they taste lousy. Here's why. Procter & Gamble and the others tried to duplicate the taste of fresh-baked cookies by treating the cookie dough with two types of chemicals that controlled the baking process. When they were done cooking, the outside was crunchy, but the inside was still soft and slightly under-cooked.

What amazed me was that they tried to get around an absolute fact of the bakery business, which is that from the time something comes out of the oven, it gets progressively worse. Cookies are probably at their absolute best between ten and thirty minutes after they come out of the oven. From there they go slowly downhill. So there is no way you can really duplicate the taste of fresh-baked cookies.

What happened was fairly predictable. Consumers wouldn't pay the extra money for an inferior product. The soft and chewy cookie business has dried up because the companies stopped advertising. Procter & Gamble is on the way out of the soft-cookie business. Keebler is, too.

Nabisco, the gorilla of the cookie business, has the bulk of what's left. But it made what I consider a famously bad decision. It took the best selling chocolate chip cookie in America, Chips Ahoy!, and reformulated it as a soft and chewy cookie. When Nabisco saw people wanted their old, stale, dry crunchy Chips Ahoy! instead, it brought those back, too. It was just like New Coke and Classic Coke. Corporate America tried to force something down the mouths of consumers that they didn't want. I think New Coke has only a tiny fraction of the market. What a disaster!

THE FEW HOME RUNS REALLY PAY OFF

The good news is that when you get a winner like Oreos or Twinkies, the kind of money that can be made is astronomical. I'm convinced, for instance, that Mars makes the bulk of its money not on any of its new candy bars but on Snickers, which has been around for years. Mars has long since paid for the development costs, so everything that comes in is gravy. Everybody is fighting for those one or two heavy-hitter winners that become cash cows.

TRY TO FIND THE HOLES

Since you have far less money than these big guys, you have
to be even more skeptical and cautious about your ideas. If
you think logically about your idea up front, undoubtedly
you can think of a lot of holes. Examine the holes carefully,
because the process can stop you from hocking your house
prematurely.

Don't worry that you are an amateur. With your common
sense, you probably know as much as the pros know. There
is a concept about business I have: nobody knows what they
are doing. My friend Steven Bochco, who produces "LA
Law" and created "Hill Street Blues," says that nobody in
Hollywood knows what people like to watch on television.
They put the new shows on the air and wait to see what is
watched. In TV, the failure rate is 90 percent. Of every ten
new shows, only one ever stays on the air long enough to
return a profit to its producers. Fortunately, they can make
enough on that one hit to subsidize their mistakes.

BE REALISTIC

Frequently, people who come in to see me with a new food
are very concerned with confidentiality. I had a guy in here
who said he wanted me to market his brownies. But when I
asked to taste them, he said I couldn't. I said, "How can I
market your brownies if I don't even know what they taste
like?" He replied, "I can't have you taste my brownies; you'll
steal the recipe and sell them yourself."

Those kinds of people are not going to make it in business because there is nothing on the face of this earth that
cannot be stolen by somebody else, especially in the food
business where recipes aren't patentable or trademarkable.
There is nothing you sell that is so special that somebody
can't knock you off.

Even if your product is unique, which is unlikely, it is not
going to stay that way for long if what you have is any good.
You have to live with the fact that people are going to knock

you off. To put it bluntly, they are going to steal ideas from you.

I have a friend who made chocolate mousse cakes that were great. He sold them to Zabar's, had 200 accounts, and then somebody came along and knocked him off. They undercut him on price, offered allowances for displays, and so on.

I was the first one to put chunks of real chocolate in my cookies, rather than chips. If I could have found a way to copyright the words "chocolate chunk" I'd be a millionaire just off the licensing. But you can't do that. Those are the breaks.

INTERNATIONAL RIP-OFFS

At this writing, there are at least six David's Cookies stores in Rio de Janeiro that are doing a helluva job. They are exact replicas of my stores: the logo, the tiles, the layout, everything. Unfortunately, I don't own any of them. There are two David's Cookies stores in Panama, presumably owned by some Panamanian. In Paris, there are stores called Le David American Chocolate Chunk Cookies, and if you ask the kid making the cookies where they come from, she says, "New York." Not from me, however.

RIP-OFFS AT HOME

There is not much I can do about those. Even if I sued and won, which would cost me a fortune, the verdicts probably wouldn't be enforceable. Here in the United States, it is a different story. There was a company called Victor's Cookies in White Plains that was a total rip-off of the David's Cookies concept. It duplicated the look of the store. It even had the chutzpah to go to the same company that made our neon signs to get them to duplicate the gorilla lettering that we used in our logo. We sued them and won a decision where we could pick out a new logo for them that was as far away from David's as we could get. Our victory was mostly moral, though, because the lawsuit was very expensive.

Another guy we went after was a Korean in Texas who opened up a business called David's Cookies. When I called him on the phone, he kept saying, "My name David, my name David." His name may well have been David, but when it applies to cookies, his name belonged to us. We sued him too and stopped him from profiting on our trade name.

The message is that while imitation is the greatest form of flattery, it is very expensive to go after the imitators. We just don't have the money or the resources to do what Coca-Cola does and police a trademark all over the world.

MORAL

There are lots of good ideas left in the food area if you want to start your own business. But stick to mainstream ideas. Try to execute them better than the other people who make them. Make sure that there is a market for your concept. Your best bet is to come out with a better quality product where the customer can recognize the difference. And don't lose sleep at night about knockoffs. It is going to happen. You just have to cope the best you can.

5
FINDING OUT IF YOU WANT TO PUT YOUR MONEY WHERE YOUR MOUTH IS

I am absolutely convinced that you can thoroughly analyze your own concept by yourself and get a sense about how you can shape it into a profitable venture without risking a lot of money.

START AT HOME

Ask yourself: would I buy this new product or service myself? I've started everything I've done with that question. I think you are in deep trouble if you have a product or service that you are not that interested in but think that somebody else will buy.

The second most important question to answer is: what is the commercial viability? That is the crap shoot. You won't know for sure until your product comes out.

WHY IT IS IMPORTANT FOR YOU TO START SMALL

It is cheaper. You need less money when you start small. If you can keep your financial nut to a bare minimum, there is a very good chance you won't be one of those who fail. You can weather the slow periods if things go badly. The people who borrow, borrow, borrow in the hope that it is all going to come out right are almost guaranteed to fail. Borrowing is even more compulsive than going down to Atlantic City and putting all your money on red.

You don't have to start big. Steven Jobs and Steve Wozniak really did start Apple Computer in their garage. The guy who founded Rubbermaid made his rubber dustpans in an old balloon factory in Akron, Ohio. It is when you want to grow and you have to borrow money that it begins to get difficult.

When you start small, you also present a smaller target. It took IBM five years to figure out that personal computers were here to stay and that it could make some money on them. So little Apple had a chance to grow.

Huge corporations are grabbing ideas faster than they used to, however. It wasn't long after Howard Head invented the oversized metal tennis racket that Wilson and Rossignol and everyone else got into the business. Today you can't even buy a regular-sized racket, much less a wooden one. So you have to be really sure you have a niche and a niche that is going to stay sleepy for a while until you can develop your business. The last thing you want is to start by competing with Coke and Pepsi.

TESTING YOUR IDEA

There are products around like the pet rock that last for one season. But they aren't really a business; they are a gimmick. How should you determine whether you have a gimmick or a business? The answer is, you have to go out there and try to get people to carry your product, get distributors, see if anybody orders the product, see if the media will take it seriously.

BUM IDEAS

A guy I know had an idea for a video dating service. For a fee, the customer can take home videos of ten prospective dates and watch them. After he or she has made a choice, their video gets sent to their prospective date. Then they get together and—bingo!

The business had one big failing: no word of mouth. Nobody is going to tell his friend that he had videotapes of ten gorgeous blondes. That's the kind of information he wants to keep to himself. My friend lost a million dollars on that.

MAKE SOME SAMPLES

Assuming you have a working drawing of a prototype, there are any number of places around the world where you can get it made. Start small so you don't get hurt. Instead of starting out with XYZ manufacturer making 100,000 bottle openers for a nickel apiece, you go to the lady around the corner who can make a dozen for five dollars apiece. It may cost you more than the retail price to make the first one, but you know that when the volume comes along the manufacturing costs will come down. If those dozen sell, great; if they don't, at least you are not out a lot of money.

LOOKING AT PRICES

Then you have to figure out what the price point is. And that is one of the most difficult things about going into business for yourself. You have to have the luxury of pricing at different price points.

To start with, you better look around at what the competition is charging and figure out if you want to be more expensive or cheaper. As you become more established, you will have more flexibility in pricing. When you are just starting out, you have to be conscious of what the market is and how much people will pay.

When I opened the first David's Cookies, I priced the cookies way up because I wanted people to know they were something special. The strategy worked. Now I have a different problem with my supermarket packages of cookie dough. Because of the volumes, which are not enormous now, and the way we are making it, the price is very high. These little packages cost a dollar more than Pillsbury's because the ingredients are much better. We've tried to sell the dough at the lower price, and we know that it sells much better. The problem is, we haven't decided to take the plunge and buy the automated equipment that will enable us to do that and still make a profit.

GETTING THE FIRST CHUNK OF SHELF SPACE

The easiest way to see if you have the right price and if the product will sell at all is go to a shop and see if you can sell it on consignment. That's a no-risk deal for the retailer. If the product doesn't sell, you take it back. You are saying to the retailer, "Look, if this stuff doesn't move, I'm not going to stick you with it." And you'll find out very quickly whether or not your product sells.

I would say the consignment business is growing because retailers are not prepared to take a risk on you given all the problems they have today—crime, high rent, and so on—to in effect finance your business. The book business operates on consignment, and a lot of other businesses do, too.

FOLLOW IT AND SEE WHAT IT EATS

Store buyers by and large are conduits of public opinion. They want to sell products the public wants to buy. All buyers will tell you the same thing: "This piece of shelf space has to return X amount of dollars, and if it doesn't, I will find something else to sell on it that does."

That hard and fast rule is mitigated somewhat by the necessity for variety. Stores have to try to appeal to a lot of people with a lot of products. They can't stock just the best-sellers. If you analyzed the numbers in a department store, all they should be selling is blue jeans, perfume, and cosmetics because those things sell more than anything else. However, the stores try to balance things out to make a well-rounded, you-can-get-everything-here approach. In that regard, if you get to a sophisticated buyer who is conscious of quality, you may be able to convince him that even if your product isn't selling well right this minute, it is giving him greater variety on his shelves.

DON'T BE TOO PICKY

There are a number of nationally known stores you can approach, but the chances are they will probably want their pound of flesh to sell your product, such as guaranteed production quantities and exclusive agreements. Hammacher Schlemmer and Sharper Image are two that come to mind.

Once in a while, that can be a good idea. A little while ago, a couple of men in their twenties came into my office with a pretty good product called America Glace. It was an all-real—I never use the term "all-natural"—frozen fruit slush. They had production capacity but no outlets except for a little stand at Fifty-fifth Street and Third Avenue. They wanted me to carry their product in my store. I said I would do it, but I wanted exclusivity in Manhattan, and I also wanted a very good price. They went back to their genius attorney, who said, "We don't give exclusivity to anybody at any price." So they went away.

Whether they made the right decision or not is up to them. But if I were in their shoes, I would have taken that deal. If you have a new product, everybody is going to ask for an exclusive. The rule should be that if somebody wants the exclusivity, he should have to pay for it. He is going to have to commit to certain volumes of business, or he is going to lose the exclusivity. If he says no, you have to figure out if he is bluffing.

When we go out to sell our cookie dough in different areas of the country and two chains are competing for the product and both will take it only on an exclusive basis, we have to decide whether it is worth it to do that. You make a thousand of these decisions every day. We usually wind up giving the dough to the biggest chain.

In Detroit, we did a deal with Great Scott supermarkets. They committed to open thirteen in-store bake-offs—we send our cookie dough into the store and they bake them— and the only thing they care about is that we don't open other bake-offs in Farmer Jack's, their main competitor. So for nine months, we didn't let anybody else have bake-offs.

A WORD OF CAUTION

If you can't patent a nonfood product, don't go near it. It's so easy to get knocked off that if you don't have that basic protection, you are dead. Food can't be patented. Most inventors don't think about marketing their own invention for just that reason. They want to take it through the patent process, then license it for manufacture, take the money, and run. That reminds me. I think success stories of inventors are few and far between. Even the ones who eventually make a bundle spent years peddling their idea.

A DILEMMA

At the same time you are prepared to run through brick walls to get your business started, you ought to be prepared to say, "Wait a minute. The idea may be good but this tactic is wrong," and retreat. A little while ago I made a presentation about my idea for shelf-stable, prepackaged nutritional food to a bunch of investors. As I was talking about it, I realized that it wasn't such a hot idea. So I dropped it and went on to the next idea. It wasn't easy and I hated to do it, but the problems all of a sudden became crystal clear.

Often you see an obvious opportunity with a demand just waiting to be filled. But the reality of being a small business is that you do not have the resources to make a success of the product, even though you have identified a niche. So you let it go.

I knew from reading newspapers and magazines that there is an almost exponential growth in health awareness these days. I also knew that a quality, prepared, take-home product with 500–700 calories would sell like crazy. The problem was that with the supermarkets selling shelf space to the highest bidder and charging outrageous slotting fees across the board, and the incredible distribution problems involved in even *getting* my product on the shelves, that fresh, healthful food—even though I know I could make and package it—couldn't get into the hands of consumers in a way that would make it a long-term success.

WHEN THE PRODUCT IS OUT OF YOUR HANDS, YOU LOSE CONTROL

One morning recently I got two phone calls from food shop owners, one in Chelsea and one uptown, who are doing take-out food. They think they have an absolute gorilla by the tail because people are standing in line to buy their take-out food. So they called me up for advice on how to package their food and expand their distribution.

I told them not to even bother, because they are not going to succeed. Here's the reason: as soon as you have to rely on somebody else to represent your product, be it a food distributor or a supermarket chain or anybody else, you have lost control of that product. When you really look at the most successful food stores and the people who sell food, they are usually individual, single-site operations. You have hordes of family members in the store, making sure that everything is up to standard. When the hired help comes in, chances are the quality goes out the door.

As soon as you lose control of distribution, it is very

difficult to move fresh food around. Campbell Soup failed miserably when it tried to introduce a line of fresh salads.

Now, that is obviously less true if you are selling Slinkies or flashlights. But to the degree that your product is special and unique, it will require special and unique methods of distribution. You can't sell a Jaguar through a Chevrolet dealer. And there is nothing more special or unique than fresh food.

YOUR BACK-UP STRATEGY

If you do get your product out there and it doesn't sell, you have to go back and assess whether the product is viable. With a food product, one of the ways to test your product is to get it to as many members of the food press as possible because, like it or not, the opinion-making working press in the food business is doing a job. They are covering the business, and they are going to give an opinion about what you put in front of them, just the way that a movie critic or a theater critic will give an opinion on what they've seen. If you send your stuff around to the five or ten most reputable food types in your community—plus some national types— and all nine or ten of them say this is the worst garbage to come down the pike in fifteen years, you've got a problem.

Food reporters don't care whether something is selling or not selling—that's not their job. They are not there to record whether you are number one in hot sauce this week. They are there to give their honest opinion about whether what you are trying to sell is any good or not. And they are going to be brutal about it. I've gotten slapped around both coming and going in this business.

WHY THE BACK-UP STRATEGY DOESN'T ALWAYS WORK

With Saucier, I got universal rave reviews from every food publication I approached in the United States. The food reporters said, "This product is fantastic; it's convenient and worth the price." But few people bought it. In retrospect, a lot of the reporters were saying subliminally that I was ten years ahead of my time with that product, and they turned out to be right. The store buyers were buying it because they wanted to keep up with the Joneses, but the customers weren't buying it.

There are very few TV shows that succeed without either ratings or critical reviews, and it usually takes both. The same thing is true in business. If you are not getting sales and you don't have any publicity, you are in deep trouble. There are a lot of products out there, however, that get no media reviews and yet get enormous sales because they tickle the public's fancy. Hunt's catsup, for one. Twinkies, for another. Nobody is going to say anything good about Twinkies with a straight face, but they keep selling and selling. If you are dealing with quality, it's especially important to get the press on your side. Otherwise, you can't convince the world that your product is worth the price you are asking for it.

FORGET MASS PRODUCTION

I think a lot of people make the mistake of jumping in too quickly. You have to realize that basically you are not going to make any money on the first batch you produce, but as long as the sales are going in the right direction, long term you have a business.

If you start small, however, you have to be prepared to get the product made somewhere in volume if it hits big. The biggest mistake I made in opening my first David's Cookies was thinking I needed only a store and a twenty-quart mixer for the dough. Now I'm in that position again with my refrigerated cookie dough. I know where to find the manufacturers to buy the equipment for a new plant to make it. But it doesn't help me to know that because I don't have the money to put into it now. I'll be damned if I'm going to invest $10 million in a plant and wait for the orders to come in, as opposed to getting the orders and growing into the plant. There is no real expertise on this issue: you just hold your nose, jump in, and hope you survive.

Aggravating though it is, I don't know any other way to do it. When you grow a business, you have to make sure that the egg you are making stays a little bit behind the chicken. Otherwise, you will expand too fast and go broke.

WRAP-UP

In testing your idea, start small. Ask your spouse or mother if they would buy it. Make a few samples and take them around to merchants. You will get immediate feedback. Talk to them about how much the product should sell for, keeping in mind your cost of production. Do consignment deals if you have to. Don't be afraid to commit to exclusives. Always be careful not to grow your capacity too fast so that your overhead doesn't overwhelm your revenues. And try to be receptive to negative feedback. If all you are getting are negatives, you may have to go back and rethink your idea.

6
GETTING STARTED THE EASY WAY: FRANCHISING

If you haven't dreamed up the next Trivial Pursuit, there is a simpler way to go into business for yourself, without suffering the pain and agony of a start-up. Buy into a franchise like Dunkin' Donuts or Dairy Queen—or David's Cookies. You don't have to devise a new product, figure out how to make it, get distribution, or go into production. You just plug yourself into the formula that the franchiser has established and follow the rules. If it doesn't work out, you can always go back to what you were doing before.

I should point out that running a franchise is not really the goal of most entrepreneurs. At our cookie stores, we find that when the best franchisees start making more than $100,000 a year, they think "Schmuck, what am I doing here scooping cookies when I could be out making real money?" They figure that if they are this successful selling cookies, they could do even better at something else.

SHOW ME A GOOD FRANCHISEE, AND I'LL SHOW YOU A GOOD BUSINESSMAN

Being a franchisee is really not all that hard. We sell you the signs and the cookie dough, you rent the space and buy the oven, and you're open for business. But to stay in business, you have to know what you are doing, and you have to have the right instincts.

I have thousands of letters on file from people who would love to open a David's Cookies for themselves, their spouse, their wayward son, or their indolent daughter. So I have to figure out how to separate the few who have the potential to succeed from all the ones who don't. When I'm interviewing applicants, I have a test I give that seems to work. How the applicant responds tells me whether that person is a suitable franchisee.

The most important thing I do is make these budding entrepreneurs find a viable location for their first store. That's crucial to the business. If you can't find a good location, forget it. It is said that the three most important things in real estate are location, location, and location. Well, it is true in the cookie business also.

What I do is tell these applicants to show me a lease and say, "This is a location that I can get to open up a store, and the terms aren't so onerous that I can't make a profit." If they can do this much, I know that part of the battle is over, because the person had the smarts to first, find a location, and second, negotiate a lease.

I then send somebody from my organization out to look at the location. Most of the time they report back that it isn't any good. We know from long experience what makes a good location and how much rent an operator can afford to pay. Rent is your biggest single expense. If the rent is too much for the location, you will probably lose your shirt.

AFTER THAT, IT IS EASY— JUST PLAIN HARD WORK

If the location is OK, we then take the applicant through the process of getting started. I have a franchise information book that is as thick as the Manhattan phone book and about as useful in running the business. The truth of the matter is that if you make sure the cookies are fresh and the ice cream doesn't melt and you are nice to your customers, you'll make a lot of money. If you are rude to the customers or start to think that the cookies will jump out of the refrigerator and bake themselves, you are going to lose your money. That's true in almost any business I know. If you do the blocking and tackling right, you will come out ahead.

It works in big business too. Take Rubbermaid, for instance. Everyone has heard of Rubbermaid. It makes rubber dustpans, dish drainers, wastebaskets, that sort of thing. Rubbermaid is a very unglamorous business, but it makes a ton of money. How does it do it? It makes the best dustpans and dish drainers around, and it is very good to its customers, in this case the K Marts and Wal-Marts that sell its stuff. It really works hard to make sure those merchants are happy. So it grows 15 percent a year.

HEAD TRIPS

I read in the *Wall Street Journal* that some franchisers are using psychological tests in selecting new franchisees. You will be amazed to hear that they are turning down people who test well for strong entrepreneurial qualities, such as creativity and independence. The story quotes Kenneth Franklin, president of Franchise Developments in Pittsburgh, who says that an entrepreneur makes a bad franchise operator because he'll probably want to do it his way and change the system.

According to Franklin, a lot of franchisers are using a 2½-hour psychological test to identify potential troublemakers. Among other things, applicants are asked about their parents, childhood heroes, favorite movie stars, and subjects they liked least in school. The tests help knock out the 20 percent to 30 percent of the applicants who don't get approved. Those who are offended by the test and refuse to take it usually aren't chosen either.

There is a grain of truth here, but mostly this sounds like

Mr. Franklin trying to drum up business for his testing service. Yes, it is true that most franchises, including mine, have lots of rules to follow, and yes, it is true that you can get in trouble if you don't follow the rules. But running a franchise and being an entrepreneur have a lot in common. You have to be a self-starter and enjoy working for yourself. And you have to have that spark—that twitch factor—that enables you to cope with adversity when things don't go right. When the delivery truck doesn't show up with the frozen beef patties or the garbage man doesn't pick up the garbage, it isn't going to help you to look it up in the encyclopedia of directions you got from the franchiser. You have to figure it out for yourself.

Does this mean that if your favorite movie star is Marlon Brando or Sean Penn, you aren't going to be able to sell Dunkin' Donuts? I have a hard time believing it.

MY KANSAS CITY COOKIE KING

Good franchisees come from everywhere. Some of them have already had red-hot careers selling something else. Others are just getting their feet wet.

You would think that somebody who had worked in an essentially bureaucratic job for a big corporation would be a poor bet to run his own business. His experience would be very narrow, he would not be good at taking risks, and he would be used to having the corporation do everything for him, from turning on the lights in the morning to ordering pencils. In general, you would be right. But not always.

One of my most successful franchisees is a guy named Charlie Barnard. He worked at IBM for fifteen years as a financial and systems guy. He came to me because he wanted to start his own business. Since he was not secure enough to conceptualize a business from scratch, he wanted to open a David's Cookies outlet—in Kansas City, of all places, a territory we weren't developing.

We told him he was all wrong for David's Cookies. He had no experience in small business, he was used to having the support of a giant corporation around him, and he was an IBM'er—he was used to doing things by the book. Besides, Kansas City wasn't the right place for cookies that then cost $5.95 a pound. It is conservative and midwestern, and we are glitzy and eastern. What plays in Manhattan often doesn't play in Peoria.

So what happened? Charlie went out there with no experience and basically took over the market. David's Cookies *owns* Kansas City. What Charlie brought to the business was, first, his own money, so he had a stake in its success. He also had some really good street smarts. He knew a lot about locations, and he brought a decency that is very important in terms of how to deal with people and how to negotiate. He became friends with landlords, and, of course, he made friends with customers.

The thing that made Charlie successful—and this applies to our other franchisees as well—is that he spent endless time attending to details. Why is the sink dripping? Why is the sign crooked? Why don't the cookies look exactly right? You don't always hit perfection because *nobody* always hits perfection. But Charlie always remembered that no matter what else he was worrying about, somebody has to open the store in the morning and somebody has to make the cookies. Selling is the easy part. If the location is right and the product is right, the cookies will march out the door.

THERE IS NO FREE LUNCH

Everyone wants a sure thing. But if you try to buy your ne'er-do-well son a cookie store, the son may decide to go fishing on the weekend. Then the parents, who put up the money for him, come to me and ask, "Why am I losing my rear end in this business?" There is a very logical reason for it. Nobody is paying attention to the details.

In the retail business, there is no substitute for being there every day. There are several reasons for that. One: Since it is your business, you are going to work harder at it than anyone you can hire. Two: The people that you *do* hire will work harder when you are there for the simple reason that if they don't, you will fire them. Three: Customers like being served by the boss. They feel important when you hand them the cookies or dish up the ice cream. And don't worry; they can tell you are in charge, even if they don't know who you are.

TAKE WHAT YOU ARE DOING SERIOUSLY—THERE IS MONEY AT STAKE

At David's Cookies, we look for decent people who treat cookies like a business and not as a joke. They don't think cookies are "cute," and they don't think it would be a party to run a cookie store. They have money invested, and they want the operation to pay off. They are not debutantes waiting to meet Mr. Right.

The cookie and ice cream business is a lot simpler than running a McDonald's. Simplicity attracts a lot of people. They don't have to go to Hamburger University, and they don't have to supervise fifty $3.50-an-hour employees. But inherent in that simplicity is an understanding that if they don't watch their businesses, they are going to fail.

ANOTHER TRUE-LIFE STORY

We sold a store at Seventieth and Broadway in Manhattan to a Saudi Arabian. He was in there working seventy-five–eighty hours a week, and he was making lots of money, well in excess of $100,000 the first year. He was a big success.

After a year, he called me up and said, "I'm miserable. I want to sell the store." I said, "Are you crazy? You've got a gold mine." He replied: "You don't understand. I figured I was making so much money I didn't have to keep working in a cookie store. So I hired a manager, and he's stealing me blind."

The moral is: don't go into business unless you are prepared to work long hours getting started—and keep working long hours once you are a success. It is true that you may find it difficult to enjoy your success because you won't have any free time. But once you start to slack off, the business probably will, too.

STAY INVOLVED

Either you have to be physically at the business and stand there, or you have to have employees you implicitly trust. That's why we don't like franchisees to have more than three or four stores, tops. Because even a very good franchisee can't watch many more than that. You have to understand that as soon as you start delegating, a lot of money is going to walk out the door.

In New York City, where many of my outlets are, honesty does not seem to come naturally to many people. Employees think that it is OK to take things home with them at night because the store is popular and nobody will notice. Even when people *do* notice, employees take things. Sometimes it is cash. The only way to stop stealing is for the owner to actually be there. This take-all-you-can-get attitude is less prevalent in other parts of the country, I've noticed, but it is rampant in New York.

That's another reason to understand your motives when you go into business for yourself. If you are not driven by something—the need to earn a living, the desire to grow and be a big success—you are going to have a hard time keeping the twitch factor.

THE DOWNSIDE OF FRANCHISES

A lot of people think that the franchisers take advantage of franchisees. Whether that is true or not, the franchisees deserve part of the blame. When they are starting out in a new venture, people have a tendency to get starry-eyed and overlook many of the less glamorous parts of running a business.

In our case, we try to cut through that in a very direct, very brutal way. We have a 125-page franchise disclosure agreement. I tell the franchisee straight out: "Regardless of what is in this document, if you don't get a good location and you don't watch the store, you will lose all your money." I can't be more brutal than that. Some people pay attention, some don't.

I can't open that store for a franchisee, I can't clean the store, I can't make sure the cookies are baked right, I can't be nice to the customers. I do have some control over where he puts that store. And nobody in this country knows anything about locations. I do know that you get what you pay for. If you pay $400 per square foot, you probably have a pretty good location, but then you have to work the numbers backward to see if you can do enough business to justify paying that much rent.

McDonald's doesn't know what it is doing any more than Burger King when it comes to picking locations. Everybody makes mistakes. If you find any franchiser who will guarantee that a certain location will make money, then have them put that in writing. One of the tenets of franchise law is that you are not allowed to put any kind of projections into the prospectus based on what kind of business you are doing at other locations. I would love to put in what kind of business we are doing at Macy's Herald Square, but that is one of the greatest locations in the world. It wouldn't apply to Des Moines. It is largely a case of let the buyer beware. And if the deal sounds too good to be true, it is.

ONCE YOU GET STARTED, YOU ARE ON YOUR OWN

Most franchisers will not give you an advertising budget. The reason is that a typical franchisee does not want to pay for advertising. Moreover, he doesn't understand that in a typical royalty deal—he pays a percentage of the gross sales to the franchiser—the money for the advertising is coming out of his pocket anyway. Where else is the franchiser going to get the money from?

The best advice I can give is that wherever you put your franchised quick-lube service, you better stand out there on the corner and see how many cars are coming by; if you are on a dirt road with no cars, you can go out of business.

There is a new game in town where the franchiser says that location doesn't make any difference. Domino's Pizza does that. A franchised outlet of a Domino's Pizza does not sell any pizzas; it is merely a preparation and delivery center. All the pizzas are home delivered.

I think these are going to be the businesses of the future, because the rent is cheap if you set up shop in an out-of-the-way location. The problem is few people know how to deliver anything in thirty minutes in busy urban environments. Domino's promises that in other areas of the country, but it won't make that promise in New York. A Domino's Pizza franchise can be interesting, but only if you are prepared to spend your life in a car making deliveries.

Whomever you are trying to sell to had better be in the general vicinity of where you are doing business. You can't do an enormous job of selling wheelchairs at a health spa. You ought to be near a hospital.

CONCLUSION

So if you think you want to be an independent businessman but aren't ready to take the big leap yet, try running somebody else's franchise. You will learn good basic business skills, and you won't be bothered with imponderables like marketing, product strategy, and growth patterns. And when you decide to get out, the exits are clearly marked and well defined. The downside, of course, is that you will be denied the satisfaction of creating your own baby and watching it grow. More about that coming up.

7
ASSUMING YOU AREN'T DONALD TRUMP, WHERE DO YOU GET THE MONEY?

Money is an impossible problem on the one hand and irrelevant on the other.

That sounds contradictory, but it really isn't. You are never going to have enough money or be able to control it to the extent that you want. But—and I really believe this—you don't have to stay up late every night worrying about nickels and dimes. If you hustle and scheme and are creative, money will become less important. It will become an instrument to get you over the barriers, rather than an end in itself.

THE IMPONDERABLES OF MONEY

A couple of things to remember when you are starting out: One, you are not going to know how much money you need. Most people don't have the vaguest idea how much money they will spend in the short term, middle term, or long term. Even people who hire an accountant to make projections are going to be wrong 99.9 percent of the time. There are simply too many variables that you have no control over. Two, however much you think you need, it won't be enough.

You aren't alone. Most people who go into business are going in undercapitalized. You either figure out a way to survive or you don't—there is no secret to it. If you don't have enough money to do something professionally, you just have to dance around and figure out how to do it yourself. If you don't, you are going to go belly up.

There is no panacea. You have to scramble. People in the street aren't going to give you money, no matter how brilliant your idea is. Nobody who has money will give you any without strings attached.

You can count on two things. Since your business is brand new, you don't know how much money you are going to need. And since you don't have a track record, you will not be able to get money from the usual sources.

So the trick then becomes how to get money without getting tied up in the string.

FRIENDS AND FAMILY

You can always raise money from friends, but it is dangerous because sometimes you make them your enemies if you don't pay them back. Relatives are a good way to start. Some of the biggest entrepreneurs got their first backing from their families: that's how Donald Trump got his, Larry, and Bob Tisch got theirs. As long as you have to borrow, it might as well be from somebody who is related to you. But that is a personal decision you have to make. If things go sour, your relatives may dislike you, but they will have a hard time disowning you.

PARTNERS

That's the classical way to go. Find somebody who complements you and, hopefully, has some money and sign him up.

The problem is you have to pick your partners very

carefully. It is the most difficult thing I know—harder even than raising money.

I'm not the only one who thinks it's hard. A little while ago I was in a meeting with a wild entrepreneur who makes me look conservative by comparison. I had an idea for his failing supermarkets that would help both of us out, so I proposed a joint venture. What does he reply? "Just what I need, another partner." I said: "Look, it is a win-win deal. You are not putting up any money, only space where you are losing money already. The worst thing that could happen is you throw my operation out and go back to being a supermarket." He said, "Nah, if you've got partners, you've got trouble." He may have had something there.

Like a Marriage, Only Worse

With a partner, instead of arguing about sex, you argue about money. There are endless stories about partners coming to no good with each other.

The most famous story about partners I ever heard was about two guys who ran a delicatessen on the East Side of Manhattan for forty years. One of them lived on Long Island, and the other lived in Westchester. Every day the guy from Westchester came to work six minutes later than the one from Long Island because his train came in later. After forty years, the guy from Long Island came to work with a gun and confronted his partner. "You son of a bitch," he said. "I added this up. Six minutes times forty years; you owe me a quarter of a million dollars." Then he shot him in the head.

The resentment can build and build and build until it explodes. The partnerships that tend to work are where both parties have distinct and defined areas of expertise. In your partners' agreement, you have to plot out what is expected. Like Calvin Klein and Barny Schwartz. Klein designs and Schwartz promotes. Other partnerships where both people have similar skills or egos or desires tend to end up in disaster.

I made that mistake twice. I assumed divisions of labor

that didn't happen. And that's why I work so well with the current president of David's, Steve Stein. It is agreed that I am the promoter/innovator out in front of the business, and he is the guy who manages the day-to-day operation and makes it work.

How to Pick a Partner

It is like getting married. How do you know who the right woman is? The major difference is that in a partnership it is more difficult to get divorced. The heavy hitters who want out of a marriage will go to their wives and say, "This isn't working; tell me how much you want, and I'll write you a check." It doesn't work that way in a partnership. People have their professional standing on the line. If they decide one day that it is all chopped herring and they don't know what do with their lives, then they are at each other's throats.

The way to make it work is for both sides to put up something that is going to hurt. It has to be money, some kind of employment contract, or some kind of exclusive devotion of time to the business—something that spells out very clearly the obligations. That way, one person can't wake up some morning and say, "Nah, I don't want to do this any more." If you are putting up the money and the guy who is putting up the skill walks away, you are in deep trouble.

It may be worthwhile to go over a what-if list with a lawyer present, where you explore all the possible things that could go wrong with the partnership. So if the thing turns sour and ends up in arbitration or a lawsuit, it will have been clear from day one that it shouldn't have been a problem. In my case, if I had known better and pinned my first partner to the wall from day one, I guarantee that (A) he wouldn't have walked out and (B) if he did, he would have known he was walking away from the deal because he wasn't doing what he was supposed to be doing.

In the case of my second partner, I did put into the

contract that he couldn't open up a competing operation, but the arbitrator didn't see it my way. What that clause should have said was "If Leonard Kaye opens up a competing business on the island of Manhattan, he doesn't get any money otherwise agreed to be paid." To collect damages from him, we had to prove how much his having opened a competing store cost us, and that wasn't easy.

Everything Should Be Out Front

You have to know where everybody stands at all times—going into the deal, developing the deal, building the deal, working the deal. That's the hardest thing to articulate and codify. It is especially tense in the beginning, because you don't know the person you are getting involved with very well.

If the partnership makes sense, there shouldn't be a lot of disagreement up front. What has kept us together with our Japanese partners for years is that the deal was structured in such a way that there were gaps that would have allowed either one of us to bail out—as gentlemen, as opposed to at each other's throats. You can anticipate time periods—three months, one year, two years—when you may have problems. You can't anticipate all the what-ifs—there may be 1,000 what-ifs out there—but you can outline how you can back out of the deal at, say, six months, if you don't like it. That can work. In terms of lawyering, it costs a little bit more going in, but it can save you a lot on the other end.

In a Partnership, Money Talks

You can argue that the person who is putting up the money should have the upper hand, not the person who is investing only sweat equity. Now, I'm not talking about making a movie with Sylvester Stallone or Eddie Murphy as a partner; their sweat equity is worth more than the average guy's. At the same time, you also want a person who is going to work his tail off for you. But if you are the one who is betting the ranch on the venture, that prevails. Your sweat-equity partner can get another job, but you can go bankrupt.

Likewise, if you have 51 percent of the business, you have ultimate control. Forget all the contracts and all the divisions of responsibility. It is your business, so you can tell the other guy to get lost. Of course, you would prefer not to have to operate that way.

Separation

When it comes to that, usually one side buys the other side out. It is better to have arrived at a formula up front. Even though you won't know what is going on when you put the details together, it will make sense if the partnership is dissolved.

OTHER MONEY SOURCES: PRIVATE PLACEMENTS

That is just a fancy term for selling part or all of your new business directly to investors. But it usually involves big money. If your father invests $50,000 in your business and gets a piece of it, he is helping out a family member. If he invests $500,000, it is a private placement.

There is an informal network of people out there who are sufficiently well endowed that they can go around making big investments in new businesses. But you won't find them in phone books or private placement directories. One of the reasons why people join country clubs, go to cocktail parties, and attend charity benefits is to connect with somebody who has money. One of my franchisees got onto the fringes of it by learning how to play golf at an early age and hustling people on the golf course. That's an absolutely viable way of getting started. It is a fact of life that most businesses get going because somebody knows somebody who knows somebody, and it all comes together with some sort of deal.

You have to work hard at these. Most of the business

connections people make happen by chance. You stumble over them. But like anything else, you have to make your own luck. If you aren't out there snooping around, you won't stumble over anything.

Making Your Pitch

To get in the door of someone who has money, you need a big thick document—fifty or more pages, lots of numbers, bound in an impressive folder—called a private placement memorandum. What it basically does is explain why your idea for a new business is a terrific one and can't miss. Since it is not a prospectus that has to be registered with the Securities and Exchange Commission, you can paint a rosy picture of your prospects.

Once you have presented your case, you get attacked by the piranhas—the people with the money. They will try to ask you questions for which you don't have any answers. Samples: What happens if there is a recession? What about the competition you haven't identified yet? Suppose all your customers die?

A friend of mine is trying to raise money for a redfish farm. He is a smart guy, there is a shortage of redfish because blackened redfish is so popular in restaurants, and the technology is accessible. Give him some money, and he will start growing redfish. But the private placement guys are tough. They ask him, "This isn't a high-technology deal, why should I invest?" or "How are you going to distribute the fish?" and "How can you protect yourself from the ruinous effects of competition if fifteen other people start growing redfish?"

There is no such thing as a perfect deal, so you have to be able to dance around the questions for the private placement guys. If you can't, they are going to tear you to pieces.

In my opinion, the kinds of questions you typically are asked have very little to do with reality. They are predictable, safe, cover-your-backside questions that don't for a minute address the kind of constant aggravation you have to deal with in business. They really don't get to the heart of the matter: whether or not the proposed business makes any sense.

When you go into business, you hold your nose, jump in, and then try to come up for air every couple of minutes. The money guys never seem to realize that. It makes you wonder there they got *their* business experience.

BUSINESS BROKERS

In theory, a business broker is someone you hire to raise money for you in exchange for a percentage of the amount. I would say that the general quality of the business brokers out there is somebody who just beat death row at Sing Sing. They are the biggest animals in business. I've never met an honest one in my life. Not that they are all crooks, but you go to them with an idea, they say, "That's great, I'll get you all the money you need in twenty-four hours," and then you find them floating in the East River.

When I was trying to sell the restaurant that preceded Chez Louis, I had at least three business brokers say to me they could move it for the amount I was asking, which wasn't a lot of money. Not one of them ever produced an offer.

Business brokers tend to advertise their services in financial magazines and newspapers. Don't bother trying to get anybody who advertises to raise money for you. Chances are, their real business is getting schmucks like you to pay them up-front finder's fees. If they were any good at raising money, they wouldn't have to advertise.

LOAN SHARKS

One of the rules of my game is that I have nothing to do with the mob. They are all over the city. You have to be out of your mind to go to loan sharks because if you don't pay, they'll kill you. Even if you are desperate, I do not recommend it.

CREDIT CARDS

They are right there in your wallet, and they can be a big help. They won't get you all the money you need, but they can sure help fill in the gaps. Some cards now have credit lines of $10,000 or more. MasterCard or VISA didn't care whether you are going to Disney World on vacation or buying inventory for a plumbing supply store as long as they get their money back plus interest.

According to June Lavelle, who runs a small-business consulting firm in Chicago and was quoted in the *Wall Street Journal*, credit card financing "is becoming enormously common." She estimates that 50 percent of the companies she deals with use them, because in many cases it is the only kind of credit they can get. One of her clients, who runs a housewares importer, uses as many as eight credit cards, with credit lines totaling nearly $25,000.

The thing to remember, of course, is that credit card money isn't exactly cheap. Most credit cards will charge you 1½ percent a month or eighteen percent plus a year. If you are able to borrow money from a bank, it will be a lot less expensive. That is a big if, as you will now learn.

BANKS

The most obvious place to go for money is a bank. Forget about it. It is still a universal truth that banks lend money only to people who don't need it. Sometimes even if you don't need it, they still won't loan it to you. The reason is simple. Banks basically are asset-based lenders, which means they want collateral for any money they loan you. Sometimes they will take stocks, or your house, or your first-born child. Your not-yet-up-and-running business isn't an asset, no matter how good it sounds to you. A bank is not going to lend you money until you are way into the game and have a proven track record, cash flow, and assets that they can grab if something goes wrong.

Hold Your Nose

Eventually, you are going to have to deal with banks. Even though they aren't about to lend you money, you might as well start early to establish a rapport. Who knows, you may need a commercial checking account. Chances are, you'll have better luck with a smaller bank. It is not true that only Citibank, First Chicago, Wells Fargo, and Sumitomo have all the money. There are thousands of banks out there on every street corner that take money in and put it out, because that is how they make money. And they aren't all doing mortgages. Every day, big banks reject 95 percent of the loan requests they get. And every day, 95 percent of the companies get funded somewhere else. Where they go represents the whole underbelly of the banking system.

I would start with a neighborhood branch office. That will give you a chance to practice your pitch. The way you apply for a loan is by going to see a banker and making a presentation. The banker will either be impressed or not impressed. If the banker is impressed, he will ask for more information. Then he will take you to the loan committee, which varies in size depending on the size of the loan. And they either will or won't make the loan.

If by some lucky chance you get a loan, here is how it works. The banks are going to be looking at the cash flow of the business because that is how they believe they are going to get paid back. While they may ask for your house as collateral, they don't really want to have to go out there and grab it if you don't pay the loan off. They are in the money business, not the real estate business.

Don't Believe Those Advertisements That You Have a Friend at the Bank

Your relationship with a bank is only as good as your relationship with a loan officer at the bank. Unfortunately, if the loan officer is any good, he or she is going to get promoted very quickly. Then your relationship is pffft, and you have to start all over again with someone else.

I heard a horror story a little while ago about a bank that loaned a lot of money to jewelers. Jewelry is a tough business because the assets are usually in somebody's pocket. One day, out of the blue, the bank decided it didn't want to be in the jewelry business any more. So the loan officers walked up and down Forty-Seventh Street, where many of Manhattan's jewelers are located, and told all their customers that they had thirty days to move their loans somewhere else. Some of the jewelers couldn't and had to go out of business. The bank effectively shut them down.

That's True Even at My Bank

Once you get started with a bank, try to pick out a banker who you believe has a future in the bank. He or she is going to get responsibility to loan more and more money as you expand, and you will *need* more and more money.

I went to a big New York bank four-and-a-half years after I got started in the cookie business. The guy I got there was a genius. He understood the volatility of my particular business, and he loaned money against my cash flow projections. He was the right guy, but I lost out. He did such a phenomenal job that he got promoted three or four times. He went up the ladder *too* fast.

The turnover at banks is enormous. You hold onto a loan officer, and then he either quits or is stolen by somebody else. Since my guy moved, there have been three other people I have dealt with. But there is no stability there, so every time a new one comes in, you have to establish a new relationship. If you can't, you become an entry in the computer system. That can kill you because the computer doesn't know what you are doing. Then it doesn't want to make you any loans. No matter what banks say, you are only a number on an account. You have to fall within various computerized criteria to maintain or increase your loan. It is really an incredibly depersonalized relationship.

From what I hear, this is less of a problem outside New

York. Regional banks are nicer, and the loan officers stay where you can always find them. In our case, we've wasted a lot of time finding an individual to talk to at a big bank.

You'd think they would treat me better. The fact of the matter is that most banks have to depend on their small and midsize business customers for the bulk of their profits. If Chemical Bank lends money to David's Cookies, I'm going to pay 1½ percent above prime, because I don't have a lot of options. They aren't making any money on loans to South America these days. And they lend money to big corporations for less than the prime rate. If I were a huge corporation, I would say, "The hell with banks." I'd be a bank myself. Ford Motor Company, with $10 billion in cash, probably has more cash than most banks.

The moral is, if you can figure out a way to use banks, good. If you can figure out a way to avoid banks, that is even better.

Find a Cosigner

One way to get a loan is to find somebody to cosign it who is good for the money if you go belly up. For example, there is this restaurant I'm thinking of backing in Aspen, Colorado. (Yes, it's crazy. I shouldn't be investing in any restaurant that I'm not running, especially one that is 2,000 miles away. But it will give me an excuse to go skiing, and I love to ski.)

It is called Lauretta's—a down-home place in a sea of glitz. It is a fantastic Mexican restaurant—all the locals eat at Lauretta's. With just two long tables in a tiny room, it does up to 350 dinners a night. The food is phenomenally good, and it is cheap. I initially became enamored of Lauretta's through the food, and then when I met Lauretta, I became enamored of her. I told her I would help her make her business bigger. So we went looking for real estate. While I was there, I said to her, "It seems to me that with all the money in this town, the banks would be tripping over themselves to loan you money because you are a known entity. You are not some bicoastal bimbo—the president of the bank and his secretary are eating in your restaurant every night." The problem is since she has been in business for only a year and a half, she doesn't have enough of a track record. So, if we find the right location, I will go in there and cosign her loan, and if she doesn't screw up, she will have a killer of a restaurant.

Shop Around

There are all kinds of loan deals out there. In truth, a small entrepreneur doesn't have a big choice. If he gets a loan commitment, he is going to want to kiss the banker's feet, not try to bargain for ½ percent less.

The typical deal is that the bank will want to amortize the loan over five years, probably with a moratorium on principal payments for the first year. That means you pay only the interest for the first twelve months.

There are all kinds of variations on that. You can amortize the loan over ten years, but take a balloon after five years. A balloon is a final payment that is substantially larger than the preceding payments. So if you borrow $100,000, you amortize or pay off $20,000 over the first four years and eleven months. When the loan is due in five years, you owe the bank $80,000—a big balloon. The bank has given you breathing room for your start-up; you have to believe you are doing well enough when the time comes to deflate the balloon. Or refinance it.

Taking that shot is basically what entrepreneurship is all about. You are gambling that some way you are going to come up with that $80,000. Meanwhile, if you are paying down just $20,000, you have room to survive. A lot of bankers don't like to make balloon loans because the money doesn't come back that quickly. But for you, it's the best deal you can get.

Projections

To get a loan from anybody, especially a bank, you have to show them some numbers that mean something. Most financial projections are baloney if they extend beyond one year, but I believe you can make some sensible ones for the first twelve months. For your loan, it is very important to come up with a set of numbers for the first year that are conservative and make sense. You want to be able to show that you have enough cash flow at the end of the first year to pay back the loan.

It really gets down to whether the banker is going to believe the projections you give him and whether or not he believes you are the right jockey to ride that business. A lot depends on whether your business makes sense to him. I'm not going to go into a banker and say, "Look, I'm going to open up a store in the middle of Manhattan that people are going to come into to be made fat. They are going to gain ten pounds as soon as they walk in." No matter how good my numbers are, I don't think too many bankers would believe there is a market for that kind of store.

On the other hand, my latest idea—selling no-cholesterol muffins out of my cookie stores—makes sense, especially to a banker who is sitting around, out of shape, overweight, and has junk in his blood. Every day he can pick up a newspaper and see a story about cholesterol. So when I approach him about my idea, he can say, "Yeah, I've heard about that."

Are the muffins a fad? Who knows? Ultimately, everything is trendy—except for Twinkies. Whoever thought they would be around for thirty years?

Tell Your Banker Everything

It doesn't help to try to hide things—if things can go wrong, it will only make things worse. The courtesy to your banker is to let him in on the bad news early. That way if something starts to go wrong, he has the ability to cover his behind with the powers that be.

Very early in my business career, my banker looked me in the eye and said, "David, never f—- a bank." You live by that.

What to Do If Your Loan Gets Called

First of all, the bank is not suddenly going to notify you one day that it is calling your loan. There will be a long series of discussions preceding that. You will get a very strong indication from the lender that something is wrong. You can try to renegotiate the loan. You can also try for a moratorium on interest payments.

Most businesses are not feast-or-famine-type businesses. It is either slow growth or slow death. For instance, we are de-emphasizing the cookie store business because the growth isn't there. At a certain point you realize that you can wake up every morning and get bashed against the wall by these franchisees and still not go anywhere. Or you can choose a different direction. That's what I've done. That's why I'm getting into supermarkets and other retail outlets. Our private label cookie program is going into Wendy's outlets. If it takes off, we could be supplying 100,000 pounds of cookie dough a week to Wendy's. That's more than we ever sold to our cookie stores. All of which is a long way of saying that you can see a trend in business long before you reach a crisis.

A Risky Method of Getting Money Out of Banks

Banks don't like lending money to businesses because if the cash flow doesn't develop along the lines of the projections, they don't get paid. They are eager to lend money for real estate because they can always grab the asset behind the loan—the building. They don't like to do that, but they can see the building and know they can sell it.

Here is how to make that work in your favor. If you can arrange to buy a building, or even your own space in a commercial cooperative, it will help you finance your business.

Let's say you have a business that needs financing as well as a place to locate. So you create a lease between the business and a building with yourself as landlord in which you agree to pay yourself, say, $1 million a year in rent. Then you take the lease to the bank to use as collateral for a loan. What you are in effect doing is securing the mortgage on the building with a retail operation.

Banks today seem to be leveraging those kind of deals between eight and twelve times. They may loan you $8 million or more on the basis of that lease, which you then use to buy the building for some amount less than that. That is not a particularly good lease because you are the only guarantee behind it. But if you say to the bank that the collateral for this lease is the building, they will lend you some money; if the business goes bad, they get the building. Presto: your business essentially now has free rent. You are able to plow the money you would use for rent back into the business. The banker can look at the retail operation and say, "Yes, you have a chance to make it, and if you don't, I'll grab the building."

The other way to do this is to buy a building with some extra space in it that you don't need for your business. You tell the banker that you will rent that extra space at a discount from the market just to give the bank another stream of income to amortize the mortgage. What's good about this is that it really does work. In most metropolitan areas there is a market in commercial real estate, and the market is highly competitive. So if you go in there and shave two bucks off the market rates, you are going to fill your building up in a hurry. So the mortgage is safe, and the bank can give you some money for your business.

The one downside of this is that you are now running two businesses: your own and the building. That's an extra level of aggravation, as you will find out from my discourse on landlords. But if it is the only way you can get financing, you ought to consider it.

BOOTSTRAPPING

As somebody smarter than I am once said, "Where there is a

will, there is a way." When I wanted to open my first cookie store in 1979, I figured it would cost me about $100,000. By tapping my father, my soon-to-be-wife, my piggy bank, and my creditors (by not paying my bills for a while), the most I could come up with was $50,000.

So I figured out a way. Back then, the construction business was very depressed in New York City. There was nothing being built. But there were contractors who wanted to keep their crews busy. So I went to them and said, "Look, I want you to build this cookie store. But I only have enough for a down payment. I'm going to give you an IOU for the rest."

In good times, that never would have worked. Those contractors want cash or nothing because if they don't get it from me they can get it somewhere else. Since business wasn't so good, they agreed to it.

Basically, I borrowed $45,000 from the contractors. I agreed to pay back those IOUs in twelve months. If David's Cookies had gone bankrupt, they would have been left holding the bag. But it was a chance they were willing to take because they had nothing else to do at the time. As it was, they got paid off. That was then. Today, contractors are so busy they won't give you the time of day. But something else will work, if you want it to badly enough.

BOTTOM LINE

Unless you have your own nest egg and are willing to risk it on yourself, there is no perfect place to get money. Friends and family are the easiest to borrow from, but being a debtor can put a real strain on the relationship. Banks aren't going to lend you money, and you don't want to mess around with the guys you meet in a bar. If you go the partnership route, check out your partners very carefully. And consider less conventional methods, such as using a lease to collateralize a loan.

8
VULTURE CAPITALISTS

Well, yes, I know they are really called venture capitalists. In the aggregate, they do do good things for entrepreneurs. Name a successful company in the past ten years that started from scratch, and chances are the venture capital was involved in the start-up: Federal Express, Apple Computer, Genentech, and so on.

But when you sit down with them face to face to try to get money, these guys are absolute tigers. Most of them are really aggressive. They have to be: they are out beating the bushes for new companies, trying to find them before their competitors do and trying to negotiate the best deal they can when they put up the money. Once you let venture capitalists into your company, you better be careful. Start to foul up, and you are out on your ear. They are absolutely heartless when it comes to dumping somebody—even if that person started the company—if the business isn't doing well. They have done it so often it is almost a cliché. Once a company gets to a certain size, they figure the guy who started it isn't up to running it because starting businesses, not running them, is what he is good at. So he goes out with a fat consulting contract, and the venture capitalist installs his own chief executive officer—sometimes himself.

THE INEVITABILITY OF VENTURE CAPITAL

Chances are, if you start your own business, you are going to wind up at some point talking to a venture capitalist. They are all over the country, not just Manhattan, and they are all looking to do deals. As I sit here right now, there is a ton of venture capital money out there. Too much money is chasing not enough good deals. With the new tax law and the inability to shelter any income—the reality is that there are no real tax shelters left—venture capitalists are looking for growth or income-producing businesses. It is not always that way. Sometimes there are too many deals chasing too little money.

Unlike banks, venture capitalists don't just lend you money over a certain period of time for a certain amount of interest. They want a piece of the action. In the early 1980s, venture capitalists were looking to put up a certain amount of money in return for a certain percentage of the business without getting any income for two, three, even four years. That was fine if the business was a hit, but very expensive if the business failed. Now they want a payback sooner. With the stock market in the dumps as I write this, it is very difficult for them to cash out with a big, prosperous stock offering.

There are a lot of books that publish lists of venture capitalists. This isn't one of them. You'll have to find one on your own. At a basic level, if you are not able to find a venture capitalist without my telling you where to look, you don't deserve to be in business.

HIGH-TECH VS. LOW-TECH

You basically find two kinds of venture capitalists out there. Meat-and-potatoes venture capitalists believe in businesses where you buy an apple for a nickel, try to sell it for six cents, and grow slowly in a nonsexy industry. Then you have the high-tech venture capitalists who want to put up a dollar and make $1 million. They know the odds are worse than shooting craps because most of their choices are wrong, and high-tech companies usually go no place but into the toilet. But the payoff when they score big with an Apollo Computer or Microsoft makes it worthwhile.

High-tech companies haven't paid off very well in the last couple of years. Lately I have been seeing more venture capitalists become interested in low-tech businesses. They know they are not going to triple their money in the first month, but they also know the business has a better chance to survive.

My no-cholesterol muffins would make a perfect low-tech venture capital deal. The muffins are timely, they taste good, they are selling, everybody seems to like them. It is a good product to pitch now, as opposed to high-calorie ice cream. Can you imagine running an ad that says "Häagen-Dazs is 1,200 calories a pint, but ours is 2,400." That would be the wrong kind of product to be pitching. Lucky for me, I am rolling out my muffins myself on the cheap, one store at a time.

IT'S NOT YOUR PRODUCT, IT'S YOU

Most venture capitalists are betting on the jockey, not the horse. They don't care much about the idea. Anybody can come up with a brilliant idea, put it down on paper, and make it seem like it is going to work. They want somebody who they think has the right stuff to make the idea pay off. One venture capitalist told me that what they are really looking to invest in is the person with the twitch factor who can build a profitable business.

HOW TO GET A VENTURE CAPITALIST TO BET ON YOU

I think people who go out there to sell their idea to venture capitalists should practice a little bit on their mother, or spouse, or dog to see if the story they are telling makes any sense.

Much like an actor or a trained athlete uses pent-up emotions, you have to get your story down so that a venture capitalist who has just met you for the first time and, if you are lucky, spent an hour with you, will get a sense of (1) whether you do or do not know what you are talking about; (2) whether the thing you are talking about has a chance of making money; and (3) whether you are the person to make it make money.

The key to selling yourself to venture capitalists, whether they are animals or angels, is that when you go in to demonstrate whatever it is you have, you better know what you are talking about and you better project the image that you are the right person to do this. You can't go in there and say, "I'm going to hire the right marketing guy and the right financial officer and the right this one and the right that one," because the person who is ultimately going to be responsible for getting this business up and running, and the person whom they are investing in, is you. If you don't know what you are talking about, they are not going to invest in some marketing person they never met before.

HOLLYWOOD COMES TO MAIN STREET

What is happening now is that venture capitalists are looking for a point guy who has some kind of track record—good or bad, it doesn't really matter—and who knows how to pull the pieces together. This person goes out and finds an operating person, maybe a manufacturing person and an accounting person, and puts them all together. Then he takes this group of people, who supposedly cover all the bases of the kind of firm they are going to run, and takes them to a venture capital firm to get the money.

It is just like Hollywood. The agent or producer packages the stars, director, and script and then takes them all to a studio to get financing. It works because people are credential crazy. As long as the people in your package have the right pedigree, you are golden.

USE CAUTION

I have heard of cases of people coming in with well thought out ideas that probably were viable, but the venture capitalist didn't think they were the right person to drive that idea. So the venture capitalist took the idea to someone else. In other words, they found themselves a new jockey.

It is not nice, but it is one of the risks of the game. If you don't have a patent, trademark, or some proprietary right when you go to a venture capitalist, you are prime meat to get your idea stolen if they don't think you are the right person.

CUTTING A DEAL

One of the psychological tricks that venture capitalists use is trying to make whatever you are talking about seem insignificant, to make you seem trivial, to make you believe that you bring very little to the party.

It happened to me. A few years ago, I decided I wanted to buy Zabar's, the famous New York specialty store, and I took the deal to a venture capitalist to raise money. I had really thought this thing out, and I figured that if anybody was going to buy Zabar's, I was the right person to do it. The guy I saw went and hooked up with another group of venture capitalists. Then they started driving down my price. They tried to make me believe that Zabar's was a start-up business because it had no track record and no audited numbers. I knew that Zabar's was making over $5 million a year. I told them, *"Schmuck*, go there and look, go stand in line. Somebody is making money there. Something is going on in that store that involves people taking food and handing over money at the cash register. If they are not, somebody is stealing a lot of money." The net result of this conversation was that they wanted me to put up most of the money while they got most of the equity. I told them to buzz off.

What I wound up doing was taking the deal to Drexel Burnham Lambert, the investment bank. Through a combination of junk bonds and some money I would put in, we figured out a way to raise $27 million. They wanted to give me 33 percent ownership. I thought, "This is silly." Then I realized that I didn't have $27 million, so the deal didn't look so bad. Even though I didn't have majority ownership, I had operational control. So it was not bad for somebody who was basically going into the deal with no money. Sad to say, Zabar's decided not to sell.

FIGURING OUT HOW MUCH YOU NEED

Recently I was investigating the purchase of a macadamia nut farm. I needed to find out only one essential piece of information: could the deal carry the financing? I didn't care if the projections for nut production five years from now were accurate. I cared only about getting over year number one, because if I got over year number one, I could look at year number two. But if I couldn't get over year number one, then I didn't have to worry about the next year because I didn't have enough money to get there. The whole analysis was based on twelve months out.

That's a guideline for any business: make it through the first year. If you can't make it through the first year, forget it. Lightning probably isn't going to strike.

ASK FOR THE MOON

In terms of what kind of deal you can get from a venture capitalist, there is no formula.

You have to make sure that you ask for more money than you actually need. Even though you may feel stupid, you need to do that to give yourself some bargaining room.

A venture capitalist will say to you, "Listen, you say that all you need is $100,000, which will get you through two years, and you won't need another shot of financing until the third year." You say yes, because all you can think about is getting your hands on that $100,000.

The guy will ask you that question four or five times, and you will answer yes each time because you want the money. What he is really doing is setting you up. If you come back before those two years are up and say you want more money, you are dead meat. He may give you more money, but he will take an even bigger chunk of your business. You are no longer partners with this guy—you work for him.

I've seen this happen time and time again. People will go in and underestimate how much money they need, and later they have to go back to the well.

What usually happens is the business is going OK but you need more money. He will say, "But I relied on your business judgment that this was all the money you needed. How can I trust you in the future? I'm going to give you another $50,000 but I'm taking another 30 percent of the business." So by the time this charade is over, you are going to end up with 1 percent of the equity and your job, if you are lucky, and he's going to own the company, with which he's going to do whatever the hell he wants.

Make sure that whatever you go in to ask for is too much, not too little. Then you can always back down. But don't go in there and say, "Oh, yeah. I can compete with General Motors for $5.53."

LEVERAGE

You don't have a lot of leverage when you are negotiating with a venture capitalist. What you have to do is follow a basic rule of negotiating: put yourself in the other guy's shoes.

The first thing you have to do is figure out whether they have tons of money or no money. As I speak, there are tons of money out there, and everybody is chasing a few can't-miss deals. What is happening is that the two kinds of deals are converging. Venture capital guys want to make a big hit, but they want absolute security, something as safe as municipal bonds. They want to make computer software profits by selling apples for six cents. That ultimately is an absurdity. A venture capitalist wants a 20 percent to 70 percent annual return on his money. To get that, he has to take a risk.

Your real leverage is knowing venture capitalists are in business to do business. They have to put their money out, or they are not going to get that return. So even though they are very cautious, they will keep doing deals. Even if they get burned nine times out of ten, they still want to do that tenth deal. It could be a home run that will pay for all the other strikeouts.

Second, when you are negotiating a deal, what you are doing is outlining a relationship. Eventually, if one party doesn't like it, he is going to offer to either buy out the other guy or sell out to him at a given price, which is usually pretty fair. Usually, the guy who is doing the work, somebody like me, has the edge. If the venture capitalists buy him out, then somebody else has to run the business.

It would be worthwhile to read business magazines before you start out to find out what kind of deals are available. Then you can always say, "Why are you offering this when I read the other day in *Fortune* that this guy is getting that?" That always works. It always slows down the negotiation. It gets you breathing room.

DIMENSIONS OF THE DEAL

The rule is there are no rules. You can end up owning anywhere from less than 1 percent to nearly 100 percent of your business.

The traditional arrangement is the sweat-equity deal: you get 50 percent of the business in return for devoting your life to making the business get up and go, and they put up all the money for the other 50 percent of the business.

There are some new wrinkles to the traditional 50–50 deal. Most of the venture money I have seen out there lately is looking to invest on a preferred stock basis. It is less risky for them but not so good for you. With preferred stock, they not only get dividends when the business starts making a profit, but they also get the opportunity to convert the preferred into common stock at negotiated terms. If the business gets bigger, the value of the common stock goes up. So from day one, the money is making anywhere from 7 percent to 10 percent on the investment. If at all possible, you shouldn't agree to that kind of deal because it is better to get the money as equity rather than preferred stock, so you don't have to pay the interest.

JOINT VENTURES

I'm going through something like this with my Chez Louis restaurant. Chez Louis is a proven winner—the concept works. People like the hearty food and big portions, and I think it is duplicatable. I think it is the kind of restaurant that I can open more of without having the ongoing problems of a very fancy French nouvelle cuisine restaurant. So I have been looking to open Chez Louises in other cities.

One of the things I refuse to do again is to become a professional debtor. Since I don't really have to, I don't want to borrow the money from somebody. So I have been talking to real estate syndicators. Together, we can buy a building to put the restaurant in, I would get a piece of the building, they would get a piece of Chez Louis, and we would probably have third parties buy in who would have nothing to do with the ongoing business and would be totally insulated from coming back to us. That way I would get some equity in real estate, they would get some equity in a restaurant, and neither one of us would have to hock our souls.

That is probably the best kind of deal, where both people are dealing from strength, as opposed to my getting on my knees and begging the venture capitalist for money. There will be more of those deals happening because of the tax laws. It is not enough any more to go into negative cash flow real estate deals to get the tax benefits. Real estate has to

generate some real income. The way that real estate developers get that income is from a successful restaurant operation. That's something to think about once you get your
business growing and want to expand.

THE SAUCIER EXPERIENCE

There are some venture capitalist stories with happy end-
ings. One of them even happened to me.

A guy named Jamie Niven, who is the head of a venture
capital firm called Pioneer Ventures, financed my first
company Saucier. I went to Jamie in 1976 with what I
realize now was a very rough and sophomoric business
plan. I had a product and I had an idea the product would
be unique and necessary, but that was all. I had no packaging and no distribution.

I got Jamie to invest in the company on the basis of a
lunch that I cooked him one day. He liked the food, so he
found enough investors to put up $150,000, which was the
only capital we ever had in the business. The deal was a
classical venture capital deal: he got half of the equity for
his money, my partner and I got the other half for our idea.

Jamie gave us the money and left us alone. We'd have
lunches every couple of months to fill him in on the prog-
ress. After we ran through the $150,000, which wasn't nearly
enough money to compete with the big boys in the pack-
aged-food business, we all sat down. We really needed $2
million to $3 million to advertise and promote and do all
the things that you have to do for a product that is very
esoteric and not easily understood by the consumer. I wasn't
getting rich, by the way. I was taking only $1,500 a month
out of the company, which wasn't very much to live on.

We realized that we weren't prepared to put any more
money into Saucier because we really didn't have a shot at
the big time. I was thinking about how to get into the
cookie business, so I dragged my brother into the business
and he took over the company. He ran it well enough to
make a little bit of money, because he cut the overhead down

to nothing. Then he sold it for $120,000. Eleven years later it is still here. It is no threat to taking over Procter & Gamble, but it is a nice little product with a niche.

And that may be all Saucier is worth. Jamie got some of his money out. With all the tax-loss carryforwards, he probably broke even. We broke up on good terms. Jamie is still a friend of mine, and he still eats at my restaurant all the time.

BOTTOM LINE

Raising money will be one of the most creative things you do when you start your own business. In all likelihood, conventional sources won't be available to you, so you'll have to be innovative. Borrow more than you think you'll need and remember that the venture capitalist doesn't have all the leverage. Most important, always try to leave yourself an out. You never want to sign your life away.

9
WHEELING AND DEALING

With me, everything is always up for grabs. My business tactics are totally unconventional. I don't do anything by the book.

As a result, I am willing to bargain for anything. If I get it, fine; I've got something I want at a good price on terms I can live with. If I don't, well, then I move on to the next project.

I was also willing to arrange crazier finances than most people. When I was starting out, I would try anything. I didn't care whether I was up to my neck in debt as long as the numbers worked. But if something looks too good and comes too easily or quickly, I get suspicious.

There isn't anybody who has to do business the way I do. But my insights and techniques should prove educational.

SEEING THE OTHER GUY'S POINT OF VIEW

One of the tricks I always use in a negotiation is that I never negotiate for myself. I always negotiate from the other guy's point of view—what he is thinking about, what he is doing, what his goals are. It is very effective in the middle of a negotiation to say, "Let me argue your side; let me tell you what you should be getting." He will say, "Yeah, that's right; that's what I should be getting," and you've got him.

Ultimately, the only kind of deals that are going to work long term are the ones that are equitable going in. It has to work on both sides. The success rate of deals where somebody pulls the wool over somebody else's eyes is not terrific.

BUYING TIME

In any negotiation, small talk works. It helps to fill in the gaps. By the same token, you should go into a negotiation with a partner, so that you can pass the ball off when things get hot and heavy. "What do *you* think, Jack?" I don't know anybody who negotiates his deals one-on-one from beginning to end.

BE TOUGH

If anybody thinks they will get everything they want going into a negotiation, they are crazy. But if you really don't care whether you lose the deal, you are better able to stick to your position. I did that when I was thinking about selling my old restaurant, Manhattan Market. I set my price and terms, and a buyer said fine. So we went to the closing, and I warned the broker that if there was any deviation from the terms, the deal was off. The buyer tried to hit me up for a couple of thousand dollars extra, and I walked. That was the end of that deal.

As it happened, it was a good thing, because I turned that restaurant into Chez Louis, and we are doing fine.

REHEARSE

Go over the negotiation in advance to anticipate the what-ifs. It is OK to write a little script in your own head. "What happens if they say this; what happens if they say that?"

BLUFF

What do you do when you don't hold the high card? You bluff, just like in poker. Here's an example. You want to buy this glass from Tom over there, and he wants six dollars for it. You also know that Jerry will sell you a similar glass for four dollars, although you don't want to buy it from him because he is a pain in the neck. But you tell Tom his price is too high and you can get it cheaper from Jerry. If he knows you can get it for four dollars the price will come tumbling down. It is this bluff, based on your knowledge of the market, that you will go somewhere else that can swing the deal in your favor.

Never be afraid of losing a deal. If you aren't mentally prepared to walk away from it, you can't negotiate success- fully. But there are no hard and fast rules about when to leave the table to look for a better deal.

GOING FOR BROKE

How do you buy something for nothing, especially when that something is worth $16 million? Here's how.

In 1988, I was negotiating to buy a macadamia nut farm in Australia. There is a world shortage of macadamia nuts, and I use a lot of them in my cookies. But owning a macada- mia nut farm is not a high priority for me, so going in I set up some absurd criteria. Besides, I knew the owners had a tough sales on their hands because the farm had been on the market over a year. Basically, I offered to buy the largest macadamia farm in Australia for $10 million on one condi- tion: they find all the money. I wouldn't put up a nickel.

Sounds crazy? Here is how it worked. I met with the two owners, and I convinced them that the deal was a good one. Since I'm 12,853 miles away from those nut trees, they would have to stay on as managers. As incentive, I would let them keep 25 percent of the deal in return for taking back a note for $2 million or so.

Then I went to an Australian bank in New York to get the major chunk of the money. The land is worth $16 million if it is developed as real estate. I got the bank to put up $8 million. So with the note from the partners and the money from the bank, I had my $10 million.

Next, I needed some working capital. So I went to my Japanese partners, who already own an interest in David's Foods, and asked for $2 million. In exchange, I would give them half of my interest in the farm. Since I was giving 25 percent to the guys who already run it, I would keep 37½ percent and give the Japanese the other 37½ percent. So I wind up with 37½ percent of a $16 million property for nothing.

To be sure, this deal is not going to be any cream puff to float. If it goes through, the farm will be carrying a debt of $10 million to $11 million. That means it will have to produce cash flow on the order of $1 million a year just to handle the interest payments. But I'm confident. Among other things, the Japanese market is ripe for exploitation. Macadamia nuts are small, elegant, and tasty—perfect as a Japanese gift item. Plus, they are expensive, and nobody likes luxury goods better than the Japanese. Right now they are buying all the BMWs and Mercedes-Benzes they can get their hands on and paying $100,000 or more to join a country club so they have some place to drive them.

HOW MUCH DEBT?

The Australian deal illustrates another important point: how much debt do you deal with? The answer: it depends. What's reasonable is how much you can stand. If you wake up one morning and say, "Oh, my God. I have only $10 in the bank. What am I going to?" then it is too much. On the other hand, I know plenty of people who owe hundreds of millions of dollars, and they sleep like puppy dogs.

The Trumps of this world probably know it better than anybody. For the amount of brain power and aggravation you put into a deal, it makes absolute sense to put as many zeros in to it as possible. In other words, grab all the debt you can. The amount of work is no different, and the rules of the game haven't changed. The trick is making sure your liability ends within the confines of the deal and you don't have your house on the line if it goes sour.

Negotiating a lease for a 10,000-square-foot warehouse is the same as negotiating a lease for a 1-million-square-foot office building. They both take an ability to wake up in the morning and say, "I can deal with this." If you owe a million dollars and don't pay it back, you can hurt really badly but no worse than if you don't pay back $10,000.

The danger sign is simple: when you are not making enough money to pay the interest on the debt, you are in trouble. You have to see a point where the cash flow will carry the interest charges. You either have to go out and get some more money or think about folding it up.

Which raises another issue: at what point do you give your debtors a piece of your business so you have less debt and are not paying so much in interest? That is a gut reaction. Would you rather own 1 percent of a going business or 100 percent of a dead one?

Debt is a very personal thing. You should take on as much as you are comfortable with. I can't tell you how much you should have. It is not like going through the steps on how to sign a lease. In theory, you should have no debt, but the only way to get rich is to use other people's money.

HOW MUCH CAPITAL?

I know people who run businesses according to how much they have in their checkbook. It is the ultimate seat-of-the-pants operation, the ultimate method of watching your cash flow. As long as you have money in your checking account, you are solvent. When you don't, you aren't.

The first year you are in business, every supplier is your partner. There is incredible tension in business most of the time because nobody pays anybody on time. So if you are paying for your supplies on time but your customers aren't paying you on time, you have a big hole in your cash flow.

What it turns out to be is a big daisy chain, and it all depends on how good your relationships are with your suppliers and customers. We try to maximize our cash flow as much as possible, just the way Macy's tries to; even the telephone company does the same thing. People are coming out of Harvard Business School trained to program computers so they don't print checks until a couple of months after they are due.

THAT IS ANOTHER AGGRAVATION

On the one hand, you can know that AT&T owes you money, and they are surely good for it. On the other hand, if they aren't going to pay you for 120 or 180 days, it isn't doing you any good because you don't have it.

A time may come when you can't pay your bills in thirty days, or forty-five days, or sixty days because you aren't getting paid. That is reality. I don't know anybody who doesn't have that problem. There isn't a business in the world that doesn't think it will be paid on time and then discovers that it will be paid late or not at all. You have to live with those aggravations every day when you are starting up. The moral is that you are going to wind up with the suppliers who give you the best terms, even though their quality may not be the best. Certainty of payment becomes the overriding consideration.

FACTORING

When your customers are late paying, you have to think about factoring your receivables. When you do that, you are in effect selling your bills for a discount. You give your bills due from customers to a factoring company, which then lends you money based on their face value. Most factoring is what is known as discount factoring, in which you get the money from the factor prior to the due date on the bills. For that, you typically pay a cash discount, plus an allowance for unpaid bills, returns, and so on. You would probably pay the factor an interest rate based on the daily balances, usually 2 percent or 3 percent above the prime rate.

IF YOU ARE NOT MAKING MONEY, HOW LONG DO YOU STICK IT OUT?

In a retail operation you have to figure out whether your market is stagnant, growing, or shrinking. I've caught only two neighborhoods on the upswing: one in SoHo and one in Greenwich Village. More often than not I either caught neighborhoods right at the top or stable neighborhoods. So whatever you are paying in rent, you better make sure you are getting that money back right away. If your monthly profit isn't meeting your monthly expenses, you are in trouble.

The other reality is that your rent is going to keep going up, so you better see some growth ahead. The way that escalators are built into leases, chances are your rent will double in ten years. If you can't see the business growing that much out of the space you are occupying, you better bail out. The reason you see so many retail stores closing is that even if their business is as good or even better than they expected, it wasn't keeping up with the rent escalation.

WATCH THE NUMBERS

One of the early warning signs that your business is in trouble is when you have nothing left to leverage against. That means you have exhausted all your capital, and your assets are fully hocked. When that happens, you better hope you start showing a positive cash flow quickly, because your margin of safety has vanished.

BOTTOM LINE

To this day, I don't have my finances in order. I deal with banks every day, pushing and pulling. But I have made a decision. I want to own the business, not the bank. I didn't sell shares to investors when I started so I could keep control. At times, I've had three times the debt I have now. That makes me nervous. But I was able to pay it off without bringing in any more shareholders. So far, I keep telling myself, so good.

10
LIES, DAMN LIES, AND STATISTICS: THE BUSINESS PLAN

I f you borrow money from anybody reputable, you are going to have to produce a business plan. All a business plan really says is that you would like to start up this operation. Most of the ones I see are garbage. But nobody is going to loan you money unless you have one.

PROJECTIONS AND PROJECTIONS

Most business plans have pages and pages of numbers generated by a personal computer. The key numbers are the ones that show projections for sales and profits.

There has to be some geometric sales growth built into your business plan for somebody to back it. Investors want to see that there's light at the end of the tunnel. If they don't see it they have no reason to invest.

Of course, the numbers are unbelievable. Most business plans have projections going out three years. When you are just starting a business, nobody knows what is going to be happening in six months, much less three years. Most business plans, if you take them off the shelf three years later, won't be within 50 percent of where you said you were going to be.

There is also this magic period around eighteen months out when there is supposed to be positive cash flow. That means there is more money coming in every month than is going out. That's wishful thinking, too. It can also come back to haunt you. You have to anticipate that your backer, whoever he is, is going to be looking at this and saying, "You're in positive cash flow at eighteen months and you're making $25,000 a month—what the hell do you need so much money now for?"

That's a real catch-22 question because the reality is you are not going to be making $25,000 a month. Assuming you were, you'd have 100 competitors by that time. The business network out there is very finely tuned. If you get a winner, then everybody jumps in.

FORECASTING

One of the trends in projecting numbers is that people give you a number and then show you pages of data that supposedly support the original calculation. But none of the numbers reflects any reality. So you have imaginary numbers supporting imaginary numbers.

As you go through the numbers, you have to ask yourself a couple of questions. Are there any margins in the business? In other words, can you make any money at it? Second, what do the numbers mean? Why do expenses go up one year and down the next, and is there a rationale behind them? Sometimes they look too good to be true. You have to ask yourself whether they are believable or not.

TACTICS

The biggest trick in the book is to come in and say you have run the numbers backward and forward and that this is your very conservative estimate about what your business is going to do. And then you look at the person and say, "Let's assume my very conservative estimate is wrong. If I cut the numbers in half, I still make money." Baloney. Half of a phony projection is still a phony projection.

I'm also very skeptical when I see business plans that say things like, "All we have to do is get distribution in 40,000 supermarkets." Well, that's the business. If you can do that, you hardly need a business plan.

People come to me and say that they are going into the all-natural baby food business, that sales are going to be $10 million the first year because their product is terrific, and that represents only 1 percent of the market. They haven't said anything about how they are going to make that much baby food, how they are going to distribute it, or how they are going to get sufficient shelf space in enough stores to sell that much.

If, on the other hand, they say that they have distribution in 40,000 supermarkets and want to grow to 80,000—that's a growth situation. But to come in and say everything is on the come is very dangerous.

LOOK AT THE SHORT TERM

To be realistic, your projections should focus on the following: what it costs to get the business started, what it costs to get the business into its infancy where it is actually producing a product, and what it costs to get the business to a level where you are competing with the big guys. Concentrate on what it costs to get the business going. That way you're telling your backer what you are aiming at.

BETTER YOU SHOULD KNOW SOMETHING

Most venture capitalists are not going to give you any money unless you have gotten a little bit beyond the business plan. What that means is that if you want to go into the business of making delicious brownies, you better have a brownie ready to put in the venture capitalist's mouth. You have to have a real product.

The point I'm trying to make is that it is more impressive to come in to somebody, put a product in front of them, and say, "This is it. This is how I make it; this is what the niche is; this is what I think it is going to cost to make; here are some rough projections," than to just sit and write a plan about the glory of what you are going to do. Your backers don't expect to see sales because you haven't started. They don't expect to see all the problems ironed out, either.

THINK IT THROUGH BEFORE YOU START

The biggest problem in most business plans is that the people have not clearly thought about who was going to buy their product or service. You can't go into the cookie business and say, "Oh, everybody eats cookies, so people are going to buy my cookies." You have to define your market and your competition.

Sometimes you can do it on instinct. I didn't know what I was doing when I went into the cookie business. I didn't have a defined market or product. All I could say was, "I'm going to make the best cookie on the market; you ought to give it a try. Some people will like it, some won't." But I did know what I was going after. I knew that I wanted to reach upwardly mobile people who are interested in better things to eat.

ESTIMATING REVENUES AND COSTS

For any nonfood business, you can't afford to pay more than 10 percent of your revenues in rent. For food, you can pay up to 20 percent, but it depends on location. So if you are not taking in five to ten times your rent, you are in trouble.

Another benchmark: you should be able to break even on a cash flow basis—having your monthly profit match your monthly expenses—within a couple of months. Save the amortization of your capital expenses—equipment, office furniture, and so on—for later. Make sure you are able to pay your help, landlord, and suppliers first.

But you are not really going to know what those cash flow numbers are before you start. If anybody comes to you with a bunch of fancy demographics and tells you that you are going to have 100,000 people waiting in line to buy your cookies, don't believe them. You've got to stand on the corner and ask yourself whether there is a need for your service on this spot. If you have any doubt about that, you shouldn't do it.

PAY YOURSELF ENOUGH BUT NOT TOO MUCH

Among the cost items you have to include in a business plan is how much you want to pay yourself. Be reasonable. Plan to take out of the business only as much as you need to live. No venture capitalist is going to be interested in your having an apartment on Sutton Place, a place in the Hamptons, and a Porsche.

At the same time, there is a very fine psychological line to be drawn. The venture capitalist wants you to be happy, motivated, and interested, because you are the jockey driving his investment. What you should do is say you are taking very little to start, but once the company gets going, you want to take more out. They may or may not agree to that, but it is a good way to begin.

That's a philosophy I have with people. If they make me money, I'll make them money. I really don't care how much they get, as long as they produce. That's why I love salespeople. They get paid for what *they* do, not what I do. If they don't sell anything, they are not going to be working here. If they do sell, they are going to be making a lot of money. There is no confusion about how much to pay somebody like that.

SOME THINGS ALWAYS COST MORE

The expenses that get underestimated early on are legal and

accounting. You'll never get away from your lawyer and your accountant when you're starting up; they will be all over you. And initially the amount of money you would spend on them is totally out of whack with what you would spend in a Fortune 500 company. You need a lot of legal and financial work at the beginning.

The good thing is that the lawyers and accountants are in business just like you are. If you find somebody who is trying to build his business, he may be willing to take you on for less than he would charge an ongoing client. If that person establishes a relationship with you, it could be long term.

Graphics, artwork, packaging—people underestimate those costs, too. If you get professionals to design a package, it costs a lot of money. Witness what goes on in the cosmetics business, where they spend most of their marketing budget on the design and quality of the packages. I'm a believer in hiring first-class designers. What they create is the public face of your product and is absolutely a key to your success.

GOING NAKED INTO THE WORLD

One of the advantages of starting small is that you don't have to go through all this stuff that venture capitalists and bankers and syndicators are going to want. I never wrote a business plan. When I started Saucier, I didn't know what one was. When I started the cookie business, I decided to do it as simply as possible. I would just make the cookie taste as good as I could. Either they liked it or they didn't like it. That was my business plan.

That's definitely a viable way to go. As the business grows, you have your hand on the pulse of it from day one keeping track of the money. The reality is that nobody is going to invest a lot of money with you. That's tough. But in general I think much too much attention is focused on business plans. There are people out there who know only how to write business plans. That doesn't mean that the plans are going to turn into money or that the author knows anything about running a business.

BE FLEXIBLE

Adjust your mental business plan as you go along. You want an ideal situation, but more often than not it doesn't happen that way.

I remember walking the streets of New York for eight months to find an outlet for my first cookie store. I rated the various locations myself because I didn't know anything about real estate. There was a location I really wanted on the corner of Third Avenue and Sixty-seventh Street, but the rent was almost four times more than I could afford to pay. So I said to myself, "Yes, I'd rather be on Third Avenue, but I can't pay that rent. And what if we don't sell any cookies?" The rent on Second Avenue was so cheap that I knew that even if we didn't sell many cookies, I could survive for a couple of months.

SUMMING UP

A business plan is a necessary evil if you are going to raise money from a sophisticated investor. But be realistic. Stay away from blue-sky projections about revenues and profits. Focus on the early stages of the business, where you understand the costs and have better control over them. The people you want to invest aren't stupid; they can see through mindless projections. Make sure you budget plenty of money to pay for professional help, and pay yourself enough but not too much. Never forget: a business plan is a piece of paper. No matter how good it is, it cannot open the store for you in the morning or make sure the customers are happy.

11
SO, YOU ARE READY
TO GO. NOW WHAT?

T he initial reception to your product has been encouraging. You have either raised the money you need or figured out a way to do without it. Now you must discover how to make your product in quantity, identify the market, build a customer base, and figure out how to survive.

HOW TO GET DISTRIBUTION

The only was to develop a market with an unknown product made by a nobody—you—is with chutzpah. That is the way I did it with my first product, Saucier. I was making it in my own kitchen, maybe a couple of gallons at a time. I'd make a lot of stock and reduce it to a thick consistency. Then I put it into little cups, and I had a very rudimentary box I designed. And I went out to sell this stuff to the typical kinds of places you'd want to sell to in New York City: Bloomingdale's, Macy's, Zabar's, Balducci's. And in every case, they threw me out.

I was getting frustrated, so I changed tactics. I sent a

Saucier sample to a reporter at *New York* magazine who, surprise, surprise, loved the product and decided to write about it. When she asked me where it was available, I lied and said it was available at Bloomingdale's. Would it be available in Bloomingdale's next Monday when *New York* magazine comes out? she queried. I said yes.

So I hustled over to the food buyer at Bloomingdale's and said, "You better carry this stuff because next Monday it is going to say in *New York* magazine that it is available at Bloomingdale's." The buyer called me a son of a bitch, but the last thing he wanted was to be embarrassed in front of customers. So he added Saucier to his line, and he did a very good job with it. The only trouble was Bloomingdale's takes months and months to pay its small vendors. So I pulled Saucier out and took it over to Zabar's and Balducci's. It was enough of a hit that I could print up some real boxes, and I could actually afford to have the product made professionally by a commercial food processor.

The business began to grow and all because I had the chutzpah to tell a reporter that it was going to be in Bloomingdale's before it was. Given the overwhelming desire by retailers to be ahead of the competition, it is much easier nowadays to get new products on the shelves of small, fine-food stores. They know that specialty-food products sell. A friend of mine had some cheesecake he was trying to peddle. I told him to go to Murray Klein at Zabar's and tell him that Macy's is carrying it, and he would be in. And he was.

INTRODUCTION TO PRICING

There are several factors in determining a price for your product. You have to know what it costs for the ingredients, labor, packaging, distribution, and overhead. Then you have to get a sense of what someone will pay for your product.

The best scenario is when you can sell for substantially less than everybody else is charging and still make a profit. That is a no-lose situation.

Example: Murray Klein of Zabar's bought thousands of pounds of Belgian chocolate that was originally destined to go to Saks Fifth Avenue. At the last moment, Saks decided it didn't want the stuff, and the importer was stuck with all that chocolate in Saks Fifth Avenue boxes. So he was running all over town trying to sell it. People were saying "I'll take fifty pounds, I'll take 100 pounds," but that didn't do him any good. Murray offered him $2 a pound for the whole lot, which was the cost of shipping and storage charges. Murray had his elves unpack it overnight and put it in his boxes, and the next day he has it on sale as bulk chocolate in Zabar's boxes for $3.95 a pound, marked down from the regular price of $30 per pound. It sold quickly.

Good for Murray. The rest of us have to work a little harder.

COST PLUS VS. VALUE ADDED

If you have to sell your product for what it costs you to make it plus a small profit, you are probably dealing with more of a generic product than you should be. With a cost-plus product you are vulnerable to being knocked off by anybody who can make the same thing for less.

But if you have a value-packed product where you are putting something special into it that nobody else has, you have a lot more flexibility. Eli Zabar sells lobster salad for $60 a pound. That is outrageous, but he figures that any jerk who will pay $40 a pound someplace else might as well pay $60 a pound at Eli's. He has convinced his customers that he is something special, and he's selling a lot of lobster salad.

Once in a great while, you can add value and boost sales just by putting a higher price on a product. When we cannot give a wine away at $14 a bottle in the restaurant, we sometimes raise the price to $20 and it sells. But there is no rhyme or reason. When you get beyond the cost-plus scenario, you are getting into areas even the professional marketers don't understand.

In the case of David's Cookies, I can charge more because I use better ingredients than everyone else, and the cookies are fresh baked. But I add value too. I promote David's Cookies as an upscale, impulse, high-quality experience. Customers are not just getting the finest cookie on the market; they are indulging themselves through luxury eating. My cookies have become known as the ultimate upscale food. I'm not fond of that description. But the "upscale" description says something about the intangibles that have come to surround my cookies and support the price I charge for them.

A PRACTICAL EXAMPLE

A little while ago, I was going through a pricing conundrum with Mitch London, the former chef for New York Mayor Edward Koch at Gracie Mansion. Mitch was making 240 cheesecakes a week that he sold to Zabar's and six other restaurants. He charged Zabar's $7 apiece, and Zabar's sold them for $10. He wanted to get to 500 cheese cakes a week, so he had to think about making them in quantity, getting financing, and so on.

Even if he got to 1,000 cheesecakes, was there any money in it? There were lots of problems. For instance, he could probably sell as many cheesecakes out of Macy's as he could out of Zabar's, but the first thing Macy's would ask is, "What is Zabar's selling the cakes for?" Because it was $10, Macy's would have to charge the same amount. But since it wanted to make a 100 percent profit, it would want Mitch to charge $5.

Basically, if you can work on a gross ingredient margin of 40 percent, you are doing pretty well. So a $5 cheesecake ought to cost you $3 to make. Even at that, I know of very few manufactured-food businesses that are bringing more than 10 percent to the bottom line pretax. Certain products don't have any food cost—bottled water, for example. It is just the cost of a cap, bottle, and label. We should all be so lucky to have a Perrier franchise.

ANOTHER PRACTICAL EXAMPLE

We have been selling cookie dough head-to-head against Pillsbury in supermarket refrigerator cases. Our ingredients cost more, but we have been unable to figure out just how much more we can charge. Recently, we decided to cut the price to $2.99, versus Pillsbury's $2.19–$2.29. Three dollars per package seems to be the magic number; above that, it dies, but under that, it jumps off the shelves. Our volume should really pick up. To get the price that low, we had to cut our profit margin a little bit, but we got the supermarkets to cut their margin somewhat, too.

Where we made our mistake was in not allocating enough money to promote the product properly through advertising. After fifteen months, we were in supermarkets up and down the East Coast. We added two new flavors: peanut butter chocolate chunk and white chocolate chocolate chunk. We need $5 million to do it right. If I had the money, I'd advertise on late-night TV to get the munchie market and after school to get the kids' market. I don't have the money, so we struggled more than we should have.

HOW DO YOU FIND CUSTOMERS?

There is no mystery to getting people to notice what you are doing. All you have to do is figure out who you want to impress and let them know you are out there. Often I will call the media on the phone or drop off a packet of information, and I guarantee they will read it. Some things they will not read as avidly as other things, but they will read it. It is really that simple. You don't need public relations agencies, you don't need image consultants, you don't need media advisers. If you believe in what you're doing, you promote it.

BUILDING A CUSTOMER BASE
THE OLD-FASHIONED WAY

If your business doesn't start off with a bang—and it probably won't—you have to do something that works every time. It is easy to describe but very hard to do: you have to impress every customer with your mission. Then they can go out and tell other people about you. They thus become your advertising vehicle.

Word of mouth is the best kind of publicity you can get. People believe more of what they hear from other people than what they read in the newspaper or see in an advertisement. So instead of spending money on advertising or promotions, we grab people in supermarkets and put cookies in their mouths. We get as close to the customer as we can.

Never lose sight of the fact that the consumer is the objective. That's who you are trying to reach.

GETTING OVER THE HUMP

There are many more companies that survive by growing slower than those that come from nowhere and sell tons of products overnight. McDonald's screwed up everything for the first nine years. They actually sold a franchise in Phoenix and told the guy he could sell whatever he wanted and still use the McDonald's name. It was nearly a decade before Ray Kroc focused on an image of where he wanted the company to be. A company like The Limited, which is an enormous success, barely grew at all at first. The same thing was true of Federal Express.

That's as opposed to a company like Herbalife that exploded and then shrank to practically nothing. Pizza Time Theater and Fuddruckers went from a lot of stores to Chapter 11.

The moral is: you are not going to figure out everything in the first week. You are going to make a lot of mistakes as the business grows, and that's OK. But if you really believe in your product, you should keep on trying. There is nothing wrong with growing slowly. You just have to decide that your product is positioned properly so that it *can* grow. And that is simply a matter of intuitive street smarts. You can't teach somebody how to get behind a product and market it.

That's where their basic entrepreneurial skill is going to have to come through.

DON'T FORGET

The first day you open for business, your mother and your grandmother come in and give you a kiss. But on the second day, you have to show up for work, and you have to show up for work every day after that for the next ten years or more.

Starting a new business is not like going out for dinner where you eat it, pay for it, and then walk out the door. Starting a new business is just the beginning of your problems. People don't understand they are going to have to stick it out. Yes, they are working for themselves, and yes, they don't have a boss, but they still have to show up for work every day. You could argue that if they don't want to go to work on Wednesday, they don't have to because they own the business—but *somebody* has to go to work on Wednesday. You can tell people that, but it goes in one ear and out the other.

When you go to work for yourself, there is a certain rush or high, but ultimately it is work. I guess the best thing is to be independently wealthy or a member of the lucky sperm club and have family money, or to win the lottery. The goal in going to work for yourself should not be getting off the hook so you don't have to do anything. In reality, being your own boss is going to get you in a lot more trouble and be a lot more aggravating. Long term, it will get you more financial security, or it will get you broke. But it won't make life any easier.

PREPARING YOURSELF MENTALLY

I don't think you can be nice in business. You can be fair but not nice. I don't mean not being nice to customers—that's a given. But if somebody who works for me can't do the job, he gets thrown out. I don't hire accountants who can't count or cooks who can't cook, because in the end it is not me they are letting down but the people they work with. They are not carrying their weight.

You have to be tough with your landlord, suppliers and franchisees. I don't know any entrepreneur who doesn't have lawsuits. When I don't have any lawsuits, I get nervous because I worry that I'm not keeping my edge.

HERE GOES

With your product in hand, use guerrilla tactics to get shelf space. Figure out a way to set your own price and not be driven by costs or the competition. Get the media involved in promoting your product, and never forget that word of mouth is the cheapest and best form of promotion. It is no sin to grow slowly. Every day will not be a holiday. You are in this for the long haul, and you have to be ready to fight to stay in business.

12
FINDING A PLACE
TO SELL FROM

No matter what business you are in, rent is going to be your biggest expense for some time. If you are in the retail business, it gets even dicier. Not only will rent be your biggest cost, but the location you choose will be critical to your success. At David's Cookies, the first thing we say to a prospective franchisee is that we are not even going to talk to you until you show us a lease.

The other thing to remember is that in real estate, there is no such thing as a bargain location. The rental market is one of the purest markets out there. There are no hidden nooks and crannies that I know of where the rent is cheap and there are thousands of people walking in front of the store. The bargains happen when your idea is so brilliant that people are going to seek you out no matter where. But except for Disneyworld, where Walt Disney built a theme park in a central Florida swamp and got millions of people to come to him, I can't think of any site where the entrepreneur adds that much value to the location.

You will never get more than what you paid for. The trick is to make sure you don't pay too much.

DECISIONS, DECISIONS

It is possible for me to get space for a store in Queens, right across the East River from Manhattan, for around $10 per square foot. And in a good week, I'd probably do $300 to $400 in sales. It is also possible to get a store in one of New York's better locations—say Broadway and Eighth Street— for $150 to $200 per square foot. In a good week, that location will gross $15,000. Will you do better with the lower rent and the lower business or with the higher rent and the higher business?

HOW TO FIGURE IT OUT

Every business has a different break-even point that can be determined by adding up costs of goods sold, labor, and fixed expenses like rent and occupancy taxes. You have to get a sense of what your product is and who it's going to be sold to, and try to figure out what kind of location is ideal for that kind of product.

Then go into the marketplace—by yourself. Go out and walk the streets the way I did for eight months looking for my first cookie store location, up and down, trying to figure how your concept will go and then how much you can afford to pay. Or how much you can afford to lose paying rent while your concept is beginning to catch on.

ONCE AGAIN, FORGET THE EXPERTS

There are any number of real estate location companies or location survey companies with very fancy demographic data—the average income of residents within a four-block radius, for example—that will pinpoint the types of people in your neighborhood, their sexual preferences, their marital status, their age, their average income, the number of cavities in their mouths, and so on. These reports are not worth the paper they are so expensively printed on. They basically are used by developers, both scrupulous and unscrupulous, to go to a prospective tenant and say, "Look, you can't miss; the average income of this area is as good as Greenwich, Connecticut."

Be suspicious when you see reams of documentation about the "perfect" affordable location. Remember, if it sounds too good to be true, it probably is.

A location consultant is a pimp. He's not working for you; and even if he is, he's not going to get paid until he sticks you into a location, so he's looking to put you in the first location he can find.

Brokers are like barracudas—they are in it only for themselves. They will arrange anything, say anything, do anything to put you together with a landlord so that they can get a commission. But they should at least be knowledgeable. The best thing you can do is go out and find a professional, well-connected real estate broker. A good one will be looking for repeat business, so he should at least take some of your interests to heart.

LOCATION, LOCATION, AND LOCATION

There are three kinds of locations. They range from high rent to low rent, high volume to low volume, nice neighbors to crummy neighbors.

The Problem with Shopping Malls

The first location everybody thinks about is a shopping mall. It can be in a downtown project like Boston's Fanueil Hall or Baltimore's Harbor Place, a regional shopping center developed by somebody like Eddie DeBartolo or Al Taubman, or a strip center, which is usually a bunch of stores that look alike lined up along a major highway. You pay more in a mall because the space is usually newer and the customer traffic is high. And you get somebody else to worry about many of your problems, such as sanitation and security.

There is one big drawback: I don't know anybody who ever successfully started a concept in a mall. They may have moved a concept in after it was successful elsewhere, but they didn't start there. You get lousy locations. Mall operators are like sheep when it comes to latching on to proven concepts, and they will not even consider you unless you have one. Plus, there is a real pecking order. The concerns that are the biggest and have been doing business with the mall owner longest get the best locations.

Be Adaptable

So you have to assume that in your first couple of malls, you are not going to get great locations. You'll probably get lousy deals on the rent, too. But the way to get around that is to look at it as a marketing problem. If what you are selling is something the mall needs to sell, as opposed to just being something *you* want to sell, you will do very very well.

The best example of that is a food concept that uses a lot of space—a restaurant. Six-hundred-square-foot concepts like popcorn and yogurt outlets are a dime a dozen. The guy who designed a restaurant for Taubman got a location on the ground floor for 6 percent of the gross, instead of up on the third floor next to the men's room for 15 percent of the gross, because he could fill up an odd section of space that Taubman would otherwise have trouble renting.

Strip Centers

Strip centers are good for a lot of stores that don't need dense foot traffic. Furniture stores, for instance. They have a higher average sale and don't need that multiple repeat business. The rents are usually lower, and you have more leeway in terms of where you can locate yourself. And it is usually less competitive. But you have to hope and pray the strip center is in the right location and people are going to come by in their cars, or you are not going to make it.

Freestanding Space: Somebody Else's and Your Own

The second kind of location is space in somebody else's building. There you are on your own, dealing directly with the landlord. The rent will vary, depending on the quality of the building and the location. You will have a lot more flexibility in terms of what you sell and how you operate, but you will be on your own when it comes to dealing with headaches.

The third kind of location is where you actually go out and build your own building, like McDonald's does. Since you own the space, you profit if your business takes off and the value of property goes up. If you guessed wrong, however, you not only have a dying business to deal with but a distressed property as well.

Since very few of you will have enough money to build your own building as well as start your own business, most of you will be dealing with the first or second kind of location when you start out.

THINK SMALL

When you are considering a business idea, think of one that will use the least amount of space. We are putting a lot of effort into miniaturizing our cookie stores. We used to take up to 400 square feet; now we can get even more products into 125 square feet of space, just by using smaller pieces of equipment and being more efficient about the customer flow. That sort of thing takes time to learn. It took us about eight years.

You can learn a lot by going to a department store and seeing how the cosmetics companies merchandise their products. They have figured out how to get incredible sales out of a very small space. Now, if you are selling auto transmissions, obviously you can't do that.

HOW I FOUND MY FIRST STORE

I basically set up my own criteria in finding a location for the first David's Cookies.

First of all, I wanted a spot where there was activity day and night. Selling food is different from selling jewelry— you want people coming by all the time. A lot of people will eat cookies after six o'clock in the evening, though they won't buy a pair of shoes or a diamond ring then.

The real estate industry ranks locations based on percentages. Harry Winston, the gem dealer on Fifth Avenue at Fifty-fifth Street, has a 100 percent location. Between the hours of 10 A.M. and 5 P.M., the foot traffic is as dense as any location in New York. But at six o'clock, it clears out. At night the street is dead. Fifth Avenue wouldn't do me any good in the impulse food business.

So I went after what the industry would consider a 50 percent location. That was fine with me because I could get the other 50 percent at night. Second Avenue between 10 A.M. and 5 P.M. was not all that great in terms of foot traffic because there were not many office buildings that far east in Manhattan. But after dark a lot of people walked down the street to go to restaurants and nightclubs. Munchie food like cookies gets bought after dinner.

Best of all, the rent was dirt cheap. It was $1,000 a month to start. These days, comparable space in the same location would cost ten times that much.

FINDING OUT WHAT THE SPACE IS WORTH

Now I have it down to a system. We go to prospective store locations three times a day on three different days, count the people walking by on the sidewalk, and then factor that into the rent. Sometimes you get really lucky and the neighborhood develops around you. But you can't count on that.

In the case of David's Cookies in New York, that has happened only in two instances.

In the last couple of years, finding the kind of space I need has gotten tougher and tougher. Everybody wants small spaces of a couple of hundred square feet in high traffic locations. Not just me and Mrs. Fields, but ice cream stores and outfits like Benetton and One Hour Photo. The competition makes the rents that much higher.

Madison Avenue has gotten so expensive—up to $500 per square foot—that I'm convinced that most of those stores are just fronts. They are in the fashion business and have to be there for image reasons, but they don't make any money. There is no such thing as an image location in the food business. I don't know of any food store that *has* to be somewhere and is losing its rear end to stay there.

At a certain point, the rents just get too ridiculous. I was looking at locations in Paris that would have cost $2 million to $4 million. A lease is an asset that you can put on your books, and it is usually not going to lose value. But to invest $4 million to do $600,000 or $700,000 a year in a cookie store just doesn't make any sense.

I still want to be in Paris some day, but not at those prices.

TOO MUCH FRONTAGE, TOO LITTLE TRAFFIC

Luckily, my first store turned out to be at a good location. Not all of my decisions have been that good. The mistakes I've made show how easy it is to screw up.

The second cookie store location I took was at Eightieth Street and First Avenue, in what is known as the Yorkville area of Manhattan. It was an up-and-coming neighborhood but not, as it turned out, up and coming fast enough.

At the time, I thought it was important that customers be able to see the cookies being baked in the store. It was a relatively new concept at the time. To do that in New York City, I needed as much street frontage as possible. My first store had twenty feet or so of frontage, and that allowed me to put the oven and the conveyor belt carrying the baked cookies in the window. People would stop to see the cookies coming out of the oven.

I thought the big, open-front store was more important than a lot of foot traffic going by the front door. The Eightieth and First location had more frontage and what I thought was 50 percent location: 50 percent in the day and at night. The rent was more than my first store but still pretty cheap because it was off the beaten path—$2,000 a month.

We opened up the store in 1979. For the first six or eight months it did pretty well. It was new, and there seemed to be a lot of action. Then the sales went steadily downhill. I finally decided to sell the store three years later.

I learned two lessons. One, the frontage was not as important as the foot traffic, which, as the business developed, became the key criterion in picking a location. Two, First Avenue, is almost entirely residential, whereas Second Avenue is almost entirely commercial. So during the day there was no reason for anybody to go out on the street because there were no other stores around. There were days we didn't sell a single cookie until 4 P.M. In the evening, because there was no action on the street, people didn't go out and walk around the way they did on Second Avenue. There have been two bakeries in our store since we sold it, and they have both closed, so the location may be jinxed.

Not only were the sales poor, but the store also had a lot of robberies. Crooks look for stores in out-of-the-way locations because that way they don't run into customers when they are escaping with the loot.

TOO LITTLE FRONTAGE, TOO MUCH TRAFFIC

The next case was almost the exact opposite. In the early 1980s, Columbus Avenue on Manhattan's Upper West Side was the hottest shopping street in New York. The place was jumping with people, new restaurants and boutiques were opening daily, and rents were skyrocketing. Stores that were paying $10 per square foot went to $150 a square foot overnight. It was at the apogee of trendiness.

I thought we had to open a cookie store on Columbus Avenue no matter what. So we took a store at Seventy-fifth Street that had seven feet of frontage—it was actually taller than it was wide. From day one we never did any business. You couldn't find the store. The landlord wouldn't let us put a sign out front. The store was cramped, it wasn't appetizing, and you couldn't display the cookies well. The only place you could see David's Cookies was from the other side of the street. People used to walk right by it. That store stayed open shorter than any other cookie store in the city— ten months. We wound up selling the lease back to the landlord because he wanted to put a dress shop in there.

Columbus Avenue isn't hot any more. The landlords killed it. "From Boom to Bust: Trendy Shops Take a Fall" was the headline in a 1988 *New York Times* story. It went on to say that "As one pricey boutique after another has closed, . . . real estate professionals are calling Columbus Avenue one of the biggest retailing busts in recent memory."

The reason, of course, was the extortionate rents. A 1,500-square-foot-store at one time commanded $200 a square foot, or $300,000 a year. A rule of thumb in retail real estate is that the rent should not exceed 10 percent of gross sales. So a merchant who was paying that much had to sell $3 million worth of stuff a year, or nearly $60,000 a week. As the *Times* pointed out, that means 300 pairs of $200 slacks every week. That's a lot of slacks. As one boutique owner put it: "The customer on Columbus is the ultimate yuppie, strapped to the gills trying to make ends meet. The only thing he can afford after paying for his co-op is an ice cream cone on Saturday. I've never seen so many dripping cones on my floor."

NO TRAFFIC

My third disaster story is a tragic one. We signed a lease on

Christopher Street in Greenwich Village in 1983. When I was looking at the store and tracking the traffic, Christopher Street was packed day and night. It looked like a sure thing.

Between the time we signed the lease and opened the store, AIDS hit Greenwich Village. The whole gay community left the streets and stayed indoors. All the businesses in the area, especially restaurants, began getting no traffic at all. The whole area was devastated economically. We were in that store for less than a year before we had to walk away from it. We just told the landlord we were leaving, and we left.

CONVENTIONAL WISDOM

One of the myths about store locations is that you should try to go into a neighborhood where there is an established anchor like Bloomingdale's or Zabar's. Brokers will tell you, "Great. It's in the Barney's neighborhood, it's in the Macy's neighborhood," but that is really more a detriment than an asset. The reason is simple: shoppers have tunnel vision, and they won't see anything else in that neighborhood other than the big-name store they are looking for. Instead of roaming around, they will zero in on that one place.

Besides, being around a big-name operation gets tricky. For instance, if you are not on the very same *block* as Zabar's, which draws zillions of people on weekends, you might as well be in Hoboken. Being in the Zabar's vicinity makes absolutely no difference. A store on the east side of Broadway across the street won't know whether Zabar's is there or not. You are, in effect, in a different neighborhood.

Another thing to watch out for: nearly every street has a good side and a bad side. One of the idiosyncrasies about Broadway is that every successful business from Seventy-fifth Street up to Columbia University at 116th Street is on the west side of the street. That's because there is three times as much foot traffic on the west side of the street. Nobody knows why. When Jim Bildner decided to open up a branch of his fancy, upscale grocery store, he went to the east side of the street despite what I and a lot of other people told him. A year or so later, he closed down. He was getting killed.

Being in a hot neighborhood doesn't work either, as we proved on Columbus Avenue. Merchants were doing good business in that neighborhood. But if you are paying $200 per square foot for rent, you have to be extraordinarily successful or you will not make any money. You could be better off doing one-quarter the business but paying $30 per square foot.

SOMETIMES YOU GET LUCKY

Take our store in Battery Park City, a big new residential development built on landfill in the Hudson River. When we were looking for a location down there in 1984, there were only two buildings up, and the rest was empty space. I had to envision what it was going to look like. Now the store is doing $350,000 a year. Buildings are going up around it, and it turns out construction workers buy a lot of cookies. Sometimes you have to just smell the air and say, "Yeah, this is going to be a good thing." If the risk isn't astronomical, then it is worth doing.

Because the area was undeveloped, I also got a good deal on the rent. I paid 10 percent of the gross for the first three years, but there was no minimum. A percentage-only deal is the best kind you can get, as well as the fairest. If you do well, the landlord does well, and if you don't do well, he doesn't do well. Landlords don't look at it that way, however. If you do well, they want to do well, and if you do lousy, they get your house and whatever else you put up for collateral.

A lot of landlords don't want to do percentage deals because they don't trust the tenant to give them a square count on the revenue. Most landlords don't care how well you do, as long as they are getting top dollar. They will rent to whomever pays the best rent, including X-rated movie theaters.

We just opened up a cookie store across the street from the

main gate of the University of Virginia. There are a lot of upper-middle-class kids with money to spend. That's the kind of store where all hell would have to have to break loose before we lost money. Any college kid who can afford to spend $60 an ounce for dope can afford $6 for a pound of cookies. So far, we have been very successful at Harvard, Yale, and Princeton. I think that students are more sophisticated these days. When I was in college, kids ate garbage ice cream. Now they eat Häagen-Dazs, Ben and Jerry's, or mine.

ELASTIC RULERS

I never look at any deal in terms of what I will be paying per square foot. Landlords lie about the space; they all are including half their garage in Scarsdale in the computation. The crucial question is: can I afford it? For example, I go to look at a store location. The broker said it has 1,000 square feet, though just by looking at it I can tell it has only 500 square feet. What I am really thinking about is what I can do with the space and what it will cost. I ask myself: "Can I afford to pay $3,000, $4,000, $5,000 a month rent?" If I think I can, then I start negotiating. "No, landlord; I don't want to pay $3,000 a month; this space isn't worth a dime more than $2,500."

HOW MUCH, HOW MUCH?

We have stores from as little as thirty square feet to 1,500 square feet. Rents range from $600 a month in New Paltz, a small town in upstate New York, to thousands a month.

Big or little, don't rent space you don't need. It can be the difference between a profit and a loss. If a store can do $500,000 a year, we can justify paying $100,000 a year in rent. Most of the stores, however, gross between $175,000 to $300,000. That indicates a rent of around $50,000. Usually, in the fast food business you do not want to pay more than 20 percent in occupancy costs—rent, taxes, the works. Every percent you pay above 20 percent is profit you are not making. And rent is only the beginning. In most other malls, common charges run 10 percent to 20 percent of the rent. In some malls, the common charges are sometimes more than the rent.

BELIEVE ME, IT IS ROUGH OUT THERE

Landlords are vicious. When they see these bright-eyed entrepreneurs coming who want to buy themselves a job, they go after them. It is brutal what they do to you. I know; I've been had. But you learn by doing.

THE RIESE BROTHERS

Take the Riese brothers, Irving and Murray. They are landlords and do business on a handshake. People say they control more retail space than anybody else in New York City. For example, they have at least one corner on every Broadway intersection from Forty-third Street to Fifty-second Street. And they fill those spaces with franchise food operations. They have Pizza Hut, Burger King, Roy Rogers, Houlihan's, TGI Friday's, Dunkin' Donuts, and Kentucky Fried Chicken.

They are very smart. When the New York real estate market was soft in the 1970s, they developed a very canny *modus operandi* that has stood them in good stead. They go to a developer who is building a new building and offer him what they claim is an unbreakable lease on the ground floor that the developer can then use to get financing for the building. So they get great terms on the lease, operate a business there for a couple of years until the location takes off, and then sometimes sell the lease at a big profit.

Since the Riese brothers have the best locations, they can attract reputable franchisers. They have so many locations they probably feed everybody in New York once a year.

The first thing the Riese brothers did to me was to get a franchise to open a David's Cookies store at a great location,

Fifth Avenue and Thirty-eighth Street. They kept the store open for about nine months, alienating all kinds of customers because they ran it so badly. Then they closed it without telling me.

The next thing the Riese brothers did was to put me in Grand Central Station. They promised me this great location right in the path of most of the commuter traffic. When the store finally opened, it wasn't where they had said it would be. It was way down at the end of the corridor where nobody could see it. Ninety percent of the traffic was turning north about twenty feet in front of the store. A supervisor of mine went to buy cookies at the store and discovered they didn't taste anything like David's Cookies—they looked and tasted like Famous Amos's. So I called up to complain, and Irving and Murray both pleaded ignorance. In fact, they were selling prebaked Famous Amos cookies instead of fresh-baked David's. So I made them close the David's Cookies. They then opened a Famous Amos. Then, six months later, they closed Famous Amos and opened a David's again at the same location. They subsequently closed the David's a second time.

The third time I dealt with them, they wanted to open thirty cookie stores. I should have said no, but the deal looked so attractive that I decided to go ahead. So they opened six of the stores, and, sure enough, they got me again. The locations were not quite what they promised. For example, they plopped down one David's store right in the middle of a Dunkin' Donuts store.

I complained, the way I always do when things don't go right. So they decided they didn't want to do business with me because I caused them "too much pain." In November 1987, they threatened to stop operating the stores. Since that was right before Christmas, I decided to get even. I ordered our bakery not to ship them any more dough because around Christmas time we are always short of dough anyway. When they called up and wanted more dough, we told them we would rather supply our franchisees who were going to still be doing business with us in January and

February, rather than those that were jumping ship. I couldn't stop myself from adding, "I'm just alleviating your pain, Irving and Murray."

It makes it tough not to do business with them when they have all those great locations. But I think I've finally learned my lesson.

IT IS NOT GETTING ANY EASIER

I think there are enormous opportunities in this country to try concepts out of town, where the rent is cheaper—just like Broadway shows used to open in Boston or Baltimore. New York has become more difficult to do retail in because of all kinds of complications with the bureaucracy and the crime, and there is a lot to be said for opening on the road and staying on the road. It is much easier for me to make money in Boston or Philadelphia than New York.

But the rules for getting a location are the same anywhere. Figure out what kind of environment you want to be in. Find a reliable real estate broker you can work with. Walk around so you thoroughly understand your neighborhood and the kind of traffic it creates. Don't be blinded by first impressions. Try not to take any more space than you need. Sign a long lease. And don't pay any more than you have to.

13
FIGHTING WITH
THE LANDLORD

A fter finding the space, negotiating the lease would seem like an afterthought.

Wrong. Your success or failure in arranging a bearable lease for yourself will determine whether you will sleep nights for the next ten years—or lie awake with worry. There are dozens of things that can go wrong with a lease and make your life miserable.

I've negotiated dozens of leases, both in New York City and around the country. As it happens, landlords are toughest in New York, because space is at the greatest premium there. But the lessons I've learned there can help you in arranging your own rental space whether you are in Miami or Minneapolis.

THE STANDARD FORM IS
MERELY A STARTING POINT

A typical retail lease is contained in a document called a standard form of store lease. In New York, it happens to be put out by the Real Estate Board of New York, an organization of landlords. That is another way of saying that if you sign the standard form, you are dead meat, and I've never seen a situation anywhere where the lease wasn't on a standard form. So you can assume you are stuck in a catch-22 situation and will have to deal with this monstrosity.

LAWYERS

The first thing you need to get yourself is a really good real estate lawyer—not just a contract lawyer but a specialist. I'm a big proponent of individual practitioners in the real estate business. All they do is real estate deals, so they know what they are doing, but they charge a lot less than a big megabuck firm does.

Find out what the lawyer is going to cost. Most real estate lawyers charge by the deal, but some charge by the hour. Some, if you have a good relationship with them, will not charge if the deal falls through. That's really the difference between using a law firm and using a lawyer; the law firms will bill you on a killed deal, but the sole practitioner probably won't.

MONEY AND TIME

You've got to fight like crazy for two things: the amount of the rent and the length of the lease.

There are plenty of good locations, but landlords want outrageous rents. It's a pure greed factor. Whereas in the old days there was some give and take, the landlords are now saying, "Screw you; I'll wait and get somebody else." In 1978, the year of New York's last bad real estate market, a lot of landlords were hurting because they had been through a down market just four years earlier. Then came the bull market, and it lasted for ten years. All the landlords were so rich, nobody had to haggle. As I write this in 1988, things have loosened up again. Since the stock market crash in 1987 on October 19, people are a little nervous.

Here's a case. Sheldon Solow, a big New York landlord, has this store on the corner of Fiftieth and Second. It's a 35 percent to 40 percent location under my grading system. The whole building is caked with pigeon dung. He wants $13,500 a month for 750 square feet. I wouldn't pay $3,500 for it. Every once in a while, brokers call me up and ask me if I'm interested. I say, "Sure, if he cuts his price by $10,000 a month." In the old days, that didn't happen. He would deal and the space would be rented.

GO FOR A LONG LEASE

Don't be shy about asking for a long lease, even if you are not sure how things are going to work out. In my case, it makes no sense to negotiate anything less than a ten-year lease. When you are first getting started, the only asset you have is your lease. If you go to sell your business and have six months left on your lease, your business is worthless. The new owner will either have to negotiate a new lease, probably at much higher rates, or move.

HAGGLING OVER THE TERMS

The thing about a lease that the landlord usually doesn't have to admit—because the standard lease form is so intimidating—is that everything is negotiable. If you go in assuming he has you beat on fifty points, he is going to beat you on fifty more points. What getting a good lease really comes down to is how much the landlord wants you, how much leverage you think you have, and how much you are prepared to pay.

If you go into a situation where the landlord has figured he wants $5,000 a month and you offer him $10,000, you are going to negotiate a pretty good deal for yourself on other important points. If, on the other hand, you try to squeeze every penny out of the deal, at a certain point the landlord will say, "Forget it; I can't take it anymore," and walk away.

He may or may not mean business. There have been

numerous negotiations where the landlord has stormed out of meetings or I have stormed out of meetings, but it was a bluff because we both thought we were getting someplace, and that was part of the act of negotiating.

BE TOUGH

If you start out by letting the landlord know that you are going to fight over every line, you are better off. Back in 1980, when I didn't know better, there weren't a lot of changes on the standard lease form. In my later deals, we have torn the standard form into shreds.

Here's an example of how you can be hamstrung by the standard lease form. On the first page, it says, "The tenant shall make no change to the premises of any nature without the landlord's written consent." That sounds reasonable, right? Except that the sentence has been held to mean that if you want to paint the walls, that's a change and you have to get the landlord's approval. You don't want to do that. Any time you have to go back to the landlord for something, there is a good chance he will use that opportunity to hold you up for more money. You want to paint; he'll charge you money. That's the nature of the beast. So make sure that everything is already in the lease.

RENT

Right at the beginning, the lease says, "Tenant shall pay the rent provided hereinafter." That's the money issue. If you read the previous chapter, you know how to take care of that.

WATCH OUT FOR ESCALATORS

Most landlords want an inflation increase in the rent, and they want to make it all cumulative. The rent may be great in the first year, but in the sixth year, you're dead.

Inflation-increase clauses are time bombs. If you can't

eliminate them, get fixed amount clauses so you know how much you will be paying. Otherwise, they will go up and up inexorably until the additional amount you are paying is more than the cost of the original lease.

The worst kind of inflation-escalation clause you can have is the kind that is based on something you can't control, like the Consumer Price Index. If you do, the increase in year two of the lease becomes the base for the increase in year three, which becomes the base for the increase in year four, and so on. The increases become geometric. This is something you are going to have to fight against because the landlord is not going to want to take it out.

A guy came to me with a proposal for a David's Cookies store location in a mall in Syracuse, and he was about to pay $50 per square foot, full-inflation escalators, and a lot of other stuff. I pointed out to him that within four years, even if inflation went up only 3 percent a year, he'd be paying $100 a foot. He'd be bankrupt unless a man from Mars came down and bought 1,000 pounds of cookies every week. All he was focusing on was fifty bucks a foot. You have to show these innocents that it's not fifty bucks a foot after four years.

WHO PAYS?

Another big money issue is who is the guarantor of the lease. Never put your own money behind a lease. That is a good way to lose it all.

I never personally guarantee any of my leases—the corporation that is doing business at that location does that. Landlords will jump up and scream and say that they have multinational companies ready to come in and rent the space, but I don't pay attention to them. What happens is that the entity in the lease that pays the rent is a shell corporation. So if business is terrible and we decide to leave the location, all we lose is a couple of months security deposit and what we leave behind on the walls. That isn't nice, but it is business. I think anybody who personally guarantees leases should have his head examined. Because if the business goes belly up, you can lose your house.

How do you get the landlord to agree to that? You have to say to him, "Look, this is a crapshoot for both of us. I'm going to go in and improve your property, try to make a living, and pay the rent. If I fail, my business goes broke, but at least you can rent the space to the next sucker." The landlord will give you a thousand reasons why that doesn't make any sense, but you have to stick to your guns.

It is one thing to go into business knowing that if you fail you can go on to something else. It is another thing to go into business knowing that you have signed your life away on some lease. You are not going to sleep that well knowing you have put your house behind the lease.

THE USE CLAUSE

On the lease form, there is room for one line to explain what the space is going to be used for. There is no way you can fit it all in. This is another critical issue. Like the rent, it is a money issue and something that landlords use to club tenants.

Basically, the use clause allows the landlord to hold you up whenever you go back to him to make a tiny change in what you want to do with the space you have rented. Suppose that along with the whoopie pies you are selling, you want to sell ice cream too. So you go back to the landlord to ask his permission. He says, "Sure, but you are going to pay me $3,000 more a month." Anybody who gets sucked into a tight use clause is putting a rope around his neck, standing at the edge of the stool, and waiting to jump.

Initially, I didn't know any better, so I signed a bunch of stupid use clauses. In the food business, the best terms you can get are "any legal use." The second best thing is "any legal food use." The worst thing you can do is what Mrs. Fields, for instance, did when she went into a bunch of shopping malls. She agreed to sell only six kinds of cookies.

That's it—no drinks, no novelty items, just cookies. If she ever gets in trouble with some of those leases and has to go back to the landlord, she is in big trouble.

Your goal is to get a use clause that allows you to make any legal use of the space. If you do, then you have a club over the landlord, rather than the other way around. Here's how: Say you want to start selling ice cream along with whoopie pies in your location. As a courtesy, you inform the landlord; who says no, so you go to a porn shop operator and get him to agree to open up a peep show in your space. It may not be tasteful, but it is legal. Then you can go to your landlord and say, "If you don't let me sell ice cream at this location, I'm going to open up a pornography store."

In the case of a regional mall, the use clause probably makes sense. It is important that there be only a couple of stores selling cookies and only a few stores selling shoes. Everybody in the mall can't sell cookies and shoes because they would cut each other's throats. So you have to specify what everybody will and will not be allowed to sell.

On the streets of New York, the use clause doesn't make any sense. Your landlord will argue that he wants control over what the space is used for because he wants to protect the integrity of his block. If there are too many yogurt shops, it will be bad for his tenants and thus bad for him.

It is not necessarily harmful to have several outlets doing the some thing in the same block. Here my Chinese restaurant theory comes into play. There are over 300 Chinese restaurants in Chinatown; they have been there for a long time, and none of them seems to be going out of business any more rapidly than any other restaurant in New York City.

ALTERATIONS

When you move into a space, you are going to be improving the landlord's property. You will be painting the walls, carpeting the floors, building shelves, and all that stuff. You have to make the landlord understand that you are going to file the proper permits with the city and get all necessary approvals so that the alterations you make to that property are your business, not his.

This is another money issue. If the landlord does not agree that you can make any legal changes to the space, it is an indication that he is going to give you trouble. If he says any alterations have to be approved by him and the building department, then he is looking to run your business for you. If he is going to run your business, he can also pay your rent. Forget it.

REPAIRS

Arguments over the repair issue fill up landlord and tenant court. The moral issue should be: if something breaks in the building that the landlord controls, *he* should fix it. If you improve a location by bringing in a piece of equipment and that equipment breaks, *you* should fix it.

In the standard lease form it says: "Landlord shall maintain and repair the public portions of the building, both exterior and interior." If you are dependent on the landlord for heat, which most small-business operators are, you better add a very tough clause that says if the boiler breaks, the landlord has to fix it immediately, or use his best efforts, or fix it in twenty-four hours, or the following is going to happen. If the lease doesn't say that, you may have to close your business down because of lack of heat, and you will *still* be liable for the rent.

Over the years, we have been forced to close the restaurant three or four times because of lack of heat. It is a real problem. Landlords delay and delay. He can say, "The plumber is on strike," or "I can't find a plumber," or "The plumber went hunting." The bottom line is: it's not your problem; it's the landlord's problem. If the landlord is not prepared to enter into a contract with you that says he has to fix the boiler pronto, you can't run your business without worrying about whether the boiler is working. You have to be able to tell him, "Look, I can't pay the rent because I can't run my business without heat; and if I can't run my business, where am I supposed to get the money for rent?"

WINDOW CLEANING

You should clean your own windows.

LOADING

This is a building-code issue. Certain buildings can carry only a certain amount of weight on their floors. You can't put ten pounds of bricks on a floor that can take only five pounds.

Most new buildings take 300–400 pounds per square foot, and most businesses don't put anywhere near that kind of load on the floor. So it is generally not a problem. You should still be aware of the legal limit, however, in case you decide you want to store ingots of steel on your premises.

FIRE INSURANCE

Landlords always want more fire insurance than they have. If they can get it out of you, so much the better for them.

Landlords want to be covered not only for your store but also for the other stores in the rest of the building that they probably haven't covered adequately. That's another issue you have to fight over. You basically say to the landlord, "Look, I'm prepared to pay $10,000 or $20,000 for $500,000 worth of insurance." If he says, "I want $10 million of coverage," he is probably tacking another $5,000 to $10,000 onto your overhead. That's money coming out of your pocket that you could have kept instead of giving the landlord more comfort. So don't give in.

EMINENT DOMAIN

The law says the government has the right to set a price for your property and take it over for public use.

If the city comes along and wants to put a highway through your store and grab the building, they can do it. And there is nothing you can do about it.

SUBORDINATION

Another money issue. A landlord will want to be able to subordinate your premise in a mortgage. In other words, if he goes to mortgage the building, he will want to put up your lease as collateral. Watch out.

That is a sneaky, backdoor way of subordinating something. Because if the landlord defaults on the mortgage and ownership of the building passes over to the lender, you are out on your ear. What the landlord is really saying is, "I don't want this little 500-square-foot cookie store getting in the way of a mortgage for a $50 million building. As long as I am financially able to own this building, you can stay. As soon as I get into trouble and have to bail out, you're getting out."

If you sign a lease, you ought to be able to stay in the space. It isn't fair for the landlord to in effect pledge his whole building as collateral for a deal and, if anything goes wrong with the deal, to let someone else come in and empty out the building—including you.

ACCESS TO PREMISES

Big problems here. It is not so much because the landlord shouldn't be allowed to get into your store if there is a fire and you are not there. That is reasonable. But you have to make sure that the landlord has very tight control over the other people who go into your store. We've had cases where building managers have come into our stores with the landlord's key and stolen all our money.

So you have to be very clear about who gets in and under what circumstances. Some tenants will agree to the clause as written and then as soon as the ink is dry, change the lock anyway.

BANKRUPTCY CLAUSE

Basically, what this says is that if you go bankrupt, the landlord gets the store back. Forget it. If you go bankrupt, the store may be a real asset. Keep the bankruptcy clause out of the lease. The landlord shouldn't care, as long as he is getting the rent.

EXPENSES

What this clause says is that no matter what you do, you pay for everything. No matter what the landlord does, he pays for nothing. Change it.

REPAIRS

This delightful clause says, "Neither landlord nor landlord's agent shall have made any representations about physical condition of the building." Baloney. If you are renting a space, you want to know the roof is not going to cave in over your head, the heat is going to work, there is a modicum of security, and so on. In a big building, you are even going to wind up paying for escalations in the porter's wage. Since the porter is responsible for the physical condition of the building, you are going to want to have some say in the condition of the building. Strike this clause.

WAIVER OF TRIAL BY JURY

That's the landlord's way of saying that if you ever get in front of a jury, he knows its members are going to side with you, not him. He's right. Landlords are among the most unpopular people on earth, right up there with bill collectors and IRS agents. Do not waive this right.

WATER CHARGES

Yet another big money issue. Never let the landlord send you a water bill. Insist that a water meter be installed on your own premises and pay the bill yourself.

We have a lawsuit on this very issue against the building where we have our original cookie store and restaurant. The restaurant never used more than $1,200 worth of water a year. Then we suddenly got a three-month bill for $26,000. We tried to point out to the city water department that this was impossible. They said we must have left the faucets on too long.

So we brought in our own engineer, and we discovered that the building was tapping into our water pipes. We were paying for our own water and also for that of Häagen-Dazs, the eyeglass store, and maybe even the air conditioner for the whole building. The landlord's explanation was that he got caught once when his own water supply wasn't working and he had to get into our water. So we were supplying water to all the tenants and paying for it to boot. The sad fact of it is that in dealing with landlords, you can't trust anyone.

So you should not only get your own water meter, you should also sign off on the pedigree of your pipes. Get an engineer to go in and locate where the water is coming into the building and find out where that pipe is going so that nobody else's pipe is cutting into your pipe ahead of the meter. You should also make sure the water meter is on your premises—your basement, not the landlord's basement. That's so the landlord can't mess with the water meter in the middle of the night, which has happened. We've been fighting for four years at one location to get the water meter moved onto our premises.

CLEANING

The standard lease says, "The tenant shall keep the premises clean up to the standard of the landlord." What does that mean? It means that the landlord has the right to come in with white gloves and say, "I'm not satisfied; I'm throwing you out." Fix the lease.

After you fight your way through the first four pages of

the standard lease form, you get to what is known as the "real deal"—the extras, or riders. Anyone who signs one of these standard leases without any riders is going to go bankrupt in the first four months. So pay attention here.

THE WORK LETTER

In most cases, there is going to be a rider called the work letter. It will describe how the landlord is going to fix up the premises before you move in. You will not be surprised to discover that this is another dollars-and-cents money issue.

What does it mean when the landlord says he is going to give you rough plumbing? That could mean he is going to bring the hot and cold water up into your space and install outlets and drains where you need them. Or it could mean that he will provide just one water outlet and make you connect all the other outlets to that one. The difference could cost you thousands of dollars in pipe and plumbing charges.

The best way to make sure you get what you think you are getting even before you have a lease is to have an architect come and do a rough plan of where you want the water outlets to be. Then you get the landlord to sign that plan. It will cost you a little more money initially, but it will turn out to be a big money saver.

An architect's rough plan is even more important for electricity. You want the landlord to run the power into your space because running a new line in could cost you $50–$60 a foot. If the power source is 100 feet back in the basement, running in lines gets expensive. If the landlord says you can bring in the power from the street, you want to make that his problem, not your problem. Otherwise, you will wind up fighting the city and Con Edison so you can tear up the street. It is expensive, and it will take months, if not years.

TAXES

The landlord is going to try to extract as many taxes from

you as he can. There are a half dozen or more, and they are a nightmare.

The best way to negotiate taxes is to get the money issues on the table first. You tell the landlord, "This is the rent I'm prepared to pay, this is the work I want you to do, these are the increases I'm prepared to pay, and these are the increases in taxes that I am prepared to pay." So you are working from your list, not his.

When we signed our first restaurant lease in 1979, the taxes on the whole building were $573,000. Today the building taxes are $850,000. Way back when I didn't know the difference, we agreed to pay 2 percent of the tax *increase* on the building each year. What that means is that this year we have to pay an additional tax of $4,300, which comes out to $373 a month. That's $373 that I don't make in the restaurant. It is just one of many escalations that were slipped into the lease. These are time bombs that just keep on ticking.

UTILITIES

Always pay your own. Never let the landlord pass on the costs. There is too much room for mistakes or plain old hanky panky.

MECHANIC'S LIEN

The landlord will try to tell you that under no circumstance is he going to allow you to have a mechanic's lien put on these premises if you get into trouble.

A mechanic's lien allows a contractor to grab hold of a house or building if he has done some work in them and didn't get paid for it. If your contractor knows that your landlord won't permit a mechanic's lien, he won't work in your space because he has nothing to grab if you don't pay him. It sounds funny, but you have to fight like hell to have the ability to have liens placed on your property.

GARBAGE

Every landlord is crazy about garbage. They will tell you, "The garbage has to be picked up around the side of the building every night between midnight and 2 A.M." If you sign any clause like that, you are basically saying to the landlord that you can control the gorillas who drive the garbage trucks. That's malarkey. The private garbage system is one of the things that works best in this city, but they will pick it up when they want to pick it up, not when you want them to pick it up. You do not want to tell the landlord you are going to put your life on the line to live up to his garbage rule.

OBNOXIOUS ODORS

A lot of my cookie stores have obnoxious odor clauses. I'm not too happy about that. The landlord knows that I am going to be opening a bakery and that baked goods have an odor—in my case, I consider it an aroma, not an odor. If the landlord doesn't want any smell, he can put a library in there. To have a clause like this where the landlord can decide you are not paying enough rent because you have obnoxious odors coming out of the store is like putting a loaded gun to your head.

NOISE

These clauses are usually pretty reasonable. You are not allowed to scream and yell unless you open a disco. Then you are going to have noise. So it better be in the lease.

CASH SECURITY DEPOSITS

One summer I worked for the attorney general of New York State in what was called the miscellaneous frauds division. One of our main jobs was chasing landlords who kept security deposits for themselves. So a law was passed that landlords have to put your security deposit in an escrow account that pays interest. At the end of the lease, you get a little something extra back in turn for having your money tied up.

You should fight like hell to get that interest back. The landlord will give you a story about how he has to administer the bank account and everything else and how much money that costs him. Forget it—just get the money.

DESCRIPTION OF OPERATIONS

Landlords are like sheep: they like to follow each other around. They like to see that the store you are about to open in their building is like a store that is already open in somebody else's building.

In our case, a lot of our leases say that our store is going to be run like another David's Cookies at such and such address. When you think about it, it is a very interesting negotiation point. What happens if you turn the first location into a strip tease parlor? Does that mean you can do the same thing in your new location? This is the kind of ruse that landlords sometimes fall for.

What landlords should say instead is, "I want the store to be like the other one as of such and such a date," but they never do. That language has never been put in a lease.

OFF-PREMISE CONSUMPTION

Money, money, money. The landlord doesn't want people eating on his premises, he doesn't want seats, he doesn't want tables. So he tells you that people can't eat in your store unless you pay him extra money. You say to him, "I want to put in seats and tables so people can sit down to eat their ice cream cones and cookies, and I can get all the permits I need to get in New York City to do that. It is none of your business whether somebody eats in my store."

In some cities like Princeton, NJ, you have to have a parking space for every seat in your cookie store, but not in

Manhattan. So tell the landlord it is none of his business.

ASSIGNMENT CLAUSE

Always keep in mind that you are in a business. A business, by definition, can be bought and sold. There is no reason why you should give the landlord the right to tell you whether or not you can sell or transfer your business, or to whom. That's like buying a life sentence—you will never get out of your business. So when you decide you've had enough or somebody makes an offer you can't refuse, you don't want to have to get down on your hands and knees to the landlord and say, "Please, let me sell my business to this person."

Basically, what you should say is that the lease is assignable and the landlord should not unreasonably withhold his permission to assign it. If the landlord is going to make an issue of that, what he is really telling you is, "Look, after you have worked your tail off, paid all this rent, taken fifteen years off your life trying to run this business, and are lucky enough to find some other schmuck to come in here and buy it, I am going to bury you because I am going to charge so much more rent that the guy won't want to buy the business and you are going to die in the store."

Sometimes landlords will insert a clause specifying that the person to whom you assign the lease has to meet certain economic criteria, such as having a net worth of half a million dollars and five years' experience in a similar business. If your business is a restaurant, they want to specify a fine quality restaurant. What the hell is that? They want to make sure that you don't sell out to Burger King. One landlord defines a fine quality restaurant as one that sells seafood, French or Italian cuisine, or steaks and chops. So you couldn't open up an Indian restaurant, for instance.

SIGNS

Very important. You have to get the landlord to agree that it is okay to put up any kind of sign that meets the building code.

We had a building at Forty-second Street and Sixth Avenue with a flagpole, where we hung a David's Cookies flag. Down the street from us was a McDonald's with the same kind of flagpole and a McDonald's flag. All of a sudden, we were getting $250 tickets from a city inspector who said our flag was sticking out too far. So we hung the flag flush to the front of the building, and we got a ticket for that, too. McDonald's, meanwhile, had hung an American flag in place of the McDonald's flag and installed an illuminated sign jutting two feet out over the sidewalk, and it wasn't getting any tickets.

We were up to about $3,000 in tickets when we found out that the city inspector just happened to be a part-time salesman for the company that made McDonald's illuminated sign. Funny coincidence. That kind of stuff goes on all the time.

FREE TIME

The landlord will sometimes give you rent-free time while you renovate your space. But the renovation process is so arduous that it usually takes twice as long as you planned. Often it is the landlord's fault. If he doesn't connect the electricity, you can't open your store. So that clause has to be very precise in terms of when the rent starts. If for any reason the landlord doesn't complete part of his work, you don't have to pay rent until he does.

EXTRAS

There is always something to throw a monkey wrench into a negotiation. I've been trying to get 10,000 square feet to expand my factory in Queens from a landlord who is actually a friend of mine. Then I find this clause in the lease that is the kind of thing you could go broke on: "If at any time during the run of the lease, the New York State taxes go up, the tenant will be responsible for 28.75 percent of the increase" (that fraction being the percentage of the space in the entire building that I am renting). That isn't so unusual. In every commercial lease, the tenant is on the hook for increases in the real estate taxes. But I said, "Wait a minute. The current taxes are essentially on an unimproved building. The landlord is in the process of improving the building from a garage to a palace. So I want to pay only 28.75 percent of the old assessment, not the new assessment." This could easily be a $15,000 a year haircut going in if you are not careful.

CONCLUSION

When negotiating a lease, hit the big points right up front. It is true that deals often fall apart on little points. But if you can't get over the big points right up front, it is best just to halt the negotiation.

At the beginning, tell the landlord and his lawyer, "Here are the parameters of the deal I am prepared to make: this much rent, this much renovation, and so on, and if you have any problems with this let me know, because I will go find another location."

One of the tactics you can use is to let the landlord lead. You get him to say what kind of deal he is looking for. If he does, you can respond directly to that.

Deals don't get any better if you sit there longer. I think a lot of people believe that once they get all the parties in the room, there is a kind of headiness about the negotiating process that will make it all work out in the end. Not so. The best deals are the ones that happen fastest. If the dickering drags out for a long time, the tenants usually end up getting screwed.

At a certain point, the landlord may say to you, "Look, I can get a better deal some place else," and mean it. At that point, you get up from the table and leave, too. The deal is off. There will always be another deal.

14
PEOPLE AND HOW TO
DEAL WITH THEM

At some point in your business career, you discover that no matter how smart you are or how hard you work, you can't do it by yourself.

Essentially, you need three different kinds of help. The first is a partner. The best time to find partners is early in the game. That's when they can do the most for you. Partners are designed to bring to the party things that you don't have. That's usually one of two things: money or expertise.

Beware of going into business with people who like the same jokes you do, who like to eat what you do, who become your friends. That can be a dangerous situation. Way up front you have to define the limits of where a partnership can go, and you have to define what can go wrong with the partnership.

It is like a prenuptial agreement. It may not feel right at the time, but there is nothing wrong with sitting down with a prospective partner, going through a thousand what-ifs, and putting them all in writing. If you sit back and say, "This deal is comfortable; it's OK. He wouldn't screw me," he will. You have to fight complacency. The only thing that can kill a friendship faster than having your friend steal your wife is losing money together in a business deal.

MY FIRST PARTNER

As you know, I had the great misfortune to be forced to start a restaurant at the same time that I opened my first cookie store. When I was putting together the cookie deal, the location that I found was part of a much larger space, and the landlord wanted a restaurant in there, too.

Even though I had worked extensively in a kitchen as a chef, I didn't have the vaguest idea about how to run the front of the house: the bar, the waiters and the waitresses, serving the customers, and making sure the money got in the cash register. So I went out and found a partner named Bobby Shapiro, who at the time was running the hottest restaurant in New York, Hoexter's Market, up on Eighty-first and Third.

Bobby and I had similar personalities, and we kind of fell in love with each other. He didn't put up any money. The division of responsibility was very clear. I was going to take care of the cookie store and the restaurant kitchen; he was going to take care of the front of the house. Then and now, Bobby is an entrepreneur out of control. Unbeknownst to me, he was into many more things than he could handle. Simultaneous to entering this agreement with me, he was building another restaurant next to Hoexter's called Uzie's with this Italian hotshot named Giancarlo Uzielli.

To see what was going on at Hoexter's in those days was beyond belief. There were gorgeous models at the bar, lines out the door from 6 P.M. to 4 A.M.—it was the ultimate New York City hot spot. And the food was not bad. I figured if Bobby could do that for Hoexter's, he could do wonders for me at my place, Manhattan Market.

Manhattan Market opened in September, and Bobby was there part-time for about four days. Then he disappeared. He said he was too busy getting Uzie's started.

So I was stuck running a cookie store, a restaurant kitchen, and a restaurant front of the house that I didn't have the vaguest idea how to operate. One thing Bobby did for me was get three bartenders. Our bar was filled from 7 P.M. to about 1 A.M., but when I went to look for the bar receipts the next day, they were way below what they should have been. I figured one of the bartenders must have been stealing most of the profits. I got rid of the bartenders, but when I called Bobby to come help me, he whined that he was too busy.

To make a long story short, we ended up in a lawsuit that is still going on eight years later. Bobby is suing me, claiming he owns a part of everything I have done in the cookie and restaurant business. He never put a nickel of his own money into the deal, and he never signed for any money. To make matters worse, he stole my idea. He took the manager out of my cookie store, went down to Florida, and opened up another cookie store called the Cookie Factory.

THE LESSON

If you are going to get a partner you must outline very precisely what your respective responsibilities are. What invariably happens to partners if the duties are not clearly defined is that the person who signed for the money and has the gun to his head does all the work, and the other person gets all the glory.

KEY EMPLOYEES

Ultimately, if you can hire somebody to provide missing expertise, it is better than getting a partner because you can control your own destiny. It is a situation that has to be looked at on a case-by-case basis. Clearly, in most instances there is one entrepreneur who has the fire in his belly. He has his flag out front and is running with the idea. That entrepreneur, whenever possible, should try to hire people.

If the people are key, you should give them options and incentives.

One way to do this is to set up the company so that at the end of five years the employees own it. That's brilliant. Ultimately, the name of the game in business is business. You don't get married to any business; you just do it. If you can figure out a way to get out of it up front and make money at it—that's phenomenal. I think there are a lot of instances where people have given equity options to key players where it worked out. On the other hand, there are a lot of instances where the key players didn't have that fire in the belly, which is the worst thing that could happen. If you are basically staking your guts on the line to make a business go, are signing for the debt, and have people out there who don't have the same fiscal responsibility you do, it isn't good.

LAWYERS

Speaking as somebody who went to law school and actually practiced law for three months, lawyers are very important—but you have to know how to use them.

As usual, I found that out the hard way. My first lease took me about two months to work out, and I got a bill for $15,000 from my lawyer. The landlord's lawyer, on the other hand, because he was a sole practitioner, he had billed the landlord only $2,500. So I decided to hire the landlord's lawyer.

I also have a corporate attorney. I stumbled onto him, too. My first lawyer was from my old Park Avenue law firm. A couple of years ago, that firm got bought up by Finley Kumble, the giant legal supermarket that was going to rewrite the laws about lawyering until it failed in 1988. When my first lawyer disappeared into Finley Kumble, his fees all of a sudden had to support a much bigger overhead. The result was that I couldn't afford him any more.

I found my current attorney, Ronald Shechtman, through

the old-girl network—he went to college with my wife. I picked him out because I felt that I could talk to him. He has since become my friend, which I think is very important. The way I do business is that I fight a lot and it helps to have a lawyer standing behind you. It is very important to be able to talk to him or her beyond the usual attorney-client relationship. I'm on the phone to him several times a day to get his opinion on business matters, not just legal ones, and to plan strategies.

By the way, I don't believe in having your lawyer write threatening letters to people on his legal stationery. People are generally smart enough to see through that. Those letters are worth only the price of the expensive paper they are written on. Putting muscle behind them takes a lawsuit. As I've said before, there is nothing like having a couple of lawsuits going to help you keep your edge.

So I demand a lot of lawyering. The business I'm in—selling food products—does too. There are agreements to be drafted, disputes to settle, and so on. Neither I nor my lawyer knew anything about franchise law when we got started, but we know a lot now. We learned it together.

What is happening in the legal business these days is that everybody is looking for the next Roy Cohn, a tough-as-nails litigator who will strike fear in the heart of your adversaries. Well, as we are now finding out, the late Mr. Cohn had about as much legal acumen as the Wizard of Oz. He was all bluster and no action. He was fine for threatening people on the phone but terrible when it came to making routine filings and court appearances.

Which reminds me. I generally don't like dealing with huge law firms because they are expensive and cumbersome. But there are times when you need them. If you are involved in something that requires the shuffling of massive amounts of paper, such as a public offering, you can't beat them. They are skilled at producing huge amounts of boilerplate expensively typed and making sure it gets distributed to the right parties in the required amount of time. That's what they have all those associates and clerks for.

You may pay through the nose for it and you may get precious little in the way of advice, but you will have no trouble meeting the requirements of the law.

ACCOUNTANTS

A legal relationship is really more important than an accounting relationship. You can find a bean counter anyplace. You pay your money, and you get your beans counted.

You actually need two kinds of accountants. The first kind is a blue-chip corporate accounting firm, such as Arthur Andersen or Peat Marwick. They will charge you a lot of money and will not actually perform any kind of useful service. What they will do is send over twenty-five-year-old CPAs once a year to audit your books and tell you where you stand. You should already know where you stand; otherwise, you run the danger of going out of business. The value of having Arthur Andersen tell you where you stand is that you have a piece of paper with Arthur Andersen's name on it that you can use in your business negotiations. Should you want to borrow money from a bank, you need a certified financial statement, and your Arthur Andersen paper will provide that. Should you want to do some sort of deal with somebody who is worried about your financial stability, he will want to see that piece of paper, too. You will pay a lot of money for a certified financial statement, but it is a good thing to have. Lucky for me, Larry Charney, my accountant at Ernst and Whinney, has been very supportive and helpful.

The second kind of accountant actually produces some valuable work. He comes in quarterly or even more often to check on your books and pull your records together. And he should be able to provide some valuable advice about how to make your accounting system work for you, where to go for various services, and so on. He can tell you who pays their bills on time and who doesn't. Typically, he is a sole practitioner or works for a small office, is located nearby, and is easy to get to see on short notice. He will also charge you about one-half of what the big-name guy will charge you.

LOCATING PROFESSIONAL HELP

There are lots of ways to find these helpers, none of them foolproof. If you don't know anybody, ask around: friends, neighbors, suppliers, maybe even a competitor. The other thing to do is call the local bar association, describe what you need, and see who they recommend. They will probably give you several names, and you should go to see them. More important than the quality of their address or the thickness of their carpet is how hard they are willing to work for you and the degree to which you are *simpatico*.

Since you are small and just starting out, you cannot promise to provide enormous billings right away. But if you can find a lawyer or accountant who is also just starting out or is hungry for new business, you can actually cut a pretty good deal. They will hope that you will grow from a small fry into a big fry, and they will treat you accordingly. That's an easy way for them to get new clients. If they try to charge you a big entrance fee up front, they probably are not all that interested in you, and you should probably go elsewhere.

Instinct is important here. You can amass all the references you want, and you probably should, but if you don't feel comfortable with the people you pick or don't think you can develop a relationship, then it is probably best to go elsewhere.

EXECUTIVE TALENT

Talent is where you find it. That is particularly important in your case because you can't afford to hire a head-hunting firm, and you can't dangle impressive salaries in front of people. You have to be inventive.

I discovered Steve Stein, now the president of David's Specialty Foods, in a law firm I was using. I was looking for somebody to run the business, he was looking for something to do besides practice law, and it worked out. We are opposites. Steve is a detail guy; I'm a big-picture guy. He makes lists every day about what he wants to get done and does them; I sit around and strategize. That's fine with me. The nitty-gritty of the business bores me to tears and is hardly a good use of my talents. I can better spend my time dreaming up new food products, promoting the company, and talking to reporters.

Steve and I even work in the same office. I hang out on the ground floor of my town house on the east side of Manhattan. My wife runs the restaurant out of there, and we have two executive assistants.

Steve came along at a good time for me because I was in the process of digging myself out of my disastrous dealings with another partner who went sour.

LEONARD KAYE

Remember the Aesop's fable about the wolf in sheep's clothing? Aesop couldn't have known Leonard Kaye, but the fable sure fits.

I first met Leonard in 1980. He had a very large electronics distribution company in Chicago that he was about to sell, and he wanted the David's franchise in Chicago to give jobs to his employees. We hit it off instantly. He was charismatic, and he loved food just like I did. In fact, we started to socialize. My father introduced him to his second wife. He signed a letter of credit so I could borrow $800,000 to buy the town house I'm living in now. I became a kind of adopted son.

The Chicago franchise deal never happened, but after I had known him for a year, he made me another offer, one I couldn't refuse. He offered to put up the money to open up lots of stores in New York that he would run and to which I would supply the cookie dough. That sounded great to me. I was short of capital and management structure, and he had both. Plus, I could make more money on my core business, cookie dough.

Leonard wanted to open ten stores in the first year, so we ran around and signed up a lot of leases. The first couple of stores did very well, but then his organization began to collapse. The people that he had doing the administrative work couldn't handle ten stores.

When cracks started developing, Leonard started to show his true colors. He came to me and said the stores that he controlled couldn't pay for the cookie dough they had bought from me. They owed me a lot of money—over $250,000—about 90 percent of my outstanding receivables. He tried to sell his interest in the cookie stores to somebody else without telling me. It was clear that he was trying to drive me out.

I felt like the only choice I had was to buy him out or he would ruin me. Many of the stores were losing money because they were poorly operated. So I went to him to negotiate getting the stores back. He had maneuvered himself into a position of strength, and I had no leverage. In the end, I had to completely buy him out for $1 million.

The price was much too high, but I figured I didn't have any alternative. He was practicing a very sophisticated form of blackmail. I would be out of business in three months if I didn't get rid of him.

Eight months later, Leonard opened a competing store called Sweet Victory selling cookies and ice cream that violated an anticompete clause in the buy-out agreement. Naturally, we stopped paying him his $1 million. It turned out that while we were still running around together, he had formed a rival organization to make cookie dough so he wouldn't have to buy it from me. He had been making a concerted effort to ruin my business. We eventually went to arbitration, and I got the amount of money I owed him reduced substantially.

Subsequently, Leonard took Sweet Victory public for $5 a share. The stock went as high as $12, but that was the ball game. Leonard couldn't run that business either, and the stock is now selling for almost nothing.

It turns out that I wasn't the only guy Leonard tried to

ruin. I've been told he did the same thing with a barbecue restaurant and a furniture company. This is not the type of person I would ever do business with again.

MORAL

The lessons for me in terms of doing deals is that you have to think through how the situation can impact on you if it goes awry. I didn't have the foresight to see that Leonard could get the kind of leverage on me that he did. He's another example of my maxim that if it seems too good to be true, it is.

Another maxim, I'm sorry to say is that, if you tend to have good human values and you are trustworthy, sometimes in business you have to fight those instincts. My experience with Bobby Shapiro and Leonard Kaye show that some people will take advantage of you if you give them an opportunity.

MOBILIZING THE TALENT

Like most good managers, I am intolerant of meetings. There are plenty of other ways to get things done without them.

We have staff meetings every Monday. I don't go to them because I can't stand sitting through them. Bob Tisch, the former postmaster general, whom I got to know when he was my landlord, told me that the reason he left Washington was that he couldn't stand the endless meetings. Since he and his brother Larry run Loews Corporation out of their back pockets, they weren't used to them. They would just talk to each other.

Instead of meetings, you give directions to various people in your organization and say, "Accomplish this." I find that if I can go up to somebody and say, "I need six things done in the next two days, and don't worry about what the other guy is doing; he's got his own problems," chances are those six things will be done. Besides, I know everybody will talk to each other without me having to tell them to.

There is another approach. Call a meeting to order and let everybody say what they have to say, shoot each other down, and kill each other. Then in the last five minutes, you say, "Let me sum this up. What we've agreed on is this, this, and this," and leave the room. Everybody is so confused, they don't know what to say. Afterwards, you put out a memo with everything in writing. Of course, "this, this, and this" were the same things you wanted to do in the first place and bore little or no relation to what was discussed. It isn't terribly democratic, but it works.

THE STAFF

Dealing with your workers is far different from coping with your executives and deserves its own chapter, full of heartache and woe.

15
HIRING, OR WHY THERE ARE SO FEW GOOD PEOPLE AROUND

I have the answers to a lot of questions, but one problem I haven't figured out is how to find and keep a steady supply of good people. If you know the answer, write me; I'd love to know what it is.

This isn't only my problem. It is everybody's problem that I know of. There are not enough young people, the ones you get are uneducated and don't have the proper work habits, and they want more money than I can afford to pay them.

As soon as you get into business, it will be your problem, too. It is one you have to solve. Ultimately, you will function only as well as your employees.

SHORTAGES

I am sure there are very nice communities in the Midwest or the South where you can find high school kids who want to work. In big urban environments, you have problems. Common sense tells you that the fast-food industry is going to

169

have to change. The first question we ask potential franchisees is, "Where are you going to get the people?" Ultimately, you are going to have robots serving the hamburgers at McDonald's.

David's Cookies has thousands of hired people. It sounds unbelievable, but out of all of those it is tough to find good ones. I don't know anybody in this business who is doing it well. I think a lot of potential workers look at these as entry-level jobs that lead nowhere. Nobody aspires to a career running a bunch of Mrs. Fields cookie stores or even a bunch of David's Cookies stores. They are putting in their time and passing through on their way to other things. They all think they can do better than work for a cookie company.

Money is not the answer. We pay as well or better than anyone else in the industry. People come into our system above minimum wage, and if they are at all energetic, they get a fifty cent per hour raise within a couple of months. A couple of months after that, they become an assistant manager making $12,000–$15,000 a year. They can go up to $25,000 or $30,000 if they run a big store and do a good job.

You don't get better people even if you raise the ante. In supermarkets, for example, a unionized checkout person, who makes the least amount of money in the store, gets $10–$12 an hour with benefits. That's pretty high for an entry-level job, yet the turnover is astronomical.

Advancement is surely not the answer because we lay out for them a very attractive performance path. We tell our employees that if they can walk, talk, and breathe, they will be an assistant manager within six months; and if they stay just a little while longer and show at least average intelligence, they will be managing a whole cookie store. They could care less. Company picnics and that kind of stuff don't work either.

It is just as bad in the restaurant business. Everybody is an actor or actress waiting to be discovered—that's their dream, what keeps them in the system. Of course, it is hard to concentrate on working in the kitchen or being a waiter when you are thinking about your next audition.

We are down to one company-owned store. Mrs. Fields is different. They have no franchisees; they own all their stores outright. As a result, Mrs. Fields has to try to develop talent internally. Mrs. Fields lives or dies on a promotion system within their stores. But it isn't successful. I understand the turnover of store managers is very high.

These kinds of low-wage service businesses eat up people and spit them out—that's a fact of life. Nobody else is having any better luck. Macy's Herald Square hires the people who work in the David's Cookies store there. During the busy season in the fall, I am constantly urging them to hire more people. They tell me they hired four yesterday, but three were fired for stealing and four more quit because they couldn't take the pressure, and on and on and on.

Macy's is a very important outlet for us. It does more than $500,000 a year and has very high visibility. So we decided to copy the cosmetics companies. We put our own manager in that store. He works for Macy's, but we pay him. Even though this guy is expensive, he's going to get the sales up substantially just because he's paying attention.

Unless you've got a situation like Balducci's where many of the sixty employees are part of the family, there isn't a store in New York that doesn't have to worry about being properly staffed on a day-to-day basis.

THE UPSIDE OF NEPOTISM

I have had a lot of family members pass through my various businesses. My wife, Susan, has been running the restaurant almost since it opened. My cousin Ann was involved with it for a while. Her sister, my cousin Ginny, was a waitress in the restaurant. Susan's older brother Rocky worked as a baker in the restaurant and as a counterperson and manager in the cookie store for a number of years. My brother was involved with selling franchises for David's. My mother scooped cookies. It worked out. Plus, they were honest. But hiring relatives can be a mixed blessing if they take advantage of their privileged position. There is no one set of rules.

HONESTY

It is an enormous problem.

When a franchisee asks us how to control the money, we say, "Look, we have very exact systems and only a few products, so it is not a very complicated inventory system. At the end of the day, the dough is in either the refrigerator or the cash register. If it isn't, then somebody took it. And if somebody took it, we can't tell you where to look."

We can't catch the thieves for them; we can only run the numbers.

What is terribly disappointing and sick about this whole environment is that often the young people who work for us are the ones who are setting up armed robberies. They have a friend come into the store and take the money out. That's the inherent problem with this kind of business. You have to pay attention. If you don't, the employees begin to believe it is their business, and they help themselves.

I think the rest of the country is better than New York City, but things are definitely headed in the wrong direction. The rip-off mentality, the lack of ethics in business, is much worse now than when I started in 1979. People see these kids on Wall Street who are barely old enough to shave either stealing or making millions of dollars. So they ask, "Where is some of this for me?" As long as we have a succession of public officials who are thieves, crooks, and robbers, it is going to be hard instilling honesty in young people.

SCREENING PROCEDURES

One of the ways we try to find good people is by screening them thoroughly in the interview process. Through long experience we have developed a set of hiring guidelines for store managers that I think are valuable. In fact, they are so good I will give them to you verbatim.

Questions you (a store manager) should ask in an interview.

1. How long does it take you (the applicant) to get to work? You need people who are within about fifteen minutes of the store. If a person works only twelve to fifteen hours a week, it isn't really worth the cost of getting to work to travel any farther than that.
2. How will you get to work? Are several family members sharing the same car? Chances are you will need the employee sometimes when there is no ride available.
   working somewhere else? That doesn't make for much flexibility.
3. Are you over eighteen? If you hire a seventeen-year-old without working papers who injures himself, you are in a lot of trouble.
4. Marital Status? A mother who brings children with her to an interview is bad news. Find out what the husband or father does. Always be on the lookout for a spouse who could cause trouble. Some occupations that can spell possible trouble for us are labor officials, lawyers, etc. Teenagers who have been involved in a parent's business are pretty good risks. What parent would let their kid stand around and do nothing?
5. Number of dependents and ages? If there are small children, who will stay with them? Will the husband keep them when the wife is at work? A housewife who really wants the job will have the answers to questions about child care already settled and may even tell you before you ask.
6. What family obligations do you have that will conflict with your job? Summer at the shore? Bowling every Friday night? Church every Wednesday night?

7. What does your spouse think of your working? If a husband doesn't want his wife to work, he will make her life so rough for her that she will quit without warning. Sometimes men feel really opposed to a wife bringing home extra money.

8. What position are you applying for? If they put "cashier," have they worked at K Mart, where they stand at a register all day and say, "Thank you for shopping at K Mart?" If they put "stock work," are they shy people who might not be able to sell to customers?

9. What pay do you expect to get? If you pay less than what they have been getting, make sure that it is agreeable.

10. How many hours a week do you want to work? A person who says full-time usually wants just that. He will work part-time only until he finds full-time work, and then you lose.

11. What times are you available? Be sure that weekends are no problem.

12. Is there a second job? If there is, we usually end up playing second fiddle and get the person only when the other place doesn't need them.

13. Were you previously employed by us? Before hiring this person, check with the supervisor.

14. Are there any friends or relatives working for us? Company policy states that we do not hire relatives. Friends working together can cause huge problems. They will want to ride together, work together, etc.

15. When can you start? We encourage people who are presently working and are leaving another job to work for us to give two weeks' notice. We would want the same courtesy from someone leaving us.

16. Do you have any physical limitations? Bad backs don't go with lifting. Bad legs or feet don't go with standing all day. Bad kidneys mean lots of time lost in the bathroom. Chain smokers just don't fit into our work routine.

17. Is past education in keeping with this type of work? Why does a person with a college degree want only part-time work? Is it to raise a family or keep income and taxes down?
18. What references are listed? Ministers and other professional people are good.
19. Are you a job hopper?
20. If you were at one job for a good period of time, did you get pay increases? You know that we give pay increases to people who do a good job. Most companies operate this way to keep good employees.
21. Is all time accounted for? Don't be afraid to ask what a person was doing between jobs.
22. Why did you leave a particular job? Not getting along with a boss should be pursued. Remember, there are always two sides to a story. Was the work too demanding? What couldn't they do, or what didn't they want to do?
23. Why do you want to work at David's Cookies? This will tell you a lot about the person. Does the answer say they just want a job or they want to work for you because they love cookies and people?

There is a lot of common sense involved in hiring. If you are hiring a baker, you don't look at credentials or references. You say, "Make me a cake." If the cake is no good, you don't hire the baker. When you hire a controller, you ask him if he can count.

References are, by and large, totally worthless. I know that for a fact because I am one of the few people who give realistic references. I got crazy taking a former employers at his or her word that so-and-so is good when so-and-so is a disaster.

DOING IT BY THE BOOK

Since most of our cookie-store workers tend to be young and have limited job experience, we find it crucial to spell out exactly what is expected of them. We have employee evaluation forms that rate them from poor to excellent on the following traits and skills: attitude, enthusiasm, speed, sales techniques, baking knowledge, scooping skill, bagging/ boxing skill, customer awareness, aggressiveness, scale and register knowledge, and availability. We also provide employee incident reports for when employees break the rules or there are security problems. The reports are designed to prevent abrupt firing by making the manager take the time to fill out the report and to make the eventual tasks of firing an employee, when it has to be done, much easier. One report has been especially effective at communicating company goals and job requirements to workers. Here's a sample.

Attendance and Tardiness

Our general policy is that from the day of hiring, job attendance and punctuality are an important part of each employee's performance record. Employees absent for any reason must notify the store manager by 8:00 A.M. that day or at least two hours before their scheduled starting time. Absence without notification is cause for dismissal, as is a pattern of excessive absence. Repeated tardiness may result in disciplinary action or discharge.

Disciplinary and Termination Policy

1. Probation Period—An employee whose work or conduct is unsatisfactory during the probation period will be terminated, but only after a warning from the manager.
2. Immediate Dismissal—An employee may be dismissed immediately and without warning for any of the following causes:
   A. Using or being under the influence of drugs or alcohol while on company property. Also, receiving, selling, or distributing medically unauthorized or illegal drugs while on company property
   B. Proven dishonesty or theft

C. Violation of corporate cash-handling procedures
D. Absence without notification
E. Embezzlement
F. Falsifying company reports or records
G. Deliberate, willful destruction or damage of company or personal property

3. Disciplinary Action or Termination—Activities that may result in one of these procedures are:
    A. Possessing firearms on company property
    B. Willfully completing another employee's time card or allowing another employee to complete one's time card
    C. Falsely claiming sick leave
    D. Insubordination
    E. Any action while in company uniform which discredits or results in loss of good will toward the company
    F. Failure to report a sale at the time of the transaction
    G. Any negligent action resulting in injury to self or to others, or damage to company or other private property
    H. Irregular attendance on the job

The work rules are not extensive, but they are direct, specific, and easily understandable. They include guidelines on eating in the store, parking, and personal appearance. We have a set of nine check points on neatness, covering aprons, blouses and shirts, blue jeans, stockings, and shoes. We even have rules on entering and leaving the store. For security reasons, everybody has to go through the front door. When in doubt, spell it out.

Customer Service

There is no substitute for treating customers right, yet you would be amazed to learn how many people we hire don't have any instinct for good service. Here are some simple guidelines:

Customer complaints must be handled quickly, courteously, and without question.

Customer concerns are David's Cookies' concerns. When a customer wishes to return merchandise, proof of purchase or a sample of the product is required.

Procedure for handling a complaint:

1. Tell the customer that you are sorry that he/she has been disappointed or inconvenienced.
2. Do not contradict the customer or argue with him/her. The magic words are, "We are sorry. What can we do to correct the problem?"
3. First, offer to replace the merchandise with fresh merchandise of equal or greater value. If this is unacceptable, offer to replace the merchandise with a gift certificate.
4. If the customer insists on a refund and has a sales receipt, give it immediately and cheerfully.
5. It does not make any difference from which David's Cookies store the merchandise was purchased.
6. After the customer is satisfied, get all the details: name, address, store, etc., so that the incident can be followed up.

Failure to treat customers equally regardless of race, sex, or color will not be tolerated.

Crime

Needless to say, there are extensive guidelines on how to deal with robberies. The most important is this: In the event of a robbery, employees should not offer any resistance. If a robber demands money and/or merchandise, the store employee should comply immediately and without resistance. The company places greater value on the safety of employees than on material goods such as cash and merchandise.

RULES GET YOU ONLY SO FAR

Of course, you could give some employees ten volumes of rules and make them recite them every day, and it wouldn't make any difference. The difficulty of finding good people is a continuing disappointment. Since I have always been driven, it is hard for me to fathom why the people we hire are not better motivated. It is a problem that I think is going to get worse, not better. Independent operators like me are having to spend more and more time scheming up ways to get people to work at our stores.

There is an endless demand for young people to work in these stores, and there are just not enough of them. In fifteen years, as the numbers get smaller, we are going to have a major crisis finding good people to work in retail selling. Not only is it a lousy job in the eyes of the public, it is becoming a dead-end job. What's frustrating for us is that we use what I think is a pretty common-sense system. We tell them, "Look, we know you are not going to stay here forever, but if you pay attention while you are here and work hard, you can be promoted and learn something." People still don't want to do it. It is a very discouraging problem.

SOLUTIONS

At a mayor's conference in New York recently I met this guy named Maximo Blake who has a company called the Court Employment Project. He takes 250–500 teenagers a year out of Rikers Island prison and tries to straighten them out. While the politicians of this world talk about all the good things they do, this guy is doing it. And he does it in a very creative way. He started a demolition company with guys who were convicted of breaking and entering. Now they run around wrecking houses and get paid for it. He started a car-stripping company with guys who were arrested for stripping cars. If they work hard, they can earn a piece of the action.

I just took back a cookie store from a franchisee at Twenty-third and Eighth Avenue, and I don't want to run it. I told Maximo that if we could figure out a way, his young people could work in the cookie store and buy it at the same time. I will sell it to them for basically the price of the security deposit on the lease. They will be responsible for the bills—rent, electricity, and so on—and they can buy the store from us for $15,000.

It was a good idea, but Maximo's board of directors turned him down. They were afraid that the young people wouldn't be properly supervised and that they could not resist the temptation of stealing from the store. I was very discouraged. If we don't do something, we are going to lose this generation. We have to start by fixing the schools. Recently, I was involved in adopting a class at a New York City junior high school. It is part of a program to introduce these kids to a more stable way of living. So I'm going to take them to my cookie plant and show them how a business operates. Hopefully, some of them will be inspired to stay in high school and get a steady job when they graduate.

LEARNING HOW TO DELEGATE

Once you have learned how to do everything, you then have to learn how to let go. The process of delegating is the process of becoming an entrepreneur, because then you can remove yourself from day-to-day details and think about the next deal you are going to get into. If you are worrying about fixing the copier or hiring a secretary, you are not using your time effectively.

I don't run David's on a day-to-day basis. Sometimes I wish I did. I'm not up to my neck in the grimy details; I am up to my neck in the strategic questions about where the company is going, what we do next, how we push this thing to the next level. Giving up control is excruciating. You are letting other people make decisions at important levels, and you have to work yourself through the tendency to second-guess everybody. Ultimately, you are going to grow only if you attract people who in effect become partners as the business begins to grow. You have to become secure with the notion that other people are going to be making decisions and you might not agree with 100 percent of them. But if you don't let them make decisions, you'll never get any bigger, and they won't learn how to take on more responsibility.

16
HOW TO
BECOME FAMOUS

S omewhere along the way during your early months of operation, you'll need to figure out ways to leverage yourself. Your product is out there. The people walking by your store who stop in to try it like it. They tell their friends, so you have begun expanding your market beyond the street traffic. But you need more customers than you can reach that way. How do you take the next giant step?

The answer is to let the media find your customers for you. And out of all the things I have done in business, this has proved to be one of the easiest.

BEING DIFFERENT SELLS

First, you must have a product that is not a me-too product; there will be other me-too products out there, and yours won't have a chance unless yours is different. Then you have to identify what makes your product different, or unique, or controversial, or sexy, so you can promote it.

THERE IS ALWAYS A GIMMICK

I don't care what kind of product you have; there is always a way to get your foot in the door.

Say you have a quick-lube franchise. You call all the newspapers, radio and television stations, newsletters, and weekly shoppers and say, "I've got the best lube store in town. It's unique; come do a story about it," and they won't listen to you.

So you need a gimmick. A gimmick could be giving something away. "The first 400 people to show up at 4 A.M. get a free lube job"—that's a story. You are going to have 400 crazy people in front of your store. "The proceeds from the first 100 lubes on Saturday will go to charity"—that's another story.

All you can expect from the media at first is that people will discover you are alive. Then you take it from there, whether you do a good lube job or a lousy lube job. But I think there is always a way to create some sort of crazy situation that will get the press to cover you. Hire an elephant and give him a lube job. The press is looking for craziness.

Everybody, from McDonald's Ray Kroc on down, got started this way. They got one break, and they got noticed.

THE MEDIA VOID

In terms of publicity, think about your product in the following way. There are ten thousands of journalists in this country. Every day they wake up and they have to do their job, just like you do. They have to fill up their pages or their TV screens or their magazine covers with somebody's story about something. They can't write about "Man Leaves Wife for Bulldog" all the time. They have to write about something that is somewhat factual because that's what their business is all about.

So you should approach the garnering of publicity with the notion that a reporter has to write about something. If you can deliver an interesting story, it is just as easy for him to write about you as it is to write about the next guy who's delivering not such an interesting story. That's 99 percent of the battle right there.

HOW I GOT INTO SHOW BUSINESS

I got lucky; I started at the top with Craig Claiborne, food editor of the *New York Times.*

Back in 1975, when I was still in law school, he wrote a story about my working as a chef at Troisgros, a three-star restaurant in France. Claiborne heard about me through the publicity department of New York Community College, where I was studying cooking while I was in law school. The reason he wrote about me is that I was the first American who'd worked in the kitchen of a top French restaurant.

Worse things can happen than being written up by the *New York Times.* It put the story on its national wire service, and the piece was syndicated all across the country. As a result, a lot of other reporters started calling me up and interviewing me.

If you want to get noticed, you can promote yourself intelligently. But don't stretch the truth too far to make your story better than it is. If your credibility is questioned, you are dead meat. In the case of Troisgros, for instance, I was absolutely the first American to get a job as a chef in that restaurant. They paid my room and board. After the article came out, everybody and their mother came out of the woodwork saying, "I used to work at that restaurant." It turned out a lot of people would go there for the weekend, and they'd put on an apron and putter around in the kitchen for three or four hours a day. And they said they "worked" at Troisgros. The bottom line is that they weren't working there sixteen hours a day for an extended period of time.

PROMOTING SAUCIER

Two years later, I started Saucier, and I was in the market for publicity. Thanks to that story that Claiborne wrote, I had an opening. Surprisingly, a lot of food writers remembered it.

As it turned out, Saucier was a product that was easy to promote but hard to sell. It was sexy, and it had mystique. The trouble was nobody knew what it was good for. Still, Saucier was a natural for TV publicity because I could go on TV programs and in seven minutes make two sauces right in front of the cameras. The story had motion, it had cooking—TV people love cooking segments. Plus, in 1977, I was practically the only one doing this. That is more interesting than going on a talk show, holding up your fingernails, and saying, "Look at this new color of nail polish I invented last week."

ON THE ROAD

So I started out on these publicity tours for Saucier, and in two months I was interviewed by more than 100 newspapers, I was on forty television shows, and I did innumerable radio programs. It was always the same schtick. I would take my carrots, onions, a piece of meat, and two saucepans, and I would go on TV. In seven minutes I would make two sauces, I would tell them my life story, I would listen to the host tell me what kind of great cook he was, how he'd made this great peanut butter salad dressing that I had to try. And then when the thing was over, I would put my two greasy saucepans in my suitcase and go on to the next city.

Often, I was selling Saucier in cities where my distributor hadn't even gotten it on shelves yet. And if that isn't lesson one, it is lesson one-A: don't do publicity until you have something to sell. That came back to whap me in the face a second time when I went out to promote a cookbook I had co-authored on nouvelle cuisine—and there were often no books in the bookstores.

KEEP IT SIMPLE, STUPID

I have done seven publicity tours. I've always had too much to do in a day rather than not enough. The challenge was not getting the space or the air time but the mere logistics of getting from the newspaper to the TV station. If you are prepared to take the incredible abuse of media tours, they will be there for you.

You have to make sure you have something to sell and your message is simple. That was my problem with Saucier. Even though to me it was clear, because I had been making the product for a long time, I couldn't in a short time period explain to the American public what that stuff was. I think that is a problem with computers now. You cannot explain how to work a computer in thirty seconds.

BE YOUR OWN BEST PUBLICIST

Why, you may ask, if I didn't know what I was doing, didn't I hire a professional to do it for me?

If you have a product that is screaming for promotion, *you* have to go out there and promote it yourself.

One of my basic rules is that you better know how to take out your own garbage before you pay somebody to do it for you. So you have to know a little bit about a lot of things to get your product to the market. If you don't have a sense of how to promote your product yourself and you just go out to a public relations agency and say, "Promote this," they are not going to know what to do unless you tell them. Besides, it will cost you money you don't have.

I really believe that you are much better off talking directly to the media. That way, they get to know you and you develop a relationship. Second, you can work on your own story by talking to a number of reporters and editors and thereby make it more appealing to them.

BE CONTROVERSIAL

These Milquetoast people who say, "he's wonderful and she's wonderful" put everybody to sleep. That's not what the media want to write about or broadcast. Part of playing to the sensibility of the media is being controversial and saying what you think. They want you to say that so-and-so is a jerk and here's why. As long as you have reasons for saying it and you don't say everybody's a jerk, you can get colorful. Being a very controversial character anyway, I say a lot of candid, real-life things about people in the food business. That's my nature: being nice to people who are genuine and skewering the phonies. Having been in the food business full-time since I quit the law firm, I think I've paid my dues enough to be able to do that.

BE JUDGMENTAL

If you are marketing a whoopie pie and you think it is better than the competition's whoopie pie—especially a competitor with many more assets than you have—and you can prove it, there is nothing wrong with saying the other guy's whoopie pie is garbage. Besides, that is the kind of thing the media will respond to. They will come after you to find out who this loudmouth is who's saying he has a better whoopie pie.

As usual, the corporate world is slow to catch on. It seems to me that the whole business of comparing people's products by name has been going full steam ahead for only the last six or seven years. Forget Coke and Pepsi wars. Now they are fighting over Raisin Bran on national television. It is a fact of life; everybody wants to be better than the other guy, and everybody is prepared to prove it. That's all-American stuff.

GO STRAIGHT TO THE SOURCE

When pitching your story, go straight to the person who

can do you the most good. I believe in the filter-down theory. If a reporter at Channel Two in New York gets a letter from Larry Tisch, the guy who runs CBS, that says, "I had the most delicious brownie in the whole world last night, and I want you to do a story about it," it is going to make more of an impression than if you, the owner of the brownie store, write to the general assignment desk. The trick then becomes how to get your brownie in Larry Tisch's mouth.

The other approach is to go directly to the person who deals with your area: the small-business reporter or the food reporter. Don't get tied up with the assignment editor or the story-development editor. You want to go to the person who knows what you are talking about and can make a recommendation to cover your story. Plus, they will do it quicker. I think you should always go to the source in any kind of situation in life. Since I'm the owner, I pay more attention to the various complaints coming into my office than the truck driver who failed to deliver my cookie dough or the man who put the person in the wrong seat in my restaurant.

FORGET SHYNESS

Unless you invented antiaging cream or some other irresistibly interesting medical process, the media will not come to you—you have to go to them. A lot of people are shy and don't like to do that. I'm shy, too, although I may not come across that way. I never sold anything in my life. And I'd probably be a lousy salesman selling somebody else's product. But I think I'm pretty good at pitching my own product because I have faith in it.

One of my rules is that you have to trust your instincts. Before you are out on your own for too long, you will have to develop the ability to sell. It won't be as hard as you think. You will constantly have to present yourself to customers, partners, employees. So pretty soon you learn to make a good pitch. If you are shy about going out and making presentations, it is almost a good sign because then you have to think long and hard about what your message is.

Since I am personally comfortable with my products, I can answer any question anybody can throw to me about them. That's as opposed to a public relations person who is used to packaging the story and isn't as familiar with it. I am less comfortable answering questions like, "What is America going to be eating in ten years?" I do better with questions like, "Why is your chocolate better than somebody else's chocolate?" It really is a matter of promoting from your strength, rather than generating a lot of hype because you have nothing that is new or different.

I don't think anybody really likes to go out and sell. That's why I think so many actors and actresses fail. They may be good at what they do, but they don't know how to go out and promote themselves. They hide behind agents, and they are just another piece of meat to that agent. That's why only one percent of the actors and actresses today make enough money to live on in their chosen profession.

There are a lot of pure salesmen out there, but for the most part they don't make good entrepreneurs. There are people who sell thousands of new cars a year yet do not own the car dealership. We have a guy at David's Cookies who calls himself a sales animal. He goes out there, establishes relationships, and works people over, and he sells and sells and sells. But I'm not sure he wants to or has it in him to run his own business.

BE FORCEFUL BUT DON'T PUSH

If you approach the press incessantly, it is not going to work. And you needn't. Word of mouth among the press is phenomenal. There's a daisy chain there. It can work for you, but it can also work against you. If *New York* magazine does something, then TV will, but the *Times* often won't because they are competing against each other.

I have never gone after a piece of publicity in my life— ever. I will never call up somebody and say, "I am doing a great cookie; do my cookie." I use the principle of putting things out there and getting people to try them. One thing I'm sure of now is that writers and editors *will* try them. They may hate them or love them, but at least they'll try them. Then they will either say, "I want to do something about this," or they don't want to do something about this.

There is one exception. When we opened up Chez Louis, we wrote a letter to Bryan Miller, the restaurant critic of the *New York Times*. We didn't say to come; we just said we were open. And then he didn't come for ten months.

IN GENERAL, BE HONEST

Hype doesn't hurt. It hasn't hurt Donald Trump. Trump is a master at publicity. If his game is to just get his name in the press so he can sell more apartments, he is doing a phenomenal job.

Trump gets knocked around a little, too. If you play the publicity game, you are going to learn very early that you are dealing with the good and the bad. Think of it as a long boxing match. You may be on the canvas in round seventy-five, but you still need to get off the canvas and go to round seventy-six. The press loves to love you and leave you, that's its nature. The press loves to build people up and then cut them off at the knees.

One of the problems is that the press is so used to seeing hype that it can't see when somebody is being very honest. There is no good way for them to check it out because they assume you are hyping. This comes back to what I really believe about David's Cookies: we use better ingredients than anybody else. When I was going around trying to get the press to understand that there is a serious difference between using fresh eggs and frozen eggs, or imported chocolate and domestic chocolate, I couldn't get anybody to pay attention.

Now, that doesn't mean that we didn't win a lot of these cookie tasting contests and that we didn't sell a lot of cookies. But I went to the press and said, "There are real quantitative reasons why our cookies taste better than their cookies and why ours cost a dollar more per pound.

Some stories are too good to be true. Take something that happened to me. For a while, we were selling French bread to the French consulate in Manhattan. That's like selling spaghetti to Italians—it was unbelievable. I didn't even know we were doing it until I got a call from a reporter who asked if it was true. I replied, "That's news to me because we don't have any special accounts, so we don't know. People come in and give us the money, and we give them a loaf." It turns out that the consulate was sending a maid over to buy the bread.

There's a limited stretch factor you can use in dealing with the media. But I would never have made up that French consulate story because it would be so easy to check out with a telephone call.

CELEBRITIES DO NOT COUNT

In fact, the stuff you could lie about in terms of promoting a product is probably not worth lying about. For instance, it doesn't really make any difference whether Ronald Reagan or Paul Newman or Spuds MacKenzie eats David's Cookies. It really doesn't.

When I first opened my restaurant, it was a big deal whether such-and-such celebrity was coming to eat. The game was really invented by certain newspaper columnists for their benefit. They would call up and say, "I'm bringing a celebrity to your restaurant; of course, we'll get a free dinner, and I'll write about it." They got a free meal and an item for the column, and I got my name in the papers.

Lately, the whole scene has become more sophisticated. Movie stars don't matter now; it is fashion designers. We are always hearing about what famous person did or did not come to our restaurant, and it doesn't make a bit of difference long term. What matters is whether the food and the service are any good.

STAY VISIBLE

If you have the option, you ought to think about the kinds

of ways you can keep yourself in the public eye. What I am trying to do now is more personal—more speaking engagements to defined groups, where I can work on my message a little better. I really hate giving speeches. I break out in a cold sweat before I go on. But I make myself do it.

JUST AS LONG AS THEY SPELL YOUR NAME RIGHT

Actually, I've been treated pretty fairly by the press. The reason is that there is so much going on in the food business that I've become a source for a lot of the stories that are printed in these magazines and newspapers. That's true in any business: you want to become known as a source. I know some people in politics who are never going to be publicly criticized because they are sources.

So just grin and bear it when they spell your name wrong. You really have to develop a thick skin. You must get used to being beat over the head occasionally. Just keep your story interesting and fresh.

HOW TO DO PUBLICITY WRONG

Chipwich is an example of how not to get wide exposure. The founder, Richard Lamotta, made a lot of mistakes. In the summer of 1981, Lamotta had the fastest-selling product on the streets of New York. It was a novelty ice cream product: vanilla ice cream sandwiched between two chocolate chip cookies, and he priced it at a dollar—back then that was a lot of money. It was so successful that he sold tens of thousands daily. Then he got greedy. The first thing he did wrong was saying he created the recipe. That was stupid. He didn't need to make that claim, and besides, it wasn't true.

Then he had one of his lawyers call me up and threaten to sue if I did not stop selling David's ice cream cookie sandwich. The lawyer threatened to put a Chipwich cookie store next to every one of our cookie stores, and if they couldn't get a lease, they were going to put a Chipwich cart in front of every David's Cookies store. That was fine with me because I was convinced mine tasted better, and the public feud would help my sales.

It was all downhill from there. He got into a fight with Good Humor over whether it had stolen the Chipwich idea. Whether it did or not, you can't patent a food product, so it wasn't against the law. Eventually, everybody was knocking him off.

To raise money, Lamotta tried to go public. The Securities and Exchange Commission took one look at his prospectus and said, "No way." It said that he used an improper accounting technique that inflated sales and profits and that he hadn't properly disclosed legal problems.

In August 1984, less than three years after he was the talk of the town, Lamotta got pushed into involuntary bankruptcy. The irony is that the two creditors who did him in were a marketing consulting company and an advertising agency. Despite all the enormous free publicity he had received, he went in hock to some professionals to get more.

By now he could have had a $100 million business because he had that kind of jump on everybody. But he started getting bad publicity, and it killed him. You don't go out and say your stuff is all natural, and then somebody reads the label and says, "Wait a minute, schmuck. It isn't."

He forgot what kind of business he was in. He should have said to himself, "Maybe this stuff isn't the most wonderful, the most natural, the most terrific product in the world. Maybe it is just a very good-selling, middle-of-the-road novelty item, and maybe I should just keep my mouth shut and put it out there at a reasonable price."

The bottom line is that in most specialty food businesses, there is some kind of correlation between value and price. The ingredients do cost more, so you have to charge more. There was nothing in his swill that should have cost any more than a Good Humor bar or any other comparable product in that price range. The customer knows—or even-tually finds out. Lamotta's problem was he started to believe his own publicity.

SUMMING IT UP

Publicity is easier to get than you think. If the product you are making or selling is novel, you merely have to alert the media to its presence. Even if you are not a natural sales-man, you should plug your own product yourself; you will be more convincing and sincere than any hired pitchman. Be generous in your estimation of its potential, but don't say anything so obviously stupid that it can be proven wrong. Don't be afraid to speak your mind either, as long as you are not slanderous—the media loves controversy. And never forget that publicity is no substitute for sales. If customers don't like your product, they won't buy it no matter how much they have seen or read about it.

17
SURVIVING YOUR FIRST YEAR IN BUSINESS

I honestly don't know how I lived through it. In 1979, I was trying to start two businesses at once—a cookie store and a restaurant. Under normal circumstances, that was something no sane person would do, but my landlord forced me into it. He wouldn't lease me the itty-bitty space for the cookie store unless I took the large space next door for the restaurant. It was too good a deal to pass up, and I guess you could say that I was too naive to realize how much trouble I was getting myself into.

OVERWORK ALMOST KILLED ME

My typical day that first year began when I took the subway in from Brooklyn Heights, where I lived, to Manhattan around 6:30 in the morning. I'd start making cookies and open the cookie store at 10 A.M. Then I'd sell the cookies for another hour until I would go next door to the restaurant and start making lunch. I was the chef. After lunch around 2:30, I'd go back to the cookie store and sell more cookies. At

5 P.M. it was back to the restaurant to begin cooking dinner. Then back to the cookie store around 11 P.M. to close it up and count the money. Sometime between midnight and 2 A.M., I'd hop on the subway and go back to Brooklyn. The next day, I would start all over again.

Lucky for me, I was too busy to get discouraged. I was winging it. I was operating on no sleep, no money, and no prospects. I was absolutely on the edge of a cliff every day— and I loved it. I made enormous mistakes, but because of the budding fame of the cookie business, we survived.

FORCED EXPANSION

In retrospect, even though I thought my world was coming to an end, the man from around the corner and his brick who I mentioned earlier turned out to be a good thing for me. That extra store that I didn't want provided me with space I needed to make more cookie dough. I turned it into a commissary. If he hadn't come along, I probably would not have started to expand when I did, and the business would have stagnated. So it got me over a big hump, the question of expansion, which is always very scary.

And that was the last time I got hassled. I'm not sure why, but I think that I had inadvertently done the right thing. It got out in the community that I bought the man out when I didn't have any money, so I was perceived as a good guy.

The Mafia picks up the business garbage in New York, and they do a better job of that than the companies that supply my food. That's surprising, because the incentives are all on the side of the garbage company. I can throw them out in ten minutes, but the Mafia owns this location. Compared to getting up every morning and beating my head against the wall with employees, suppliers, and city bureaucracy, I'd rather deal with the Mafia garbageman. I know the garbageman is always going to pick up my garbage at a regulated price.

In fact, the organized crime community is into drugs and women, not cookie stores and restaurants. The reason is simple: cookie stores are not high-grossing businesses. Oddly, nobody cares about my restaurant either. It doesn't do a big bar business, and that's where the cash is. Ninety-seven percent of the food business is American Express charges, and the Mafia doesn't steal from American Express.

Once some guy did try to shake me down in the restaurant, promising to destroy the place if I didn't pay him off. I physically threw him out, and he never came back.

FROM SECOND AVENUE TO HERALD SQUARE

After the *New York Times* article declaring my chocolate-chunk cookies were the best in the city, Macy's called. They wanted a cookie store. So I went down, and we had an hysterical meeting with the senior vice president in charge of food. He was a pure Macy's animal. If Macy's was burning down, he would throw himself on the building and try to put out the flames. He was skeptical about cookies in general, even though we had gotten that good review. His concern was that the cookies were going to smell up his store. He kept asking me what I was going to do about the cookie *odor* all over his Herald Square store, I kept on telling him that it was an *aroma*, not an odor.

We didn't open at Macy's until late October 1979. We replaced a jelly bean store that in a good week was grossing $1,200. Very quickly our store began doing $4,000 *per square foot* annually, or about fifteen times more business. So the odor magically turned into an aroma.

In a good week at Macy's now we do $15,000. In fact, David's has been at that same spot in the Herald Square store ever since, even though everything around it has changed. We don't own the location; we just supply Macy's with the product, the way that Calvin Klein supplies it with blue jeans.

We're in numerous Macy's now. I'd love to get my hands on that Herald Square outlet; we'd do much better if we managed it ourselves. Still, it is the best department store location we have ever opened. It shows that it doesn't do anybody any good just to get their product into a store. It has to be in the right spot or it won't sell and they will have to throw it out, which is embarrassing for both sides.

TRANSPORTATION

Expansion caused lots of headaches. I was shipping dough to Macy's in these expensive plastic buckets. Macy's was slow about returning them, so I never had enough. When the buckets did show up, it was always at lunch hour, when we were busiest and had the least room. The elevator in the basement was broken, so we had to carry the buckets up the stairs. The business was totally out of control, and the only thing that kept it going was that I was there all the time trying to make it work. And, of course, the product tasted good.

After a while, I figured I had to solve the bucket problem. So I devised a cardboard box with a plastic liner that we could use to pack the dough instead. You cannot be afraid of adversity; you cannot be afraid of making things up on the spot.

WATCHING THE TILL

Keeping the restaurant employees honest was a huge aggravation. There are 4,000 ways a bartender can steal from you but only 2,000 ways you can catch him.

Dishonest bartenders short customers on the drinks. If you specify a two-ounce drink and the bartender pours a one-ounce drink, he can steal half the money. Some bartenders bring in their own bottles so they can sell drinks out of them and pocket the receipts.

Crooked bartenders are very hard to catch. What some people do is hire observation companies that have employees who look like regular customers. They come in and drink and observe the bar to see if any of the money is not rung up.

There was a hot East Side bar where the absentee owner was absolutely convinced that the bartender was stealing $100-$200 a night. But he couldn't prove it. He would go to the restaurant and look around but couldn't see anything. Finally, he couldn't stand it any longer, so he hired one of these observation companies. They went in and studied the place but could not come up with anything either.

In desperation, he told them to hand in their report. It read: "From our constant observation of this bar, all of the liquor sales are being rung up in one of the three cash registers," Bingo. The restaurant owner had his man. There were supposed to be only two cash registers behind the bar. The bartender had brought in his own cash register.

CREATIVE CASH FLOW

There is an art to paying your bills that I learned very quickly. There are people you can pay right away and people you can delay. Some of the biggest corporations are the slowest payers. IBM and AT&T take up to 180 days to pay their bills.

We have had some of our suppliers from day one: the flour and sugar guy and Frank, the egg man, who has a chicken farm in New Jersey. Frank knows that when we get paid rapidly, he gets paid rapidly; and when we don't get paid as rapidly, he doesn't either. One summer he came to me and said a heat wave had killed one quarter of his chickens and he needed all the money he was owed plus a small loan to buy some chickens. So we gave it to him. It worked out.

PLANNING FOR THE FUTURE

By the end of the first year, business was so good that I opened three more cookie stores. I thought I wanted to stop right there. My office was this hole in the basement. The business was growing through osmosis.

Every day I had a major crisis. Where do I get enough chocolate? How do I put cookie dough in a box? How do I buy a truck to ship stuff to Macy's? I didn't have the luxury of sitting down and saying, "Let me see whether I'm on page three or page four of the business plan."

People were coming in to buy franchises for Long Island and Iowa and Japan, and I didn't know how to take their money. I had no interest in and no knowledge of franchising. So I had to hire a staff to screen the franchisees and set up the new stores. Lucky for me that it all turned out OK. What it taught me was you learn how to do business by being in the middle of colossal crises all the time. God knows, I couldn't afford to hire an outside consultant.

TAKING IT EASY

One thing I tried to be was very conservative. Excessive expansion can kill a small business. You start to get stars in your eyes and think everybody is waiting out there to buy your product. So you borrow a lot of money to expand, and then you find out that the market wasn't as strong as you thought. Presto! Your sales can't pay your borrowing costs. Debt can kill you right off.

Some people will argue that if you *don't* expand quickly, your competitors will and they will lock you out of new markets. That is true only part of the time. There are a lot of tortoises, as opposed to hares, that win these races. Some fast-food chains grew slowly in the face of this conventional wisdom and have done very well. White Castle is a perfect example. It seems to be on a thousand-year plan. It just keeps grinding out the stores. It doesn't seem to matter whether Wendy's, McDonald's, or Fuddruckers got there first; White Castle has a way of doing business that isn't hurt much by competition. Its market niche is unique.

Part of the expansion conundrum is a function of figuring out what your business is all about. Do similar companies compete against you or just complement you? I don't care where Mrs. Fields is going anymore, because I don't think Mrs. Fields and I are in the same business. We both sell cookies, but as time goes by we are selling cookies in a different way.

DE-EMPHASIZING RETAIL

Mrs. Fields still sells exclusively at retail through her stores. We, on the other hand, are developing broader methods of distribution. We now bake and sell cookies in supermarkets and department stores. We are beginning to sell cookies through national fast-food chains under the chains' labels. We also sell our cookie dough in supermarket refrigerator cases as well as to other bakers as private-label merchandise.

Quite honestly, we are de-emphasizing the 400- to 600-square foot retail store. In New York City, Häagen-Dazs and Everything Yogurt, as well as David's, are getting out of retail stores. At least this week, all these little stores don't seem to be the way to go. I could be wrong, but the way we are going to push our business in the future is either as very small stores—30 to 50 square feet—or much bigger stores. Or maybe we'll try totally new concepts like David's for Kids party places and zero-cholesterol baked goods.

NEW PRODUCTS

You have to walk a very fine line. On the one hand, you have to watch your competition very carefully. On the other hand, you don't want to get trapped into the game of duplicating what the competition does just for the sake of covering yourself. Mrs. Fields made a decision a year ago to go into soda: diet chocolate chip macadamia nut soda. That soda was offered to me two years ago. The promoter was putting together brand-name chocolate-flavored sodas. He tried Famous Amos, which fell on its rear end, and then he came to us. He wanted to do a licensing deal, where we would put our name on his soda. I thought to myself, "Wait a minute. just because Mrs. Fields and Famous Amos are going into the soda business doesn't mean that I have to go into soda, too." So I decided not to.

As it turns out, chocolate chip macadamia nut soda is not exactly taking the country by storm right now. In fact, I don't think it is even sold anymore. In the meantime, I can still sleep at night—occasionally.

PRACTICE, PRACTICE, PRACTICE

Not only did I know nothing about the retail business when I started out, I didn't know enough to know how tough it was. If there has been one disappointment of my business, it has been my foray into New York City retail stores. If I had grown up in a family of retailers, as so many successful store owners have, I would have known better. Murray Klein of Zabar's once told me he would have shot his son in the head if his son had ever told him he was going into the retail business. I never got that message. The landlords, the crime, the employees—you really have to be prepared for the aggravation.

MATTERS OF TASTE:
THE HONEY-OATMEAL AFFAIR

I had a cookie whose flavor I didn't like. It was honey oatmeal—the sixth cookie we introduced. We had chocolate chunk, pecan chocolate chunk, peanut butter, oatmeal raisin, and coffee walnut espresso. Honey oatmeal wasn't special. It looked like 100 other health-food cookies you can get at 100 health-food stores anyplace in the United States. I didn't think it was up to the same standards as the others. I was into making statements about what cookies should look like: irregular shapes and chunks, not chips, and this one didn't look like that. It looked like it was made with a cookie cutter. I thought it was horrible. So I dumped it.

Very soon afterward, I began to get hate mail. "How dare you take that cookie out? It is my favorite cookie," and "I'll never patronize your store again." People who wanted honey cookies wouldn't eat anything else. That's all they wanted. They would come into the store and say, "You have to put the cookies back; you are killing me." What could I do? I put it back.

There is an important lesson here. Listen to the customer. If they don't want to eat it, you can't jam it down their throats. In the meantime, I've changed my mind. People want healthful food right now, even if they kid themselves about what is really good for them. Honey isn't quite the right stuff—it is as fattening, if not more fattening than sugar and has the same effect on your body.

That's why I've developed this line of no-cholesterol muffins. Now there is this question of whether or not I am playing on people's paranoia about their health by luring them into a cookie store with the promise of healthful muffins in the hope that they will buy cookies instead. But the idea is to get them to buy *something*. Both products have a huge market.

MATTERS OF TASTE: THE INTRICACIES OF SHORTBREAD BAKING

We had a shortbread cookie that was phenomenal. It looked great and tasted great. But it was too complicated for the employees to bake. That's another lesson: given the general ability of the workers, the time available to train them, and the turnover, you have to keep it simple.

Early on, I realized that to make the cookie-baking system work, it had to be mistake free at the lowest common denominator: idiot proof. That's why we developed a conveyer oven instead of using the standard convection oven. With a convection oven, somebody has to remember to go to the oven and take the cookies out. With a conveyer belt oven, the cookies pass through the oven automatically and out the other side. The help has about ten minutes to remember to take the cookies out of the cooling area before they start backing up into the oven.

To make the oven system work, we had to develop a uniform cookie that would bake at the same temperature no matter what flavor it was because we couldn't expect the operator to keep on changing the temperature for ten or fifteen kinds of cookies.

That worked until the shortbread cookie came out. It is a hard, crisp cookie that has to be cooked for a much longer period of time. That entails lowering the heat on the oven and lengthening the time it goes through. What happened more often than not was that the operator would forget and burn the cookie or do it properly and then forget to set the oven back for the other cookies. So forget shortbread.

McDonald's is clearly the leader in terms of having whistles and bells to constantly remind the workers that they have to do something. And you have to make it as Pavlovian as possible or it doesn't work. In other words, the people have to respond to the signals automatically, practically without thinking.

MATTERS OF TASTE: THE FINAL CHAPTER

Now we are up to twenty-seven cookies. A lot of them are somewhat similar: chocolate chunks in place of pecans or macadamia nuts. Even if a particular cookie is not selling in some part of the country, we'll keep it in inventory so we can make it special order if there is a demand. Just give us two days' notice.

The most sophisticated cookie we make is coffee walnut. Mimi Sheraton, the former *New York Times* restaurant reviewer, said it was unforgettable. But it was too sophisticated for the cookie-consuming public. The taste was too subtle. So it didn't sell much. In fact, it may have been the worst-selling cookie ever.

Other flavors have been instant hits: coconut crisp chocolate chunk. Our butter cookie does great in the South, but you can't give it away in the north. We tried to sell pecan chocolate chunk in Japan, but we couldn't give them away because Japanese don't eat pecans. So now we have almond chocolate chunk, and it is their second biggest seller.

KEEPING THE EDGE

By nature, I have a very pessimistic personality. I am always prepared to cope with disasters, under the theory that if the disasters are fixed, the business will go forward under its own momentum—assuming it has any credibility or viability.

That's a lot different from people who don't look behind them and just keep on steaming ahead at a thousand miles an hour, hoping the blood will dry up on the way there. I don't believe in that. I believe you have to stitch up the gaping wounds as you get them. I never had one. I don't know what I would have done if things hadn't worked out. I don't believe you can go into business with an escape plan. You have to go until you crash. If you go at it halfheartedly, expecting to fail, you will.

It is not a very nice way to live—I'm often lousy to be around. But it is a realistic approach, and nine years later, I am still here.

Overoptimism can be dangerous. I think if I were the endlessly optimistic type, I could have gotten into trouble. There were a lot of times over the last nine years that we had major problems that had to be fixed right away. I could have said, "So what if the Mafia just threw a rock through my window? That's not so bad; I'll go out and buy some eggs tomorrow and throw them at the Mafia." But that's not how you deal with problems.

I *am* incredibly optimistic about the fact that David's cookies taste good. If they tasted terrible, I would have a problem. The excellence of my product allows me to try approaches that may be a little more radical or more controversial. In 1987, for example, I sold a piece of my business to some Japanese investors. It was a major milestone. It demonstrated the international appeal of the business that I have built and the fact that somebody besides me thinks it has some staying power. Plus, I got a nice price for it.

Nissho Iwai, these Japanese bankers, gave me a check for $1.5 million. I gave the check to my lawyer, told him to deposit it in the bank, and I turned to Steve Stein, the president of my company, and asked, "How many times did we get robbed this week?" The whole deal was anticlimactic. I think you have to keep that what-can-go-wrong mentality until you get rid of the whole business. At that point, when you cash it in, you can sit back and stop worrying.

THE DANGERS OF OVERNIGHT SUCCESS

Becoming famous in six months was both good news and bad news. The business survived, which was the good news. The bad news was that I believed I could walk on water. Every day when I went to work, I would have to fight my way through fifty customers waiting in line waving ten dollar bills to get to the front. It was unrealistic. The press blew it all out of proportion. It was Andy Warhol's fifteen minutes of fame come true. I didn't have any organization to handle the instant success, and I couldn't because I was making the cookies every day. I didn't have the down days that I could have used as a reference point five years later when the whole thing was falling apart because of crime, weak stores, and bad partners.

Now when I go into a new venture, I look at all the bad news, and I am very hesitant about blowing things up too early. Take my no-cholesterol muffins. I get daily calls from television, newspapers, health organizations, doctors, all wanting to talk about my muffins, and I'm just keeping my mouth shut. In the old days, I would have wanted 4,000 people in front of the store clamoring for the muffins. But long term it doesn't work. Until I can figure out how to produce and distribute the muffins efficiently, I don't want more business than I can handle.

Looking back over my first year in business, I realize how lucky I was. So many things could have gone wrong. I was really just living from day to day and using every bit of wisdom I had acquired by that age to stay afloat.

But I think people really make their own luck. I believed in what I was doing, I took chances where I saw opportunities, and I worked my tail off. Can anybody expect to repeat my experience? Probably not. Still, if you have the right gizmo and can find the right market and get it out there without being bled to death by landlords and suppliers and everybody else who is out to get you—you have a fighting chance. Just keep running through walls.

18
GETTING UP STEAM

There are a few rare people who start a business just to buy themselves a job. Once they get one location up and running, they stop. People who twitch a lot like me never stop. We always have to have something going, and that usually means expanding.

Expansion is good for a company if it is done right. It infuses an operation with excitement and energy and ensures that management stays on its toes. It provides the cash flow to develop new products and to diversify.

Of course, as I have pointed out, rapid growth can kill a company. You also may be disappointed to find out that your business is so specialized that it can't support a second outlet. So any expansion plans have to be well thought out in advance. Helping you do that is the purpose of this chapter and the next one.

HARD DECISIONS

If your product starts to sell, you will go through a tap

207

dance of anxiety for a long time as the business grows. There will be an ongoing question about whether you have enough production capacity to meet sales demand and whether you will have enough sales to meet production capacity. There is no way anybody can predict what you are going to sell, and there is no marketing consultant who can tell you that in 1993 you will be selling four times as many whoopie pies as you are selling in 1989. You are just going to have to figure it out for yourself, and that, in effect, is what being an entrepreneur is all about.

If you are lucky, you won't have to invest in more space or more machinery; you can just add people. One of the great successes of the 1980s is the Dove Bar. The way you make them is to have fifteen old ladies stand there hand dipping ice cream bars into a vat of chocolate. The process simply can't be automated. The finished product sells for $2 each. Dove Bars was sold for more than $47 million to Mars, the cheapest people in the world. So those old ladies must have been doing something right.

THE FLIP SIDE: FIGHTING THE GROWTH DISEASE

The other side of that is you may want to stay small. If all you are trying to do is buy yourself a job, you may have defined the parameters of what you want to be.

I didn't set out to build a company that would be selling food in a lot of different states. I started out to sell cookies out of a store at Fifty-third Street and Second Avenue. Sometimes I think I should have just stopped there. I could sleep better at night.

The way I did it was backward. My experience was in baking and marketing. To get my product before the public, I chose the individual retail store route. When I started, I really was not thinking about getting a second store. I was so fixated on that one store the idea of expanding didn't occur to me at all at the time.

If you are happy selling your whoopie pies out of your

one whoopie pie store, great. But remember: one of the sicknesses I see cropping up among people who want to go into business is that if they sell 100 whoopie pies this year, they want to sell 1,500 of them next year. Everybody has this growth disease. It may just be part of the game, part of the internal makeup of somebody who wants to be in business for himself. But if you don't think you can play that game—which is crazy all the time—then it is OK to just set a goal for yourself and say you'll be happy selling this much and you don't want to sell any more.

There are a lot of businesses that do that. Zito's Bread in Greenwich Village could sell a lot more bread if it had a bigger production space, but every day for the last thirty-odd years, Zito's has been putting out whatever number of loaves it makes, and then the owner goes fishing or whatever and forgets about it until the next day.

DECIDING IF YOU CAN HANDLE IT

Once you have decided that you *want* to expand, you have to figure out *how*. Do you add more space at your current location, or do you find a new location? Do you stick with your original product line, do you extend the line, or do you do something entirely different? Who will you get to run the store? Will you try to handle it all yourself, or will you hire someone to help out?

The big issue, of course, is money. How soon after you open your first outlet do you open your second one? You need not wait until you are profitable. If your sales are headed in such a way that you can project them accurately and see a point where you will break even, then you are probably in pretty good shape. The issue then will be deciding how to finance the second store. Chances are, you will not be generating enough cash yet to do it yourself. You do have a track record now, which will help you find new capital.

You still won't have any better luck borrowing money from a bank. That's because you won't have audited figures, which you will try to avoid until you have to have them because they are expensive.

There are no rules about when to expand vis-à-vis breaking even. Even though you are not profitable, you can keep going—as long as your money holds out. Eventually, your business is either going to start making money or it will go belly up.

At some point, you are going to have to sell somebody else on your idea. There are a lot of deals around like Federal Express that kept losing and losing and losing and losing, but the concept made sense to enough people to get it over the hump. Compu-U-Card, a computer home-shopping system, went through seven financings and lost money for ten years before it started to break even.

Be careful about false signs of economic health. The second store that I owned, at Eightieth and First, had all the earmarks of a hit, but after the novelty wore off, sales deteriorated. You have to watch out for unrepeatable patterns of business. Beware of false blips. If you should get lucky for a few months and decide to expand, you could find yourself in a deep hole if the experience doesn't repeat itself.

You open up your second store when you have to open up—when the opportunity presents itself and when you can afford it. The clock is always ticking. Once you go to two, it is very difficult to stop. I don't know anybody who went to two and stopped. Then you are buying into the theory that more is better. If two is good, why isn't three better? The answer is: you have to have the product.

LOCATING A SECOND STORE

Until you have the management structure in place and can deal with a widespread retail empire that is more than an hour away by car from your central location, you should cluster yourself in one community as quickly and completely as possible. There are several reasons for that. Staying in a defined area will give you a solid base. It will also help you find out if your business has legs—that the separate entities won't cannibalize business from each other. Finally, it will serve as a deterrent to your competitors. You will look far more formidable with two stores than one.

HOW CLOSE?

I think there is a lot of misunderstanding about how much space to put between your stores. Manhattan provides an exaggerated example of that. There are so many people and so much shopping is done on foot that stores can be much closer together than would be possible anyplace else. But the general theory is applicable anywhere.

The store we opened on Fifty-ninth Street between Lexington Avenue and Third Avenue across from Bloomingdale's had a severely negative effect on our first store only eight blocks away, at Second Avenue and Fifty-third Street. The reason is that a lot of people who bought cookies lived near Bloomingdale's. When only the first store was open, they would walk all the way there. When the second store opened, they naturally started shopping closer to home.

But another store that we opened at Fiftieth Street and Lexington Avenue—five blocks from the first store—didn't hurt it at all. Those five blocks put us into a completely different neighborhood. The people who lived at Fiftieth and Lexington were used to doing their shopping around their home all the time and hadn't been going to Second Avenue at all.

Deciding where to put your stores requires an instinct that you have to develop about where a store will hurt you and where it won't. Of course, a little walking-around research won't hurt.

THE CANNIBALIZATION EFFECT

Experts will tell you that opening a second store expands the total market. If one Banana Republic store gets 100 percent of the safari-clothing market, opening a second store won't split that business in half. It will probably increase the market to 120 percent or 140 percent of the original size because it will attract new customers.

Sometimes the reverse is true. Zabar's, which at one time had six little stores, does a lot more business with one big store. The single store has more cachet than a chain of stores because it is unique. Can you imagine Tiffany branches everywhere? Also, people seem to like the crowded, frantic atmosphere at Zabar's.

I think in the specialty food business, as opposed to the mass market business—hamburgers, lube jobs, rug cleaning—you would do better with one big store rather than three or four little ones. There are such economies of scale; you can hire a better manager and assistant manager, pay your employees more, and provide better service.

THE AGGRAVATION FACTOR

Running two stores, your headaches don't just double, they triple. With one store you can deal with the ongoing problems; you can cope with the crises one at a time.

But when you have two locations, the first store can blow up while you are solving a problem at the second. Not only are you not there to deal with it, the situation at the first store may deteriorate while you are coping with the second store.

That's why I've been so reluctant to open another restaurant. My wife, Susan, takes most of the aggravation now. Restaurants are such crazy, detail-oriented, minute-by-minute businesses that I can't imagine what the headaches with another one would be like.

In the cookie and ice cream business, one of the reasons to open more outlets is that you have to take your product to where the people are. Since these are impulse items, the customers don't come to you; it is the other way around. There also comes a point, assuming you are growing, where you have reached the capacity of the location you are in and have to expand to relieve the pressure. When we had only one cookie store, it was like a riot every day. We couldn't make the cookies fast enough. It was fun, but it wouldn't have lasted because customers wouldn't put up with the aggravation. The number of stores like Zabar's or Fairway, a popular fruit and vegetable market on the Upper West Side, where people go in to be abused are few and far between. The typical consumer is not a masochist.

PROMOTION POTENTIAL

A second store builds your brand name identity. That's an asset worth a lot of money. Lots of stores are just one of a kind, but with two, you establish yourself as a force to reckon with. Your visibility factor goes way up.

QUALITY CONTROL

As we expanded, I made sure I controlled the product. We make cookie dough in very small batches on digital scales calibrated to one one-hundredth of a pound. We have all kinds of checks and balances. We know that if we put 100 pounds of ingredients into a mixer, we have to get 100 pounds of cookies out or we forgot to put something in. I knew that short of somebody taking the dough and not baking the cookies at all, or putting them in the oven and baking them for four hours, the cookies were going to be pretty good. Are they going to be perfect all the time? No, but when I made them all myself they weren't perfect all the time either. The system always works: control the raw ingredients and everybody got the exact same product.

The big problem is controlling the employees and keeping the stores clean. I had other problems too: getting the right kind of chocolate, finding enough nuts, getting enough eggs. We never had enough space, so we couldn't store anything. Juggling the deliveries was a big nuisance.

KEEPING AN EYE ON THINGS

We have set up an elaborate system of reports for our store

managers to ensure that the stores are being run right. It is probably more elaborate than necessary because the reports take a lot of time, and a manager who is really on top of things doesn't need them. They include:

- a store visitation report
- a bake-off store visitation report
- a weekly profit and loss statement
- a daily inventory control form
- a year budget model
- a daily itemized food cost chart
- a form for waste, consumption, and leftover sampling
- a form for each delivery of cookie batter and packages
- a nightly batter inventory form
- a daily cash flow and sales sheet
- a payroll report

The waste, consumption, and leftover-sampling form is a toughie. There is really no way we can keep track of the ice cream inventory. Our budgets are based on getting fifty scoops out of a tub of ice cream. If the workers get only forty-six scoops per tub, we can't prove that they are eating the other four scoops or giving them to friends. The other problem is that ice cream melts. If it is a hot day, there may be only forty-six scoops in that tub because the last few scoops in the tub melted. Who can say?

The most valuable of the forms is the store visitation report that our inspection teams use. It creates four different categories on which to rate the stores, with twenty-seven separate items. They are graded on a score of one to five, with five the objective. Here's what it looks like:

Service

- friendly
- aware
- greeting

- packing procedures
- suggestive sell
- speed
- appearance
- uniform
- money handling

Cleanliness

- sidewalk/aisle
- windows/door
- floor/wall/ceiling
- back room customer view
- correct point of purchase/signage
- customer comment cards available

Product Qualities—Cookies

- appearance/shape
- weight/size
- freshness/taste
- labels
- display
- variety

Product Quality—Ice Cream

- appearance
- taste
- ice free
- labels
- scooping procedures
- variety

There are a total of 115 points available. After we have added them up, we have a four step follow-up. It isn't perfect, but it helps.

INTANGIBLES

There is no one right way to deal with expansion. Some people want to polish one location into a jewellike operation. Others want to grow like crazy. Sometimes I think the best thing to do is to open one store, work your tail off to make it a success, and then sell it at the peak. I had $26.5 million in cash on the table to pay for Zabar's. That's a helluva price to pay for one store, even one that was grossing $26 million. But in Zabar's case, it was worth it, and I am still prepared to buy it.

In my case, I believe that even though I am dealing with what are perceived as dessert, or fattening, high-calorie products, it is basic human nature to want to eat them. If need be, I can develop cholesterol-free muffins that don't have any sugar or salt in them, which I'm doing now. I'm adaptable. So the business is never going to go away, and it is always going to be profitable. It is a low-gimmick business based on the quality of what people put in their mouths. I am really in the business of buying apples for five cents and selling them for six cents.

GOING WITH YOUR GUT

In essence, you learn how to handle growth through trial and error. A lot depends on the people. The people in a small entrepreneurial company are not the same kind that want to sign up with IBM. It is a different kind of mind-set. To work with them, you have to have a trying-out period, because there is no ready-made structure you can put them into. You are going to make a lot of mistakes and hire a lot of wrong people. I've never heard of anyone who never missed with people, but that's the game. It is a gigantic puzzle: you are putting in and taking out pieces.

You look for good people and you try to reward them well. As I've always told them, you make me money and I'll make you money. Give them incentive potential in the business so they have a bone that they can grab. As long as they understand that you haven't grabbed the bone either, and you have your house on the line, you will all work well together. You will all have a lot at stake.

DEALING WITH ADVERSITY

I don't know any entrepreneur who doesn't do lawsuits. You fire with lawsuits; you posture with lawsuits. There is no way not to be adversarial in small business.

In a perfect world, your customers would all pay you on time, your suppliers would all deliver on time, and you would pay them on time. But it isn't a perfect world, and things don't work that way.

You are always scrambling. I guarantee there is going to be conflict—yelling and screaming and lawsuits—doing what you have to do to stay alive.

IN CONCLUSION

I can't really tell you when to expand your business. It is a decision you have to make yourself, based on how the first store is doing, how hard you want to work, and whether you can get the money. Stay close to home with your second outlet, and don't worry about cannibalizing your first operation unless you do something really stupid. Chances are, you will be expanding your total market, not just carving it up.

19
SWALLOWING A GROWTH HORMONE: FRANCHISING

You have another option when you decide that it is time to expand: selling the rights to your name and the knowledge about your operation to a franchisee, who will open the stores himself. It worked for McDonald's, it worked for me, and it might even work for you.

MONEY

Franchising is cheaper. In its simplest terms, the decision can be made on a money basis. Do you have enough capital to own your second outlet? If you don't, then it makes sense to expand with somebody else's capital by letting them own the second outlet.

Most quick-lube operations that start in Dubuque do not have the capital to expand on their own. They would have to set up a management organization and borrow money to build more service outlets. It is easier to hang out a sign that says "franchises available" and let others put up the money.

REAL ESTATE

If you are dealing with a product that uses real estate, be it a quick-lube operation or frozen-custard stand, you can also expand better through franchising. Your local franchisees will probably have better real estate connections and a better feel for the market in the areas where you want to expand.

That's important. There is no such thing anymore as going into a new area and getting the best locations by paying the top dollar. You have to know who to go to, and that means you have to know the old-boy network.

MANAGEMENT

One of the arguments in favor of franchising is that it makes it easier to motivate people. If you are Banana Republic, your headquarters is in San Francisco, and you have an outlet in New York, you are going to find it difficult to manage. How motivated will some manager be who makes $25,000 a year and is 3,000 miles away? But if the owner of that store is a Banana Republic franchisee who lives in New York and shows up every day, the manager is going to be a lot more motivated.

Now, it is true that you could probably fire an errant store manager faster if he works for you than you could shut down the franchisee if he started selling button-down shirts instead of safari jackets.

It is also true that some companies with all company-owned stores have circumvented the motivation problem. Luby's Cafeterias in Texas, one of the most successful company-owned operations, lets selected good managers earn up to 20 percent of the equity in their stores. Money is a great motivator. I think that is the wave of the future. Otherwise, the employee at a company-owned outlet will wake up one day and say, "Wait a minute. Why am I working for Mrs. Fields for $12,000 when I can go open a David's Cookies franchise and gross $400,000?"

It is also true that a manager in a company-owned store

can set higher goals for himself if the company is large enough. He can move into the corporate hierarchy as an area supervisor or vice president. Sometimes that doesn't represent real advancement, however. We have hired vice presidents from Mrs. Fields who had responsibilities for up to eighty company-owned stores, and they were making less than $40,000 a year. There is only a very small salary gap between the manager of an individual store and a guy who may be supervising twenty or thirty stores, even though his responsibilities are much greater.

In the end, however, there is no substitute for having the boss on the premises, and the best franchise operations have realized that. They are moving toward a totally pure system where the franchisee really runs the business and does not report back to the franchiser every five minutes.

So the realities of owning your own store are that you either have to figure out a way you can comfortably motivate all these people or you must have a lot of very honest family members, so you can put one of your fifteen kids in each of your fifteen stores.

AGGRAVATION REGARDLESS

Whether you franchise or expand yourself, you are creating a lot of aggravation. If you try to expand yourself, your overhead will have a tendency to grow faster than your sales because you will need a management structure to keep track of everything. That, of course, is a prescription for disaster. With franchises, you can control more outlets with fewer people and add overhead more slowly.

Franchising will ultimately be simpler. The big headache with franchising is that no matter what kind of business you have, the 80–20 rule applies. The 20 percent of your franchises that are doing the worst job will consume 80 percent of your time. It is a common problem. Human nature is to plug up the leaks. It is very difficult to take a step back and say, "How do I help the guys who are doing well as opposed to taking care of the people who are bitching and moaning?"

MACY'S CAME FIRST

I didn't think about franchising when I opened my first store. I was so busy making cookies for seven million people in Manhattan with one twenty-quart mixer I didn't have time to think about it. Probably, I would never have done anything if people hadn't starting coming to me with franchise ideas.

When I did get around to thinking about it, I operated, as usual, from my gut instinct. Instead of thinking about it or studying it for a great length of time, I jumped in. One of the reasons I am so critical of consultants is that by the time you get an opinion by McKinsey about whether David's Cookies is viable as a franchise, the opportunity has passed you by. Sometimes you just have to hold your nose and take the leap. If your batting average is above 50 percent, you will survive.

When Macy's came to me about setting up a store in their huge Herald Square operation, I said sure. It was a unique arrangement. They owned the space and I sold them cookie dough; I was a supplier. The store did well and I was happy.

At one time, I considered operating the store myself and leasing the space from Macy's. That would give me control of the store and make me more money. What changed my mind was this: Macy's has a very long document for people like me who want to lease space in the building. I looked at the document and made a very fast decision. For me to negotiate my side of the document would cost me money in legal fees that I didn't have. Furthermore, if Macy's wanted to throw me out, they would find a way to break that document. As long as the dough was selling, Macy's would keep me in the store. As soon as it stopped selling, they would throw me out. I could hire lawyers to fight it, the lawyers would get rich, and I would still be thrown out.

FINDING FRANCHISEES

Since then, we have received more than 17,000 letters from all over the world inquiring, "How can I franchise David's

Cookies?" Only a few have panned out. I have gotten to the point where I have to see a modicum of sophistication in the applicant or I am not going to let them even start. The typical letter will not be from somebody who just escaped from a mental institution but somebody who says, "I have a wife/daughter/slow relative who needs something to do. The cookie business looks easy; I like cookies, so send me all the information."

So you have to rigorously screen applicants. Rule number one is don't go looking for franchisees. One of the litmus tests for whether your concept is franchisable is whether anybody writes you letters asking if they can have one of your stores. I don't know of any good system that didn't start with the franchisees coming to the franchisors.

The next thing is to be honest with the applicant about the risks. No matter how terrific the concept is, there are always problems running a small, thinly capitalized business. So they have to know that up front.

MAKE THEM COME TO YOU, NOT VICE VERSA

We have never used franchise-gathering companies. These guys usually just got out of Leavenworth or some other similar institution in terms of their credibility, and they try to play both sides. The franchisor pays them, the franchisee pays them, and by and large they are gigantic con artists.

That doesn't mean you don't have to hustle. If you are franchising a mundane service like window cleaning or key cutting that basically is available everywhere, your success will depend on how aggressive you can be with the concept, how quickly you can run with it, and how fast you can sign up the franchisees to let the world know a lot of people are jumping on your bandwagon. So you have to move quickly.

If you don't get 250 inquiries about franchises in the first six months, you probably don't have a viable idea. That is a high standard. But it may save you some grief later on.

SCREENING FRANCHISEES

When we get a letter from somebody asking about owning a franchise, the letter is put in one of two categories. If they don't mention real estate, we send a form letter back thanking them for their interest, and then we put them in a hold file. There is not a franchise company that I know of that assists franchisees in finding locations.

If they have a specific location in mind, then we can talk. Once we have looked them over and see they don't have any obvious deficiencies, we inspect the location. That knocks out 90 percent of those applicants. The location often turns out to be a mall being built near their house, and they don't have any knowledge of the traffic or the rent. Once we clue them in about what those are likely to be, they discover they are not going to become overnight millionaires and drop out.

The ones that survive this process are then taken through a comprehensive computer analysis of how much business they will have to do to pay the rent. The trouble with that scenario is that you don't have an accurate fix on how much business they will get. It is a function of several factors: how good the area is, how good the mall is, and how good they are at selling the product.

THE CHINESE RESTAURANT THEORY

Neither you nor your franchisee should be worried about neighborhood competition. Competition is irrelevant almost everywhere. I cite my Chinese restaurant theory again. There are hundreds of Chinese restaurants in Chinatown, all competing with one another—and they all thrive, more or less. The important variables are whether or not the location is viable, the store is well run, and there is a market for the product. Your franchisees are not going to sell ice in Alaska. But they will sell a lot of ice cream in New Orleans in the summertime, just like all the ice cream stores there do.

Malls are different. Since they are enclosed, they are cities unto themselves. Clearly, if there are two cookie stores in the mall already, you definitely have to analyze the competition before you try to open number three. First of all, the landlord may not want another cookie store. Second, the location he may give you is so ridiculous that you'll go out of business in the first month.

FRANCHISING FOR INNOCENTS

The first thing you should do if you are thinking about multiplying your quick-lube operation is to get a franchise lawyer. That's easier said than done. A lot of lawyers say they know about franchising, but the rules are complicated and change a lot. For example, the whole notion of full disclosure for franchisors is relatively new.

New York and California have very stiff regulations. Other states don't require anything in the way of disclosure, so you can go out and sell a franchise to anybody. But you better find out what the requirements are because if you don't do it right, you get into a lot of trouble.

Second, your franchise disclosure document or your offering memorandum is as complicated and as detailed as an SEC filing. All the bad news is up front. You have to tell the franchisee that your business is not unique, that you have lots of competition, that the net worth of the company is negative, and that it is probably a horrible idea anyway. You want the franchisee to read the whole thing, know what the risks are, and say he wants to do it anyway.

It is imperative to leave flexibility in the standard franchise agreement. That is so you don't have to go back to the state every time the market changes. If you lock yourself into certain numbers and then try to do another deal, you have to refile, and that can be expensive. And the details can kill you. We have filed with the state of New York for seven years in a row, and we get letters back saying things like,

"You used the wrong staples to put the booklet together. The margins are too wide on Page 54," and so on. Those are the kinds of problems a good franchise lawyer will charge you $150 an hour to fix.

DISCLOSURE IS A PAIN, BUT IT IS GOOD FOR EVERYBODY

Franchisees do not get screwed as much as they used to because the franchise disclosure laws have really worked. The good franchisors are getting so realistic that their offering statements exude incredible pessimism. They load up their franchise document with every conceivable piece of bad news they can think of because they don't want some glowing forecast coming back to haunt them in the form of a lawsuit. But it works. People know that there isn't any genie in the bottle out there that is going to make life wonderful by buying them a quick-lube franchise.

Our disclosure document reads like the Bataan death march. Really. We try to scare the franchisees out of the deal. Unless somebody badly wants to run a cookie store, they are not going to sign up. These days, you can get better information about the risks in franchises than you can about almost any other kind of investment. I think the typical schmuck small investor on the New York Stock Exchange doesn't have the vaguest idea what's going on, but in franchises they really do because the business is right there for them to see. Either they work terribly hard at it and make it go or they will fail, and that is all written down in black and white.

IGNORANCE IS BLISS

One of the beauties about when I went into franchising was that I didn't know any of the basic rules. I made them up as I went along.

I came up with a very simple program for franchisees. I charged only $25,000 per store on the street ($12,500 for a store within another store). That was a one-time fee that included help with the site selection, design consultation, construction, training, help with the media and local publicity, my appearance at the opening, and business advice. If the franchisee's workers ever need a refresher course—and they do because the employees turn over so often—they come to New York and we train them. It is good for us also, because it helps us get a handle on what the labor situation is where the franchise is located.

The next part of the program is the product that I sell them. In the beginning, I wanted to make sure they used only my products, from cookie dough to paper cups. But you have to be careful. There have been a lot of lawsuits by franchisees who claim they are being sold a product that is generic in nature at huge markups. That was part of the Carvel ice cream case that went all the way to the U.S. Supreme Court. The decision was that Carvel had the right to sell a proprietary product like the ice cream mix, but the franchisee was free to buy the cups and napkins elsewhere if they were cheaper.

The reality is that franchisees do buy paper goods from us because we buy in such quantity. And they have to use our dough. The thing we police avidly is their use of David's Cookies dough. If we find them using somebody else's dough, we will do anything short of going in there with a bazooka to shut them down immediately.

Since we are less well known in ice cream, we try to get the franchisees to use ours exclusively, but there are a lot of stores out there that are half David's and half Steve's or Ben and Jerry's. They have the option of selling brownies or French bread, but if they do, they have to use ours.

You have to exhibit a certain amount of common sense. If you try to run your franchises too tightly and aren't pragmatic about what a franchisee can sell, you will find the franchisee on your doorstep with a summons saying you are trying to choke him. The examples of that are legion. Take Häagen-Dazs changed the rules.

THE OVERHEAD

Here are what the occupancy costs of a typical franchisee look like. Franchisees should expect to pay 20 percent of their projected gross sales in occupancy costs: rent, taxes, and so forth. If they choose to spend more than that, say 30 percent, the ten extra points they pay to the landlord will come directly out of their profit. If they do everything right and bring 22 percent of gross sales to the bottom line, and their occupancy costs are 30 percent instead of 20 percent, their profit is only 12 percent. In that case, they are not working for themselves; they are working for the landlord.

Numbers like that scare a lot of people out of the business. Even if you do well, you may not make a living. Most franchisees don't see that. They think, "My god, I'm selling cookies for $7 a pound, so there must be something in there for me." There can be something in there for them *if* they are not paying their profit to the landlord.

ADVERTISING

We don't provide advertising because a lot of our franchisees don't want to pay for advertising. Since it would come out of their pocket anyway, we save them that expense.

The other reason we don't have advertising is that I haven't figured out whether it is possible to come up with a singular message to promote what is basically an upscale, impulse item. Yes, I guarantee you that if I had a $600 million budget like McDonald's and put the message on the tube, we'd sell a lot more cookies. But I don't have that kind of money. So I rely on word of mouth and promotion.

This really goes to the heart of the issue of what kind of franchise it is and how well developed it is. Advertising is only going to hurt the franchisee. He is going to pay for it, but he is not going to make enough profit for it to make any appreciable difference. I am absolutely convinced that the only kind of advertising that makes a dent is multimedia saturation advertising including national television. Everything else is meaningless because you are not creating enough of an impression to make a difference.

Here's an example of what I mean. In New York, Nestlé is introducing frozen, precut cookies. You take them out, put them on a tray, and bake them. This is competition for us. I would say Nestlé's cookies are not as good as our refrigerated cookie batter, but they are certainly better than Pillsbury's. To sell its product out of 1,800 New York supermarkets, Nestlé is going to be spending somewhere between $5 million and $6 million. They are paying enough so that 97 percent of the shoppers in this area will become aware the product is available. They are having massive in-store giveaways and double and triple coupons, just to get people to try their product. It will probably work. It will probably be a very successful frozen-food product.

But the typical franchisee can't afford that kind of exposure. Then what happens is that even if a franchisee thinks up front that it is a good idea to be part of a national advertising program because it is going to make his business better known, as soon as the business runs into trouble, the first thing the franchisee stops paying is the advertising allotment, whether it is 3 percent, 4 percent, or 5 percent. And when the franchisor sues for the money, the franchisee asks, "Where is the advertising?," and the franchisor will say, "I can't buy it if you don't pay me." Somebody has to pay for it, but the franchisor is working on so little margin that he can't afford it, and if he can't pay for it, it isn't going to happen.

Even though McDonald's and, to a lesser degree, Burger King have been very successful advertisers, the franchisees are paying a lot of money for it. If you really look at a Burger King deal, with the financing for the building, the advertising, and so on, you are paying 16 percent to 18 percent of your gross sales back to Pillsbury. Granted, the franchisee gets a lot for that. But it won't work in a David's Cookies deal because the business isn't big enough to support it.

20
MAKING FRANCHISING WORK FOR YOU

Everything in life is a deal. In selling franchises, there is a moment of truth in the negotiations when the franchisee says to you, "I want to take your product into an area where it is not known. I'm prepared to take the risk and put up the money to build the stores. In return for that, I want some sort of protection to prevent you from coming in and in effect using my hard work to promote your name by selling other franchises in my area. In other words, I want an exclusive."

If he's smart, the franchisor says, "Wait a minute. Let's do these things one at a time until we see if you can hack it. If you do a good job, I have no problem letting you open up a second, third, or fourth outlet, but without the exclusive protection you are looking for." That's what Dunkin' Donuts does; they allow franchisees to open up one outlet at a time.

That's the basic issue: how much protection the franchisee is going to get vs. how much freedom you retain for yourself.

JUMPING IN

My decision to franchise basically came out over the question of who could control various sales territories. People were coming to me wanting to buy my dough and sell my cookies. But they also wanted territorial protection, and that doesn't work if you are just selling dough. The important part of a franchise deal is called a roll-out agreement. It commits the franchisee to opening up a certain number of stores in a certain amount of time in order to keep his territory exclusive. If he fails, he loses his exclusivity.

I made my first franchise deal after I had opened my first two stores in Manhattan. I gave a fellow an exclusive on Long Island to open ten stores, six of his own and four to other owners as subfranchisees. Right away there were problems. First of all, the sales were disappointing. Long Island does well in the summer but not so well in the winter. Second, the idea of subfranchisees stunk. It created a middleman between us and the store operator; that boosted costs for the operator but lessened our control. We wound end up buying back the territory from the original franchisee.

THAT IS ONE OF THE PROBLEMS WITH EXCLUSIVE RIGHTS

Ultimately, if you are selling somebody an exclusive franchise, you are selling somebody part of your business. Even though you think you have all these wonderful protections, and even though you think you can throw the franchisee out if he looks at you cross-eyed, the reality is that you can't. He becomes the public face of your business in that territory, and he practically becomes your partner.

The other reality is that if he goes into a market and screws it up, it is very difficult to come back in at a later date. You can almost never go in and pick up the pieces.

The good news about the cookie business and other small retail businesses is that you can overcome a lot of ill will in a very short amount of time. We have seen it happen time and time again. Somebody has run a store into the ground, and the customers hate it; but you install an "under new management" sign and some smiling employees behind the counter, and you can get your goodwill back almost overnight.

If you have a big business, like a car dealership, that isn't so easy. People have a lot of time and money tied up in their purchase. A restaurant might have a similar problem. But cookies and ice cream represent less of a commitment by the customer. They are willing to try you again if it doesn't cost them much.

KEEPING YOUR FRANCHISEES HAPPY

You have to listen to the franchisees. If a franchisee brings us a good product that is at the top of its class, we let them sell it. Colombo yogurt is an approved product at our stores because franchisees pushed for it. The other side of that is working to keep unapproved products out of the store. We had a franchisee in Port Jefferson, Long Island, who thought that running a David's Cookies store included hanging chocolate penises, breasts, and vaginas off the ceiling. We had to go in there and make him change his ways. As upsetting as it is to me to sell chocolate penises in the cookie store, it is even more upsetting to other franchisees who see what one of their brethren is doing to hurt the corporate image.

You are right on the razor blade though, because if the guy is making money selling chocolate genitalia, he is going to keep doing it. The other franchisees who are complaining about it are also probably trying to find out who distributes chocolate penises because they want to sell them too if the guy is making money. The franchisees will go for whatever works best for the moment.

MAINTAINING THE EDGE

Part of the job of keeping the franchisees happy is the ability to keep evolving the franchise. McDonald's didn't stop its product line with hamburgers, french fries, and milkshakes. It expanded way beyond that.

You have to keep putting in new products. A lot of them won't work, but it keeps the franchisees happy. We were playing around with this customized ice cream mixing machine that would mix ice cream and ingredients like M&Ms right on the spot. It was a good idea, but it was too expensive for the franchisees, so we dropped it.

SECRETS OF SUGGESTIVE SELLING

What really makes any business go is making sure the customer gets a good reception. It takes something called suggestive selling. It is easy to tell franchisees about it, but it is very hard for them to get their sales help to follow it. Here is an example. Let's say you walk into a delicatessen and order a quarter pound of something. The counter man plops it on the scale and says, "It is a little over a quarter of a pound. Do you want to take it, or shall I take a little off?" Only one out of a thousand customers says, "Take a little off." So when somebody comes into one of my cookie stores and orders a pound of cookies, you want the clerk to say, "Would you like that in a tin? We have a special on tins today." or "Have you tried our brownies?" and so on. It doesn't sound like much, but it can mean an increase in sales of 25 percent to 30 percent. Then you suggest other things to regular customers—giving the product as gifts, for example. When you go to somebody's house for dinner, take cookies instead of wine or flowers. Roses are $50 a dozen; for $7 you can bring a pound of cookies.

If you remind people of that, the sales go up. If you can make the atmosphere in your store so pleasant that people think it is fun to shop at a David's Cookies, you are ahead of the game.

NOBODY IS HAPPY ALL THE TIME

You are never going to keep all your franchisees happy.

Everybody I speak to—Häagen-Dazs, Famous Amos—the franchisees are always complaining about something. The franchisor tries to hold their hands, but ultimately this is a business and you can't make money doing that all the time.

Part of the reason why I am eternally pessimistic about this is a conversation I had with Harris Cooper, who was head of Dairy Queen, the largest franchisor in the world with more than 6,000 outlets. I was sure he had all the answers, since he had undoubtedly figured how to keep all those franchisees happy. Wrong. Within the first twenty seconds, he was complaining about "those blank-blank franchisees, I could kill them." He was jumping up and down, ranting and raving like a madman.

Franchisees are never happy. If they are making money, they want to make more money. If they are not making money, it is your fault because you put them in the business. You can't win.

WEEDING OUT THE BAD APPLES

Part of the contract with franchisees is that we don't guarantee a location. Nobody I know guarantees a location. If anybody in this world says they can guarantee 100 percent success at a given location, they ought to be committed to Bellevue, because it is just not possible.

Regardless of where they locate, a lot of your franchisees will just run these stores into the ground because they don't know what they are getting into. So you have to live with the fact that you are going to have to move stores and close stores. You will feel like you are stabbing a knife in your heart, but it is a reality of life.

McDonald's does it better than anyone. When McDonald's closes a store, they have a demolition crew that comes in and just levels the store. Twenty-four hours later, all you see is a parking lot. They don't want any McDonald's around with plywood over the windows. They can do that because most all McDonald's are free-standing structures. Plus, they can afford to.

ONE FROM COLUMN A, ONE FROM COLUMN B

As I look back at the great argument that has gone on in a lot of businesses about whether it is best to own your own outlets or to franchise, it comes down to this: the most successful companies have done a combination of both. That's what McDonald's and Burger King do. It all depends on what kind of direction you want to drive your business.

A quick-lube company that can grow only by opening up more quick-lube outlets around the country is going to rise or fall on the notion that whoever is lubing those cars is doing a good job at it and will be there three months from now when Mrs. Harris comes back to get her car serviced. Probably the best way to do that is to sell the concept as a franchise to somebody in that community who already knows Mrs. Harris and is intent on doing a good job on her car because she will spread the word to her family and friends. If the local franchisee isn't doing that, you have to be prepared to step in and buy the store back from him to protect your business's good name. Thus, you inevitably have to be prepared to own some of your outlets.

GETTING BIGGER BY GETTING SMALLER

In addition to our traditional David's Cookies stores, we have more than 300 bake-offs. These are small outlets with ovens but not much else which are mostly located in supermarkets, malls, or retail space that has been subdivided. We expect to open more in 1989, most of them owned by people who already have one or more.

The reality is that it is better to have dozens of smaller outlets in supermarkets and department stores than to gamble on a couple of big franchisees to do a lot of business. I'd much rather open twenty supermarket bake-offs than one traditional David's Cookies store. They are easier to run, and they produce a lot more sales for a lot smaller investment.

You have to be careful about quality in some of these stores, though. You can assume nothing. I was walking through a Burdine's department store in Florida and saw six different varieties of perfectly scooped David's cookies sitting on trays—raw. They hadn't been baked. So I went to the person who was operating the kiosk, and told him who I was and that he was selling raw cookies. He replied, "Nobody told me you have to bake them."

RUNNING THE NUMBERS

You have to give it to the franchisees straight; they are getting into a tough business.

Given the reality of the marketplace today, small individual stores are getting more and more expensive. With the onerous taxes, daily hassles, intense competition, crime, kids who don't show up for work—it is tough out there.

On the other hand, I am much more optimistic about situations where I can control several thousand square feet and divide it up into several different food outlets. That way, I can spread my risk and not put too much of the overhead on one operation. So you have a cookie store next to an ice cream store next to a yogurt store.

The other way to go is with a kiosk that uses only 50 square feet of space, a fraction of the size of a regular store. Then every square inch is being used productively, so you can afford to pay $200 per square foot in rent.

FORGET FOOD COURTS

To capitalize on the success of kiosks, landlords are creating space for dozens of them, all grouped together in food courts. Don't get suckered into a location like that. They are awful; they don't work. What do you suppose it smells like when you have greasy Chinese food served right next to greasy Mexican food right next to greasy seafood? Customers walk in and lose their appetites right away. A lot of our franchisees have gotten burned in food courts.

We were in a food court in the PPG building in Pittsburgh that opened with twenty stores in 1984. Now it has just one left.

UPS AND DOWNS

One thing about the franchise business, you'll never get bored. Just when you think things are going great, a crisis erupts.

In the early 1980s, we were on a hot streak. Everything was going great. Franchises were opening up all over the place, and everybody was doing well. Then we were hit by a double whammy in 1983 and 1984.

Number one, suddenly the stores in Manhattan were getting robbed all the time. I calculate we have lost more than $1 million in stolen money or products on the island of Manhattan since we opened eight years ago. Number two, not only were the franchisees losing money, but they couldn't get anybody to work in the stores. I had the same problems in my company-owned stores. There were weeks on end when I couldn't find teenagers to put in these stores. It was too dangerous.

In the old days mothers would say, "Please let my son work in your store because he will make money and learn responsibility." The next thing I knew, the mothers were dragging their children out of the stores because some robber had put a gun in their mouths.

It was a free-fall situation. We had to take over some franchises and close others. We even put a guard in a store at Ninety-sixth and Broadway. The guard cost us $20 an hour and almost ruined the business. Having a guard looking around for the next guy to come in with a needle hanging out of his arm and a gun to rob the place didn't exactly contribute to the fun atmosphere of buying a cookie.

One person who ran the store at Seventieth and Broadway called me one night and said he was locking the door and going home. And he did. He was too scared of being held up again. It was an invaluable experience for me because I saw what the bottom looks like. Believe me, it isn't pretty. Since then, we have solved most of our security problems, and the crime wave has abated.

THERE ISN'T ANYTHING THAT EVERYBODY LIKES

The specialty-food business comes down to a product that consumers are going to either like or not like. When we open up decent locations and people don't buy the product, that means to me that the market wasn't right for that product. There is really no way of knowing that ahead of time.

Take Long Island. It was our first franchise deal, and we wound up having to buy back the territory. Stand-alone cookie stores were not generally successful on Long Island. I'm not sure if it was a function of demographics or shopping patterns or that people spend so much time in their cars, but it didn't work.

Recently, we've decided to go back to Long Island, and I think it should work better now. The store in East Hampton makes a lot of money in the summer, when all the people are there, though it gives most of it back in the winter. The store in Great Neck was just sold to a guy who doubled the business in the first week he owned it. And we have installed bake-offs in Waldbaum's supermarkets. That will help our brand-name identity. A good supermarket will sell thirty to thirty-five pounds of cookies a day in the deli alone, which translates into $200 a day in sales. That creates massive public relations and good will.

For some bizarre reason, we had the same problem in San Francisco. The residents don't seem to like cookies. The year we opened up there, 1982, we followed Mrs. Fields, Famous Amos, and Unknown Jerome. A lot of them are closed now. Who knows what happened?

We can't do business in Ohio, either. Ohio residents just didn't get the program. I think our cookies were too sophisticated and too expensive. We had phenomenal franchisees out there, really good guys, who came to me with a proposal to open up a lot of stores quickly. They went in fast to grab the market. The only competitor was the Original Cookie Company, which was a low-end cookie. Our guys opened up eight stores, and within a year they were nearly all in trouble, even in big, supposedly cosmopolitan cities like Cleveland and Cincinnati. Maybe people in Ohio don't care about imported chocolate. Of course, it wasn't just David's Cookies, either. Häagen-Dazs stores went out of business in Ohio.

Why do we do well in Charlottesville, Virginia? Because our store is across the street from the main gate of the University of Virginia? Then we should have done well in Cleveland near Case-Western Reserve. We didn't. I guess engineering students don't like cookies, either.

Someday, I'd love to open a store in Harlem. It would do phenomenally well. Some 60 percent of our customers at Macy's are black, and they spend two to three times as much as white customers. That's true in Macy's meat department, too. I'm convinced that blacks are very well informed about quality and value in food.

Here is the moral: specialty-food products, cookies included, do not have universal appeal. Nobody in the upscale specialty-food business is successful everywhere. You have to go for the very safe middle ground with a consensus taste to be a fifty-state success. That's not for me. I have no aspirations to be in every state in the nation. It would give me absolutely no jollies at all to have a store in North Dakota. I wouldn't even want to fly there to open it.

Nor will I try to make my product more palatable just to make it more appealing to a greater number of people. I won't change the recipe or change the name of the stores to Mrs. David's just to sell more cookies. I probably should, but I can't bring myself to do it. The same thing with the restaurant. I want to serve the kind of food that I want to serve, not to try to appeal to the greatest number of people.

LESSON NUMBER 697 IN NOT BELIEVING THE EXPERTS

No matter what the experts tell you, your experience will always contradict their best advice. I can get detailed demographic information on the twenty biggest markets that have the right income and sociological characteristics for my product, open stores in those markets, and have them fall on their face. The reason: the consumers just don't understand the program. It has a lot to do with the social environment: is it acceptable to eat these products or is it considered conspicuous consumption? It is an ongoing educational experience. I suspect that one reason we flopped in San Francisco is that eating cookies is considered conspicuous consumption and doesn't fit with the lifestyle. We should have had a health-food store instead.

INTERNATIONAL INTRIGUE

At the same time, I think it is interesting that our products do well in Japan. We have numerous stores there now. The cookies are *very* expensive—$16 per pound—and we still do well. We are going to open up in Israel next. I think we'll do well there too. Israel is one of the places where the population spends a disproportionate amount of its income on food.

In England cookies won't work. Why? Because in general English are not sophisticated enough about what they eat— at least not yet. They spend less of their disposable income on food than any other country in the Common Market.

The biggest disappointment I've had is being unable to open a store in France. We've come very close three times, but the deals have fallen through. I think we could do well in France, Germany, and Italy if the situation is right. The Italians know more about food across the board than any other people in the world—including the French.

Right now, we're looking at Taiwan. And the People's

Republic of China has offered us a location in Beijing right next to the Kentucky Fried Chicken. The trouble is we would have to sell our cookies for about three cents apiece. Most Chinese do not have a lot of disposable income. Everybody talks about the one billion Chinese as representing a huge untapped market, but it looks problematic to me.

There are twenty-five or thirty countries in Europe and South America where our concept would work. We could open up in those countries tomorrow; but many of the stores would fail, and I'm not ready for that. It is a matter of finding the right partner. If you have limited resources, you cannot just barrel into a country pretending you know everything about it. If you do, you end up getting the wrong locations. Nobody can succeed in bad locations.

Even under the best of circumstances, it is hard to find good spots to sell from. I think I know as much about retailing on the island of Manhattan as anyone, but I can't make that statement about Brooklyn or Queens, which are just across the East River. I certainly wouldn't make that comment about Israel. Some people are arrogant enough to believe that they can just call up the best real estate broker and get the best locations. Baloney.

CLOSING

By the end of 1988, David's Cookies will be sold in thousands of locations. But we're doing less franchising because of all the headaches involved, mostly having to do with finding acceptable locations at reasonable rents. That is one advantage we have over chains like Mrs. Fields that own all their own outlets. If a franchise store isn't making money it will be sold or we will close it. Mrs. Fields owns all its stores so it has to carry its losers.

Still, if you want to expand, you ought to investigate franchising. The best way to test whether your concept is viable is to see what kind of walk-in interest you get. Be careful when you start out. Hire a good lawyer and screen your potential franchisees carefully. Be wary of sure things. Consider whether to expand your company-owned locations at the same time. Look for new formats. I tend to be pessimistic, and right now I'm down on traditional food outlets. But if your franchisees work hard and keep the customers happy, there is no reason why you can't succeed.

21
MARKETING AND OTHER MEANINGLESS CONCEPTS

There are a lot of business buzz words, but the one you hear the most that means the least is marketing. The next time you meet somebody at a cocktail party who calls himself a "marketing expert," try to get him to describe what he does for a living. I can tell you in two words: spend money.

That said, it is important to understand what marketing supposedly consists of. That way, you can figure out for yourself what you want to spend money on and what you want to ignore.

WHAT IS IT ANYWAY?

We're trying to hire a marketing person now. We've seen people making from $65,000 to $1 million per year. We ask them all the same question: "What is marketing?" The answers are all the same, and none of them mean anything. In every case, it is a variation of a theme about positioning and niches and I don't know what-all.

What it comes down to is the amount of money you spend

242

to "position" your product or, in other words, develop an identity and a group of customers for it. No marketing person I've met has ever come up with one idea that is free. I ask them if they can do marketing without money, and in every case they get up and leave the room.

WHAT DO PROFESSIONAL MARKETERS KNOW?

We interviewed one woman who had an impeccable background. She had worked for all the right companies. I asked her to give me an example of anything she had done where her marketing had raised sales. She said that while she was the head of marketing for a large food products company, another brand came on the market. Her boss was so worried that the new product would cut into their market share that he gave her $4 million to fight back. She told me, "I thought I did a good job at it." So I asked her: "How long did it take you to earn back the $4 million?" The answer: she hadn't yet. She called herself a successful marketer, but her bottom line was negative.

Another guy came in who was proud of taking Benihana frozen food from nothing to $60 million in annual sales in two or three years. To do that, he spent $18 million on advertising—far more than the total profit of the line. The minute Benihana stopped advertising, the sales went into the toilet.

The same thing happened with the soft and chewy cookie. When Nabisco advertised, it did just fine; but the sales didn't last beyond the advertising. The products had no legs, no intrinsic appeal. That's not marketing; that's buying sales. That would be like my packing a dollar bill in every quarter pound of cookies I sell. But that's the kind of stuff you get from corporate animals. It is the antithesis of what I do for a living. To me, marketing is merely a way to distinguish your product from the other guy's or promote it as being different or better. I think the guys who are best at it can do it for no money.

WORSE STILL, *NOT* HAVING A MARKETER CAUSED ME PROBLEMS

I wouldn't care about marketing except that a lot of venture capitalists like to ask you about your marketing skills when you go see them about money. In 1986, we were looking for money to go into a whole new business: packaged food sold in supermarkets. We decided we needed money to design our packaging and in-store kiosks as well as to redesign our corporate logo and upgrade it from the cutesy gorilla lettering we were using.

But when we took our proposal around to various money sources, the glaring hole all these smart guys saw was that we didn't have a marketing professional on the staff. I kept asking, "What would a marketing professional be doing that we aren't already doing?" They didn't know, but they insisted we had to have one.

The whole money-raising process took about three months. We finally turned down the deal the venture capitalists offered us because it was too expensive. It all came apart one night when a venture capitalist told us, "You haven't got a marketing person, you haven't done focus groups, you haven't given McKinsey a quarter of a million dollars to flush down the toilet. How do we know that people are going to buy your product?" How do you find out? You go up to them in a supermarket and ask them.

We were in two different worlds. By the time we said no to the money people, we were already doing all the marketing things that we thought we needed money and a professional for. We had gotten our refrigerated dough into more than 1,200 supermarkets. We had gone from a company that sold only baked cookies out of cookie stores to one with a whole program of small 50-square-foot ministore kiosks in place. We had gotten where we wanted to be without the benefit of professional marketing advice.

Still, it was a very frustrating experience. Six months later the money people came back and said they wished they'd done the deal. By then it was too late.

I STILL DON'T KNOW WHAT MARKETING IS

So we haven't bought into big-time professional marketing yet. We keep asking marketing people what they'd do for us, and they keep saying, "Well, we'd take however much money you give us and position the product." To my mind, any money I would give to a marketing person to "position the product" would be better spent doing baking demonstrations in the aisles of supermarkets or hiring people to stick cookies in customers' mouths. That's smart marketing. And you are staying close to the customer, which is where you ought to be.

GUERRILLA MARKETING

Rather than spend money on traditional marketing, I would rather invest it in such things as locking in distribution channels. For instance, I would much rather know that I had merchandise on trucks going to 1,200 different Gap stores than know I was spending millions of dollars on television advertising that somebody may or may not be watching.

Modern distribution techniques have really redone the food business. In the old days, if you wanted to sell a frozen ice cream bar, you had to find a frozen-food distributor who would mark up your bar 30 percent to 35 percent before it went into the supermarket. Now the distributor's markup is only 8 percent to 10 percent because these new super distributors are so huge. The problem is that the more these big companies grow, the more they are going to start squeezing the little companies like David's. They won't be able to find room in their warehouses for a few cases of our products because Sara Lee will be taking up all the space.

BESIDES, I CAN'T AFFORD IT ANYWAY

The only way marketing can be done is full-steam ahead.

The marketing community is not geared to distinguishing a Rolls-Royce from a Chevy. They either go in a Rolls-Royce or they don't go at all. Unless you are prepared to pay at a Rolls-Royce level, your money is being thrown away.

In a small start-up business, you are not going to have the luxury of doing marketing, other than promotion, which to me is marketing. Getting a good piece of publicity in a major publication or on television is the purest form of marketing to me because, ultimately, the best kind of marketing is editorial marketing, where somebody else is saying you have a good product. It is more authoritative, and it doesn't cost you anything.

To me, what Ben and Jerry's did recently was smart marketing. When Pillsbury ordered its distributors not to carry Ben and Jerry's ice cream because it competed with Häagen-Dazs, they went out with the placards to Minneapolis to picket Pillsbury with signs that read, "What is the Doughboy afraid of?" They got lots of coverage, and it cost them only two airplane tickets. I'm sure if they had taken the problem to McKinsey, the marketer would have figured out how to spend $1 million of their money and not got the same result.

This fixation by venture capitalists and financiers on having the right marketing people or program in place is the antithesis of what small business is all about. You have to learn how to make it up as you go along. Improvise, be creative. Short of having endless money, which is what marketers need, you will not be able to tap into professional marketing.

DAVID HATES DEBBI

Part of marketing is making yourself different from your competitors. That is why I play up the rivalry between myself and Mrs. Fields cookies. The David-hates-Debbi Fields phenomenon helps our products get noticed in a very inexpensive way. So I invented this feud for the press to play up with my number one competitor.

The funny thing is, Mrs. Fields has begun to take it seriously. The other day, I got this letter from her corporate lawyer:

Dear Mr. Liederman:

It is reported to us after initial investigation that a David's Cookies corporate employee by the name of Danny Krisher may have approached one of your store employees, who is a former Mrs. Fields cookie employee, with an offer to him of a payment of money if he could acquire for David's Cookies by whatever means bags of our dry cookie recipe ingredients.

We also have reason to believe that Mr. Krisher may have offered to provide funds in the event that the acquisition of these ingredients required the bribing of some Mrs. Fields cookie employees.

Fortunately for both of us, this employee who was allegedly contacted by Mr. Krisher had the good sense to recognize the possibility of illegal activity. He denied the request and subsequently left the employ of David's Cookies.

It does not take too much imagination or intelligence to recognize this purported situation as one that could have evolved to the level of corporate espionage. As you might imagine, Mrs. Fields Cookies is appalled that this activity might have taken place and intends to treat it with the utmost seriousness.

If in fact these conversations took place, and we believe they did, and if there is any further-reported such activity, or threats of such activity, Mrs. Fields Cookies will spare no time or expense in moving for civil or criminal prosecution against the perpetrators. Mrs. Fields Cookies intends to continue its investigation into this matter and to alert all its employees with regard to potential attempts by third parties to steal our federally-protected trade secrets. Let this letter serve as a warning to you of the seriousness with which we regard this report to us.

Govern yourselves accordingly.

The letter, of course, was too silly for words. Our cookies are superior to hers. I know that because I have known for years exactly what she puts in them. So I sent the following letter back to the lawyer:

> Dear Mr. Clissold:
> I was appalled to read your accusation of high-level espionage in the ongoing cookie war between our respective companies. Rest assured I would never condone such obvious and unnecessary behavior.
> For your information, you should know that the dry bags of Mrs. Fields ingredients have been offered to us repeatedly by former employees of yours who must help themselves after being terminated, and by various Mrs. Fields distributors who want to prove to us they work with your company.
> Of course, we have no use for the dry bags of flour, baking soda and salt, the dry bags of white and brown sugar, the frozen egg yolks, vanilla extract, and chocolate with vanillin, so I always decline.
> If and when I decide to start Mrs. David's cookies, the procedure of mixing these ingredients together and baking these ingredients for 30-35 minutes at 225 degrees to 240 degrees Fahrenheit will be helpful. However, right now I like David's better so I always tell the sources who attempt to force your mixes on me, "No, thank you."
> P.S. I loved Debbi's book. Perhaps the next time she comes to New York, she could come to my restaurant and we could engage in a rousing chorus of "Chippidy Do Dah" [the Mrs. Fields company song].

PROMOTION

Basically, you have to be a promotion animal.

The best way to get yourself noticed is to become totally identified with your product. I think in my case I have become totally identified with the food business in general. I've tried not to be linked to just cookies because as I get more involved in other specialty foods, it could come back to haunt me.

But I am up to my neck in food, and I think this total involvement should be true of anybody who goes into business. You have to understand your industry, not just your product. Then you get into the inner mechanisms of whatever makes that industry tick.

What that does for you is this: you get invited to become a member of industry boards and participate in certain charities, judging contests, and so on. You keep letting people know that you are there. That's the best kind of marketing you can have. High visibility can help jog a journalist's memory when he writes about an area you are associated with. I don't want to be known as a big guy around town or a celebrity who goes to all the right parties—just a food maven.

MARKET RESEARCH

The foundation of market research has to be your instincts. Once you have the feeling that there is a need out there for the product you want to bring to market, there are a couple of things you can do to quantify that feeling. Your goal, of course, is to do them cheaply.

FOCUS GROUPS ON A BUDGET

Take focus groups. A group of people sit around a table and discuss a product or service while you watch from behind a one-way mirror. There are companies that specialize in running focus groups, and you can pay them $1,000 to find a scientifically selected sample of people to focus on your product and then write up the results. At that price, you will not be surprised to find out that the markup on those focus groups is astronomical.

But you can do it wholesale. Go to ten friends or friends of friends and pay them $20 apiece to sit in a room and talk. You have a moderator there and you listen in. For literally a quarter of the money, you can get nearly professional results.

What comes out of focus groups is sometimes very surprising. Occasionally, you go into one thinking that your idea is ninety-nine percent of the way there and you just need to refine it, and the focus groups will say, "This is a ridiculous idea. I'd never buy this." So you go back to the drawing board.

THE TROUBLE WITH FOCUS GROUPS

One of the problems I find with focus groups is that there is no way to guard against the one or two big mouths in the room who will begin to sway everybody else for all the wrong reasons. That's why it is sometimes interesting to compare individual one-on-one interviews with group responses. You often get very different responses from the same people.

Let's say there is a very attractive woman in the room, and the guys in that room want to impress the woman. The woman will say, "This pizza is the worst garbage I ever ate in my life," and a guy will say, "Yeah, you're right; it's the worst garbage I ever ate in my life." He doesn't care about the pizza; he wants a date. You have to guard against that.

SEAT-OF-THE-PANTS RESEARCH

The idea of paying a company to do any kind of serious research is ridiculous. In my business there are endless numbers of publications that purport to identify trends in customer behavior. One of these reports costs anywhere from $2,000 to $3,000. What you get is academic nonsense. The information is basically out of date, inaccurate, and, on the whole, worthless.

HOW BIG COMPANIES DO MARKET RESEARCH

The typical way that Nabisco develops a new product is to do endless interviews with consumers to determine if there is an overwhelming need for peanut butter with sardines in it. Then it will set up focus groups, and the focus groups will tell them, "Yes, we love peanut butter with sardines in it." Then it will go to its advertising people, and the advertising people will develop a jingle. Then the marketing department will pull the whole thing together and decide what the advertising budget is, who should sing the jingle, whether Michael Jackson should dance on this stuff, and on and on. As the last step, the company goes to the poor slob in the plant and says, "You've got to figure out how to make this garbage."

The way I run my food business is first we figure out if it can be made. Then we figure out whether it tastes good. Then we figure out how to mass-produce it. Then we worry about how to sell it. That's the exact opposite of how big companies do it. And it is the only way to do it if you are not operating with an unlimited budget.

REAL POSITIONING

The positioning that really counts is where your product gets displayed in the supermarket. Location sells. If you do not get the right kind of shelf space, you are going to get killed no matter how good your product is.

Take our refrigerated dough. In the supermarket refrigerator case, we are right next to Pillsbury, which has 96 percent of the business. No matter what we say to supermarkets about where to put us, they put us in the Pillsbury case. So Pillsbury has become our competition.

The problem with that is that in a pure intellectual sense, we are not being positioned correctly. We are not competing against Pillsbury because Pillsbury has nothing to do with what our product is all about, which is cookie dough made with no chemicals and all top-quality ingredients. Where we *should* be positioned is next to the Nestlé chips, because the Nestlé chips customer is somebody who insists on buying real eggs, real butter, real flour, and real sugar with no chemicals to make his own chocolate chip cookies. That's our kind of customer. We just want him to buy our already-mixed, all-real dough rather than make his own.

From a pure marketing point of view, we want to make

the following argument: Hey, Nestlé chips buyer. Why not buy David's Cookie dough for the following reasons: The ingredients we use are as good or better than the ones you will buy in the supermarket. The chocolate is definitely better. The time you will save by not having to mix this stuff up in the middle of the night when you are having a cookie attack is between twenty-five and thirty minutes. We think our cookies taste better than ones you can make at home. And by the way, they are also less expensive."

Well, we don't have that luxury because there are no refrigerator spaces near Nestlé chips, which are sold off the shelf. In fact, we were thinking of coming in to the supermarkets with a little refrigerator that would stand by the Nestlé display. That would be the perfect position.

So we are being positioned against our will next to Pillsbury. The people who are looking for refrigerated cookie dough are given the opportunity to go upscale and buy ours. At the same time, they see it costs more than Pillsbury. Even though we don't compare ourselves to them because of the quality of the ingredients, a lot of the consumers are making that comparison because of the positioning.

Looking at this from an objective point of view, you could say we were dead before we started. But I was counting on the quality of our product and the recognition of the David's Cookies brand. And sure enough, in six weeks Marian Burros of the *New York Times* wrote an article comparing David's to Pillsbury's and said that David's was clearly superior and worth the higher price. That helped launch the product.

PRICED POSITIONING

How much you charge for your product is important. But the perceived value is even more important. Here's why:

Cookies don't seem to have any price resistance. People either buy them or they don't, regardless of the cost. We've sold them as low as $4.95 on special to as high as around

$18 a pound in Japan. It doesn't seem to make any difference. Ice cream, on the other hand, has to be priced closer to its real cost. That's because a customer can buy it in a carton nearly as easily as he can buy it in a cone. So if you start charging $6 per cone, you are going to get in trouble.

A typical dipping tub costs $22. If every cone is perfectly dipped and every drop goes into a cone, you can make forty-five cones. So each serving that you sell for $1.30 has about fifty cents' worth of ice cream in it. If you add in the cost of the cone, the food cost is more than 40 percent of the selling price. That is about right. Ice cream is not like popcorn or soda, where the cost of the goods sold is practically nothing compared with the selling price. Popcorn is so cheap it is practically free. Whatever they charge for it is gravy. In a typical fast-food store, soda in a cup costs the store a nickel, and the consumer pays fifteen or twenty times that amount.

All specialty-food products involve a value-for-money scenario. Anything with real ingredients in it, with bulk in it, has to cost what the food costs, plus a markup for overhead and profit.

THERE IS NO SUCH THING AS INFINITELY UPSCALE

It is not true that people will pay anything for status. The other day I was in Saks, and they were selling gift caramel apples. They were impressive looking things, for $12 apiece, marked down to $8. They looked like they were worth $12, but nobody is going to pay that much for a dipped apple, no matter how good it is.

I suspect that the bloom is off the rose in terms of spending $2 or $2.50 for an ice cream cone or $1.50 for a little ball of gelato. In fact, I think gelato is finished. It came and went in three years. The value for the money wasn't there. People look at this little ball of nothing and don't want to pay $1.50 for it.

I would be curious to know how Häagen-Dazs is doing with those three flavors of upscale ice cream they recently introduced, like the macadamia nut ice cream. They charge a quarter more a scoop for it, and I would be willing to bet they are not doing that well because at this moment consumers are not willing to pay a premium above premium for a product. Right now there is price resistance out there.

MARKETING 101

That's the end of my marketing lecture. Forget fancy reports, professionally run focus groups and overpaid consultants. They aren't any good, and you can't afford them anyway. You are much better off following your own instincts and doing your own grass-roots research. Stay close to your customers and question them endlessly about what they want. Don't be afraid to change your approach if your original direction doesn't pay off. Promote yourself through the news media. If your product makes sense, sells for a reasonable price, and has some sort of unique appeal or selling proposition, you can probably make it a success.

22

FIGHTING WITH THE LANDLORD AT SOUTH STREET SEAPORT

There is one business lesson I keep learning over and over again: if it sounds too good to be true, it probably is. It usually applies to real estate, because here you are the target of some of the world's shrewdest—and sometimes slimiest—sales people. Each time I learn the lesson over again, it hurts.

The latest to teach it to me has been the Rouse Corporation. Rouse is among the best known developers in the United States. Back in the sixties it built one of the first new towns, Columbia, near Washington, D.C. In the eighties, it has become best known for its so-called festival shopping centers. Rouse goes into picturesque but decrepit inner-city neighborhoods, spruces them up, lures well-known national retailers, mixes in a few local merchants, and generally creates a big success.

The formula was devised in Boston. Rouse put 100 commercial tenants, ranging from restaurants to folk art to—what else—cookies, into Faneuil Hall, a ramshackle waterfront neighborhood near Boston's historic district. The result was, in my opinion, the biggest single shopping hit in American history in terms of attention and publicity.

Faneuil Hall also charted a direction for the development of inner cities and ways to attract well-to-do people. By so doing, Rouse proved there was another way to build shopping malls and merchandise goods. Even better, they did it cheaply and passed the savings along to the tenants. I think the average rent was $7 per foot when Faneuil Hall opened up.

HOW I GOT INTERESTED

I first became interested in the Rouse Corporation in 1981 when I got a call from somebody who told me that a merchant in Faneuil Hall had ripped off my cookie store concept. I went up there to have a look and, sure enough, somebody had duplicated the design motif. The tile was white, the counter was brown, the oven was the same, even the cookies looked like mine. It turned out that the guy who owned the cookie store was John Kerry, who is now the junior U.S. senator from Massachusetts. I told him he had stolen my idea, and he replied, "You're absolutely right. I am a politician; I shouldn't be in the cookie business, so let me sell you my store."

Ultimately, I couldn't buy Kerry's store because he was operating it illegally in violation of the use clause in his lease. He was supposed to be selling jams and jellies, not cookies. But I was so intrigued by seeing the crowds at Faneuil Hall that when Rouse announced plans to open South Street Seaport in New York City, I decided I had to have a piece of it.

GETTING THEM INTO THE TENT

Like everything else Rouse does, the announcement was smooth and professional. They contacted all the major New York City retailers who might be interested in renting space and sent out leasing teams to talk to them. Then, having decided who they really wanted for tenants, they went back

to a few of the retailers and told them they had been chosen
for South Street Seaport.

The Rouse organization negotiated the leases in a fairly
sophisticated way, too. Rouse had its rental office on a
barge in the East River near where the port was going to be.
Every time a tugboat went by, the barge would bob up and
down. Like me, most Jews can't stand water anyway, and
here we were trying to negotiate leases with these goyische
guys from Rouse. Every time the question of how much
arose, the boat would start to rock, and I would get nau-
seated and feel like throwing up. It wasn't too long afterward that I signed the lease.

TOO GOOD TO BE TRUE

The Rouse people flattered me outrageously. They told me
that there were sixty or more cookie companies that wanted
space in the Seaport, but since they wanted me the most, I
would have an exclusive. I felt great. I could open a store for
a song and get rich. Since we would operate as one of two
dozen stores on the second floor of a huge shed, the walls of
the store would already be standing, and there would be no
need for a big expensive plate-glass window in front. The
contractor told me that the store would cost only $60,000 to
build, compared to the usual $125,000, and I estimated we
would be grossing $30,000 a week.

Some friends of mine—Henry Lambert, who owned
Pasta and Cheese, the specialty-food store chain, and Alan
Stillman, who has the Smith & Wollensky steak house—also
signed leases. By the time it was over, we were floating on
air. It looked like a can't-miss deal. The fact that I had just
committed to paying more than $100 a square foot in rent,
not to mention as yet undefined common charges, had not
sunk in.

THE FINE PRINT

Under the terms of our contract with Rouse, we were required to have our store finished by July 23, 1983. That was

the date the Seaport would open, and Rouse wanted to have all the stores ready to go. The opening would be very splashy: Governor Mario Cuomo and Mayor Ed Koch would be there; there would be bands, a big hullabaloo.

Of course, we couldn't finish our stores until Rouse finished building the Fulton Market shed we were going to be in. That project was complicated by a noble attempt of Rouse's. Little did we realize that Rouse was trying to rewrite the rules for Manhattan construction. They let it be known that unlike every other developer in New York they weren't going to play games with the mob. They were going to build South Street Seaport their way, with no payoffs and no featherbedding.

Well and good. Nobody likes the mob. New York builders pay 30 percent more for concrete than anyone else in the United States, have to hire all kinds of extra people, and pay a lot of protection money to keep the union construction workers from striking or the project from being vandalized. That just drives up the cost of doing business in the city. But I would rather some savvy New York builder try to change the rules, not some out-of-town guys from Baltimore. And I wished they hadn't tried it on a project that I was involved in.

HURRY UP AND WAIT

The long and short of it was that as July 23 approached, Fulton Market wasn't getting built. We would call Rouse to ask how we were supposed to construct our store if there was no floor to put it on, and they would tell us not to worry. Finally, near the end, there was a big flurry of activity. We later found out that Rouse paid off everybody left and right to meet their schedules—double, triple, quadruple overtime.

In the rush, the plans were changed so that the space we were given didn't match our specifications at all. For example, a column was built right up through the middle of the front of our store. We had to reformulate our blueprints and redesign a lot of our equipment. We wound up spending $220,000—four times what we had budgeted. Friends who had planned to open up a $125,000 hamburger store spent $750,000. The pizza guy's budget went from $250,000 to $750,000. The ice cream guy, who had expected to spend $175,000, spent almost $600,000.

The other reason for these overruns was that Rouse insisted to the very end that everybody had to open on July 23. If we went back to them once, we went back twenty times to say, "Look guys, if you can't open on the twenty-third, just tell us. It's OK with us if you have to open two months later because we won't have to spend all that hurry-up money." To make their deadline, we paid an electrician quadruple overtime on Saturday night, $100 an hour, to wire up the store.

On the morning of July 22, I got a call saying that South Street Seaport wouldn't open on time after all. I replied, "Unprintable, you just cost me $80,000." They said they would make it up to me.

GREAT EXPECTATIONS

When we did finally open up nine days later, it became immediately clear that the business wasn't there. Rouse promised us we would get a minimum of 35,000 people every day. We got that many on opening day and never saw that many again. Six months later, we got the second piece of bad news. Rouse announced that it was going to build phase two of the Seaport a couple of hundred yards away on the East River. All of us in the original shed in a less desirable, inland location knew we were dead meat.

By then, more than half the original tenants, including myself, either had stopped paying rent or sued Rouse, or both. Everybody had the same beef: they had not been compensated for the extra money they spent to get their stores open. We went back and forth in meetings with Rouse officials.

The other bad news was that because Rouse couldn't get a

handle on the operating costs of the Seaport, our common charges skyrocketed. Our usual common charges in malls across the country were $6–$8 a square foot. Common charges at South Street Seaport were close to $100 a foot. We were paying $15 a foot for garbage and $15 a foot for security. Even worse, the garbage wasn't being picked up on schedule, and people were getting mugged in the bathrooms. It was an unmitigated disaster. All this time, meanwhile, I was reading in the newspapers about what a wonderful success the Seaport was.

After seventeen months, I hadn't paid a dime of rent. Finally, in February 1985, I couldn't take it any longer. I threatened to sue, and we finally worked out a deal where they paid me to leave. Under terms of my deal with Rouse, I can't disclose how much it was. I cleared out in forty-eight hours. We were about the eighth or ninth tenant to go. The fact is that by late 1987, only three or four of the original twenty-three or twenty-four tenants on the second floor were left. Rouse says that this is a normal shakeout for a project like this, and they are remerchandising the floor anyway. Translation: everyone who hasn't gone is going.

LESSON

The moral of the story? It is a fool's game to chase these developers' projects. Every time you think you have a deal on space that is in short supply like a Rouse project, you get in trouble. I sure did. The one exception to that is EPCOT Center at Disney World. Restaurants there do great. But there is only one Disney World, and unfortunately I don't have a cookie store there.

23
KEEPING THE POT BUBBLING

O ne of the ways I keep my twitch level up is by constantly thinking up new products and developing new concepts. Nothing is worse than stagnation; it is the first step toward death. In the late 1970s, General Motors began to think it could do no wrong and that it was so big it could coast for a while. So it did. Around the same time, Ford almost went belly up so it had to hustle and the Japanese always work hard. Now Ford has the Taurus/Sable car and the biggest profits in the industry, and both Ford and the Japanese are eating GM's lunch. GM is finally beginning to wake up, but it hasn't started to twitch yet.

One of these days I am going to branch out of the food business. We already sell a lot of merchandise in David's Cookies stores—T-shirts, cookie boxes, stuffed animals, and so forth, and I would like to do more of it. The profit margins are better and the shelf life is longer. T-shirts never go stale.

ONE OF MY NONFOOD IDEAS

Last year, I thought I had a pretty good idea for diversification—David's for Kids. Here's how I went about dreaming it up.

We have two Manhattan cookie store locations that are not viable as cookie stores. The sales are going south, and they cost too much to run. So I started looking around, and I realized that among my contemporaries, everybody is having kids. Statistics indicate that people are going to keep having kids for a while. That means kids can be a business for me.

Kids and cookie stores go together. The question is, how? Then I thought about what I do with my kids when they have birthday parties. To get them out of the house so they don't wreck it, I take them to something called Jeremy's Place that seems to have a monopoly on the East Side of Manhattan. The kids come into this store, Jeremy clowns around with them for ninety minutes, and he gets paid a couple of hundred dollars. In addition, he sells them a lot of cake and ice cream and party favors and makes money there, too.

So I said to myself, "I should turn these cookie stores into party places for kids, so kids can come in and bake their own cookies and play cookie store."

This is a great idea. First, there is not a lot of competition. Second, there seems to be an endless demand among parents for these party places. Third, I have two perfect locations.

Voilà! David's Cookies becomes David's for Kids. Question: do I do it cheaply or do it right? I figure the idea has potential for franchising, given the success of KinderCare, the nationwide day-care center. Moreover, there is a lot of secondary space you can get in shopping malls, either in the basement or out of the way, where you can rent a couple of hundred square feet for a couple of bucks a square foot. So if I can come up with a viable concept and do it right, I can franchise it.

So I went to a company that designs packages and things for me and I told them, "David's for Kids." They said,

"Great, we have this guy Murray who designed Sesame Place, an amusement park based on the Sesame Street TV show." So I went to see Murray, who is the mad scientist type, and said to him, "This is our budget; I want you to help design David's for Kids." He asked, "What kind of environment?" I said, "Very simple. I want it to have a sales environment, meaning everything in that store, short of the air conditioner and the toilet seat, can be sold."

While all this is going on, a guy happened to walk into my office who wants to develop a character for me called the Chunkster—as in the chunks of chocolate in my cookies. The Chunkster is a human being who runs around in a cookie outfit. As I envision him, the Chunkster is a party animal who drinks milk and is opposed to drugs and sex. To go along with him, we need something for kids, so we invented something called the Chunkster Youngster.

Now we have this guy who is developing a character like Spuds MacKenzie, the Bud Light mascot, who is going to be the focal point of David's for Kids. The Chunkster and Chunkster Youngster are going to be clowns who take the kids to the various stages of the party. So I said to myself, "How can I extract the maximum amount of money from this environment?" I have a video guy, and we're going to wire up these two stores so that when little Johnny is baking his cookies, the video guy will be making a tape recording of the whole thing, which I then sell to the parents for $75 or so.

I've observed the market, and I know there is a real market out there; being a city person, I know that parents are constantly looking for places to take their kids. Kids love to bake. And there is something inherently appealing about taking over a David's Cookies store—sort of like the lunatics taking over the asylum. The parents get a chance to relax because their apartment isn't being torn up. And we make money in some less-than-vibrant cookie stores. The only competition for birthday parties is that the clowns of this world like Jeremy open up more operations; but I have the name recognition and it's a word-of-mouth business, so I can get there first.

WHAT IS WRONG WITH THIS IDEA?

As much as I loved David's for Kids, I decided to go more slowly with it than I first planned. It is OK, but it is not a superhit. The major reason is that the upside potential is limited. You can cram only so many kids and so many parties into a given store. I can already visualize what the maximum revenue per store is going to be.

You have to ration your time and energy and focus on your ideas with the biggest potential. There are only so many hours in a day that I want to work—twenty at most— and I can go after only so many opportunities. I have to pursue just the best ones.

MUFF CAKES

A little while ago, we decided to come out with our own muffin. Most muffins are air and baking powder. So we developed Muff Cakes, which were muffin tops made with all-real ingredients. They were hefty: weighed three ounces apiece. To keep the price reasonable, we had to work on a very small profit margin. We sold the ingredients to our franchisees at a small profit; they then resold them to the public. But it didn't work—we couldn't make any money.

We run into those kinds of problems all the time. Unlike companies that find out what the market is and at what price they can get the highest volume of and still make a profit, we do it differently. We make our product the way we want to make it and then try to figure out if we can sell it at a profit. That was our problem with Muff Cakes. If the world had been ready for a muffin that cost a buck and a quarter, we would have been in good shape. But the world wasn't and I suspect it is not going to be. It is not true that people will pay anything for food.

NICHES

If you can come up with endless twists on a basic idea, you get an idea of what my product strategy is.

If you have any young children, you have no doubt heard of gummy bears candy or even the Gummy Bears television show on Saturday mornings. Gummy bears are a kind of tastier, less-chewy version of the old Juju Fruits, made in the shape of a bear, rather than a piece of fruit. I decided there is an upscale market for gummy bears, based on only one piece of information: gummy bear sales are increasing at an annual rate of more than 20 percent.

We surveyed the market and discovered that every single gummy bear available had some sort of chemical in it. Since there wasn't an all-real gummy bear, we created a niche and brought one out. We introduced children's gummy bears first in the traditional five flavors, such as lime and tutti-frutti. There is a market for that kind of product.

I thought there might be a more refined niche for adult gummy bears. The country had been in a craze, which is now dying down, for jelly beans. Jelly beans went from being a children's product to being a very upscale adult product. They had kiwi jelly beans and cappuccino jelly beans. I looked at that market and saw there were a lot of adults eating jelly beans who might eat gummy bears. So I planned a line of gummy bears with adult flavors, such as cappuccino, raspberry, peach, and so on.

It turned out I was wrong. I think that whole market, including jelly beans, is not as strong as it was, primarily because people are concerned about sugar consumption. At some point, this fanaticism about low cholesterol and dietetic eating is going to catch up with the general population. It may not be this year and it may not be next year, but eventually. It is like the antismoking movement.

PLENTY MORE IDEAS
WHERE THAT CAME FROM

Instead of fighting the health and diet trend, I decided to go with it. Here is how: some months ago, my doctor told me I would have to lower my cholesterol or I wouldn't be around to see this book published. I have this intense sensual relationship with food, especially good food; I own a restaurant and a cookie store, and I eat all the time.

There are two ways to lower your cholesterol. One is by giving up butter and other rich dairy products. I did that—it hurt, but I did it. The other way is by consuming soluble fibers that absorb cholesterol, specifically oat bran fiber, which is twice as soluble as any fiber on the market. So for four months, I ate oat bran flakes for breakfast every morning.

The problem with oat bran flakes is that after you pour the skim milk on them, they turn to sludge in about thirty seconds. One morning I was looking at this stuff, and I said to myself, "There's got to be a better way."

So I came up with the idea for oat bran muffins. Eat two in the morning and you've had breakfast, plus you've helped lower your cholesterol.

Since I'm in the food business, my customers can eat what I eat. So we've started selling these muffins at my cookie stores in six flavors: peach, grape, cherry, and so on. We make them without sugar or oil.

There is an enormous market out there: 40 million to 60 million people have a cholesterol problem. The beauty of my plan is that after all these years of selling fattening food, I can tell people that they will be healthier if they eat my muffins.

The muffins are going to be incredibly easy to sell. They are a holier-than-thou product. You eat this stuff, you get well. You are going to lose weight, stay regular, lower your cholesterol. The hard part is to make these muffins taste like anything; we have to be very careful with the recipes and the preparation. The muffins taste good, considering what is in them, but they don't taste as good as an 800-calorie muffin. This isn't snack food; this is health food. Still, I can't wait to start staring reporters down when they nag me that the muffins don't taste as good as chocolate chunk cookies. A lot of people don't have a choice—I know I don't.

There is also a subtle marketing problem. In general, if given a choice between dietetic ice cream and no ice cream at all, people will choose the latter. They don't like diet foods.

Nor do people like to admit they are on diets. They hate to walk into diet restaurants. So you have to try to sell them a diet dish in a nondiet environment.

I've managed to do that in my restaurant. I have two diet plates on the menu, but I don't call them diet dishes. I call them "club cuisine." They account for 50 percent of all the lunches I sell.

Eventually, I envision following the muffins with low-cholesterol sponge cake and two kinds of low-cholesterol cookies reminiscent of the "gorp" mixtures that hikers eat, and selling them all in supermarkets in their own low-cholesterol section. There is a money-back guarantee; the muffins will make you regular in four hours or your money back. We'll see.

24

WHY YOU DON'T WANT TO GET INTO THE RESTAURANT BUSINESS

I 'll bet at least 50 percent of the people I talk to who want to go into business for themselves say they want to go into the restaurant business. Forget it. Right now.

It is a buyer's market for restaurants at the moment. There is no shortage of places to eat.

Besides, it is no business for amateurs. Period. It isn't even a very good business for professionals. I don't know anybody who should be a hands-on operator in the restaurant business. I can debunk the myth of the people who think it is the greatest business in the world because they can impress their friends, go up to their bar and get a free drink, and meet nineteen-year-old models who say, "Take me home."

WHAT'S HOT, WHAT'S NOT

There is a sickness growing in New York City about the hot new restaurant. In the old days, you opened a restaurant and after three, four, ten years, you had a good restaurant.

As you got better, you developed a stable clientele that stayed with you. Here restaurants are opening up and are supposed to be great immediately. The fashionable crowd rushes in and the restaurant turns up in the society columns. After a month the chic set goes on to the next new eating spot. Since the first place never had a chance to get its act together before it became fashionable, it is not good enough now to cultivate any kind of permanent following. So it goes downhill fast. In this quick-hit society we live in, a restaurant is like a hot movie or a hot show—people go once and that's it. And unlike the movies and the theaters, the restaurants can't stay in business long enough to pay back the $3 million invested to open them.

BIGGER IS NOT BETTER

The game is you can't just open this charming little restaurant. You've got to put the money in the walls—build something special. That means construction costs of $400 a square foot to build the facilities. Since the kind of restaurant you need to make an impression in Manhattan is 4,000 to 5,000 square feet, you need $2 million just to open the doors. And the money doesn't come back, because the landlords want this and the city wants that.

I am terribly wary of people who come in and tell me these schemes that can't miss. The best examples are these big-hit restaurants. They put a host at the door who has a big following, put $3 million on the walls, hire a chef who can't cook, get a bunch of models who are light hookers and put them at the bar, and say it can't miss. If you look beyond the glitz, it is a disaster.

If you don't make a mistake and do everything right, you may be able to bring 15 percent to the bottom line pretax. The margins are tight and the potential to screw up is great. If restaurant critics Bryan Miller or Gael Greene get a bellyache, you're dead. If Woody Allen or another big name comes in and walks out, you're also dead.

The other kind of restaurants, the kind that have neighborhood clientele and build slowly, aren't allowed to live anymore. If you are not hot and new, people don't want to go there.

THINGS BREAK

Restaurants are not only the ultimate detail business, they are also a push-pull business. You live and die for your physical plant. The restaurant has all these gadgets that have to work on a daily basis to get the food on the plates. Since space is at a premium in a typical city environment, everything is tight. Hot stuff is running next to the cold stuff, and when the hot stuff breaks, it screws up the cold stuff.

It is an ongoing problem that can't be fixed. We all live with these ice machine guys and refrigeration guys on call twenty-four hours a day. So at any given time, you could be doing everything perfectly: the chef is on time, everything is glistening, the waiters took a bath for once . . . and your stove blows up. Disaster.

PEOPLE BREAK

Then, in a 100-seat restaurant you are typically running fifty to seventy-five employees, or anywhere from half an employee to one per customer on a seven-days-a-week basis. To compound that, there is not a lot of talent around in either cooking or waiting on tables. In New York, you have a choice between going with the old-time union waiters or the neophytes. The old-time waiters are high on expertise but low on enthusiasm. The novices are all waiting to be discovered by Hollywood or Broadway, which is fine. But they don't know a lot about wine, and they don't know a lot about service.

In our case, since we opened our first Manhattan Market and first David's Cookies on Second Avenue in 1979, we have had 600 aspiring actors and actresses working in one place or the other, and not one has made it big. Not one. So you have a lot of employees with dreams that they are only this far away from being a major television star. They are out on casting calls when I am serving lunch.

The other employee problem is the chef who wants to be a superstar. The trouble is that not very many of these superstar chefs learned how to cook along the way. They come in and start doing these bizarre things, and they develop attitudes. But you are stuck. If you hire a chef and he starts running food costs that are 50 percent of the menu price, when they should be only 35 percent, that's bad enough. Suppose he quits. What are you going to do? If you have 150 customers that night, 148 of them are happy, and only two of them say they are going to sue you or kill you, you are in bad shape.

CELEBRITY CHEFS

It is absolutely a media phenomenon. The best chefs in the world are at their ranges every day, cooking. Celebrity chefs are never in their restaurants. They spend more time exhibiting their talent on the road somewhere than they do in their own kitchens.

Right now, on a celebrity scale of one to ten, New Orleans chef Paul Prudhomme is an eleven. He is a very nice, unassuming guy—who is definitely going to die if he doesn't lose weight. He can't even walk anymore; he has an electric cart that he has to be schlepped around on. Somebody should grab ahold of him and say, "Save yourself. Stop eating; it is not worth it." He could lose 250 pounds and would hardly miss it.

What's interesting about this is, with the exception of Prudhomme and perhaps Wolfgang Puck, the Los Angeles-based head of Spago, very few of these guys make any money. If you are a celebrity chef, it just means that you are living out of suitcases and going from one banquet to the next, but you're not adding anything to the bottom line. None of these guys have any other way of cashing in, short of going to a restaurant, working that restaurant very hard, and making that restaurant very successful. And not one of them is doing that—not one. I don't know what the phenomenon is all about. It may be they like getting their pictures in the paper, or they don't want to go home, but it sure isn't about making money.

OVERBOOKING

I am sympathetic to other restaurant owners. A customer who calls up, makes a reservation, reconfirms the reservation, and then doesn't show up is a thief. It is just like stealing money out of your pocket. He is not playing by the rules. The way we run our restaurant, we honor reservations. We don't overbook ever—except on Saturday nights. We made that an exception because we know we are going to get stuck by 40 percent of the people anyway.

It drives me insane when people play "my daddy is bigger than your daddy." Two or three couples will get together on the weekend, and the big shot will say, "Where do you want to go tonight? I have reservations at Lutece, the Quilted Giraffe, Le Bernadin, and Chez Louis. Which one do you want to go to? I'll just call and get us in." When they do that, they are sticking it to the three other restaurants.

There is no solution. Short of calling up customers at 3 A.M. and saying, "We are still holding your table for you, if you'd care to come," there's nothing you can do.

I try to look at things from a customer's point of view. It is very rare that somebody waits more than fifteen minutes for a table at my restaurant. We don't take 300 reservations at eight o'clock the way many restaurants do. We say, "Look, if you come at eight o'clock, you are going to stand at the bar for an hour. If you come at nine o'clock, you may be able to sit down right away."

PRICING PROBLEMS

The cost of the ingredients in an entrée vary all over the place, but the prices on the menu have a range of only a few dollars or so. The reason is that tradition and good business practice dictate that you can't price a meal by what it costs you to make it.

Here's why. Most quality restaurants that I know try to keep food costs to 35 percent of the menu price or less. But we have a veal chop in which the hunk of meat alone costs us $14, forget whatever else goes onto it. At the same time, the food cost on the raw chicken is only a couple of dollars. But we can't sell the veal chop for $50 and the chicken for $7 because it would throw everything out of whack.

As it happens, we charge a little more for the veal than the chicken, and we sell the same amount of both chicken and veal. People know a bargain when they see it. Likewise, you make a lot of money on Boston lettuce, and you don't make anything on the foie gras. Even at $14.95 a slice, we lose money on foie gras.

MONEY IS TIGHT

There is so much pressure on restaurateurs to pay their bills that the worst business to be in is that of a restaurant supplier. If the wholesalers ever called in their chits, the whole thing would collapse. We have a fish supplier— Albert the fish guy—who gets paid every Friday. He comes up here and gets his check. And because he gets paid every week, we are probably saving 20 percent on fish. Most restaurants don't have that luxury. I know some that owe $1 million to suppliers.

PROFIT MARGINS

The most you can expect to make is fifteen percent. Out of that, you are paying American Express 4¼ to 5½ percent to in effect cash your chits. A typical upscale New York restaurant does at least 80 percent of its business with American Express. So when American Express sends you a letter saying "Dear Partner," it means it. And American Express doesn't have to deal with the dishwashers not showing up and the ovens blowing out. It is small charges like these that can eat you up.

EVEN FAMOUS RESTAURANTS HAVE IT TOUGH

21 has one-hundred-fifty to two-hundred employees or more. And it was doing almost capacity business at ridiculous prices. So Marshall Cogan, the owner, shut it down to renovate it and poured what I hear was $9 million into redecorating. So even if he raises the price of a hamburger from $21 to $23.50, it isn't going to make any difference because he has no place to put the bodies. He is already doing all the business he can do. The restaurant will be a hobby. And there are a lot of places like that.

SMART OPERATORS

My friends the Riese brothers might not know much about food, but they know plenty about how to make money with restaurants. Take these examples of their operating style, which you won't find in any Harvard Business School case study.

What do you do if you have a restaurant with 125 seats and you are consistently filling up only 100 of those seats? Simple. You put up a wall around the twenty-five seats that aren't selling and you lease the space to someone who doesn't need very much, like a taco-stand operator.

What do you do when you have 100 seats and you have 200 people a day who want to eat at your restaurant? You keep raising the prices until the line goes away.

The Riese brothers also invented daily menu pricing. They leave a blank space on the menu next to a description of the food and fill it in with whatever crazy price they figure they can get away with on that day. On a Saturday with a lot of people out and about, they charge $9.95 for a hamburger. On a rainy Monday, the price goes down to $6.

SMART HELPS

The Riese brothers are evidence that if you know what you are doing, it is possible to make money in the restaurant business. The problem is trying to define what it is you have to know. To this day, I'm not even sure. For example, I can think of a couple of things that Susan and I know that enable us to sleep a *little* bit better at night than the average restaurant owner. In Susan's case, she is the best floor person in New York. She charms everybody in the room. I am horrible at that. She also has an incredible understanding of what wines sell at what price points. That is something people overlook a lot, but in our restaurant, wine accounts for at least 15 percent of our sales. It is a function of getting a good return on your assets, because the biggest chunk of money you are going to spend after you have outfitted your restaurant is building your wine cellar. I would say 99 percent of the people going into the restaurant business serve wine as an afterthought. They will bring in one of these guys who does wine lists and festoon the list with seemingly well-known wines that may or may not sell, but they could wind up giving away half their profit if they don't do it right.

GET THE MESSAGE?

Save your money and your sanity. Do something else.

25
WORMS IN
THE BIG APPLE

I may be the quintessential New Yorker, but I am getting fed up with the city. There are enormous opportunities here, great creative people, thousands of potential customers. But the hassles are just too much. I have to fight with everybody: landlords, employees, suppliers, police, bureaucracy. It is a tough place to do business in, much less start a new one. Think twice, if that is your idea.

If I had to do it over again, maybe I wouldn't do it here. All the external pressures, all the garbage you have to deal with is not worth it. It is much easier to run a business anyplace else in the country. New York City represents less than 4 percent of the population now, and there are a lot of other people in the rest of the United States who eat and buy things. If I had any kind of motivation, I would get out of Manhattan. Sometimes I wonder why I don't live in Aspen. I like to ski; I like the outdoors. I'm sure I could open a health-food store, the Zabar's of Aspen. I wouldn't become a trillionaire, but I'd do just fine.

LANDLORDS

By now, you have figured out that landlords aren't my favorite people. Well, the news is they are getting worse. I've never seen such greed. Whereas in the old days there was some give and take in lease negotiations, the landlords are now saying, "Screw you, I'll wait and get somebody else." In the last down real estate market, in 1978, a lot of landlords weren't that rich because the last down market before that was 1974. But now they have been living high off the hog since 1980. They have become incredibly arrogant. Since the crash of 1987, the real estate market has loosened up a little. But there are still some ridiculous deals being done. My friend Mrs. Fields is spending $13,000 *a month* for a rat-hole location on Second Avenue that has been vacant for years. It also happens to be just one block from my office. It has maybe 780 square feet. If they make twenty-five cents a cookie, which is a lot, they will have to sell 144 cookies per hour, twelve hours a day, every day of the month, just to pay for the rent. Take it from me, that is a lot of cookies. There is no way they can make a go of that location. The cost of doing business has just gotten out of hand. Rent, taxes, labor, everything. The cost of your break-even point goes up and up and up. So you have to fight like hell to boost your volume, which means jamming even more people into your store.

THE CITY'S ANTIBUSINESS ATTITUDE

The city of New York has taken an attitude of benign neglect toward small businesses, even though we provide 80 percent of the jobs in the city. There is no differentiation in terms of taxes and energy costs between big and small businesses. If anything, big businesses get a break on energy costs because they buy in greater quantities. Plus, they have this marvelous leverage when it comes to getting cushy tax breaks. Since they are big and well known, they can just whisper that they are thinking of moving to New Jersey, and the city hands them this big basket of financial incentives, like tax abatements, and low-cost financing and so on. Look at the deal NBC got to stay in Rockefeller Center. One hundred million dollars or more. Contrast that with my situation.

I have a small plant in Long Island City, which is in Queens across the East River from Manhattan, where I make cookie dough for stores across the country. It is an awful place to do business. Transportation for both goods and workers is horrible, costs of operation are off the wall, working conditions aren't great, and harassment by city agencies, such as getting a sanitation ticket for not putting a lid on your garbage can at 3 A.M. when a bum was sleeping in it, is continual.

I've complained about the situation for years. The city pays lip service to programs to help the small businessman. But the Department of Economic Development, which is supposed to work out the problems of small businesses and keep them in the city, has become blatantly two-faced. They listen to us gripe that crime is out of control, occupancy taxes are too high, energy rates are too high—but the programs they offer us don't work. I've been trying for years to get my energy rates down, and I can't do it because the area isn't depressed enough, even though I'm a small manufacturer, the kind the city wants to keep.

So where does that leave me? Since we are out of room where we are in Long Island City and industrial revenue bonds have basically dried up, there is no way I can consider building my next facility here. There are better deals elsewhere, in New Jersey or Pennsylvania. Or even in the state of New York, if you want to move into rural areas. It is almost impossible to do business in the city anymore.

EMPLOYEES

Everybody has trouble finding people who want to show up for work two days in a row and are honest. A friend of mine runs a messenger company. He can bond his employees to protect customers against theft, but his problem is that he fires messengers and they keep making their rounds. Instead of delivering the merchandise they pick up—they steal it. He didn't find out about it until one of his customers, a jeweler, called up and said none of the jewelry he had shipped in the past week had reached its destination.

FORTY-SECOND STREET FOLLIES

We had an office on Forty-second Street between Fifth and Madison. A Dutch businessman comes in to sell us cocoa. He is sitting in the waiting room for his first meeting. One of the trainees in the cookie store above the office comes down, sits down next to him, and steals his wallet and his jacket, stashes it away, and then goes back upstairs and continues his training. This guy doesn't realize it until several hours later.

The second time the cocoa guy came in he was mugged in front of the store. A guy used to come in and rob the Forty-second Street store every couple of nights around 7:30 P.M. The first couple of times he used a gun, but after that he would just go up to the kid behind the counter and say, "Remember me?" The kid would then fill up the bag with money. The cops figured out that if he was coming in at the same time, he must be doing something else in the area. It turns out he was attending school down the street at City University of New York. He was finally arrested in his college classroom.

One night a guy with a gun came in to rob the store. The clerk in the store got so mad that he jumped across the counter and chased the guy out onto the street and north two blocks. The employee tackled the robber, dragged him back screaming into the store, and sat on him. They got a cop off the street who said, "Do you have any witnesses? If you don't, this guy could sue you for unlawful restraint." In fact, we got a customer who saw it all happen, and they finally arrested the would-be thief.

CRIME

That's far and away my biggest headache. At Broadway and

Eighth Street, four crooks came in, locked the manager and two helpers in the refrigerator, put on aprons and worked the store for four hours. They baked the cookies and made change out of their pockets. Everything was fine until a cop walked in to buy cookies, and they panicked. They jumped over the counter and ran away. The guys in the fridge were all right.

We've had people actually rip the cash register, which is bolted into the counter, out of the store. We had a guy drag it out into the street, where he got so mad when he couldn't get it open that he started bouncing the thing up and down. Two plainclothes cops came along and arrested the guy for beating up a cash register that didn't belong to him.

There is a Häagen-Dazs at 112th and Broadway where some guy backed a pickup truck right through the front window, hooked a winch up to the safe, and dragged the safe out of the concrete and up Broadway until he was caught.

That's not all. There are the con artists who try to quick change you. Counterfeit money is all over the place. We've had people call my stores and say, "Hello, I'm David's cousin. My car broke down and I'm out of cash. Would you take the money out of the cash register and put it in the garbage can out back where I can pick it up." And the managers do it. Of course, they wind up paying the money back out of their own pockets.

TRYING TO KEEP CRIME FROM PAYING

When I can, I try to prosecute people who steal from me. But it is very frustrating. I've had cops tell me privately that it doesn't do any good to catch them; you have to throw them in the East River because the court system isn't so terrific. We had an assistant manager who was caught walking down the street at 3 A.M. with an armload of teddy bears and $1,200 in cash. He was caught red-handed. He said he was headed for the bank or something. It turns out he was the son of a cop, so he got off by plea-bargaining.

We have tried everything to cut down on crime. But what we sometimes wind up doing is just diverting a robber from holding up my store to holding up the guy next to me. Under the theory "better thee than me" I've installed live video cameras in some stores. Sometimes we put the surveillance monitor in the window of the store, so if somebody sticks it up, he goes on Candid Camera.

One week, our stores in Manhattan were robbed thirty times. So we hired a security company to put armed guards in all the stores. At one of the stores, the guard pistol-whipped one of my executives when the executive came in to collect the money.

Some people are putting in these drop safes, where employees deposit the cash at night into receptacles they can't get into. I think those safes are incredibly dangerous because most of the robbers are drug addicts who get so mad when they can't get the money that they shoot the employees. What we do is bleed the cash registers regularly, every fifteen minutes, so there is never more than $25 in the till. A new thing coming in that seems to work is the exploding money packet. When the word gets around that you have them, the crooks go someplace else. They don't want to get a face full of red dye from that wad of bills they just grabbed out of our cash register.

The hard truth is that it is very difficult to protect the money. If you scream loud enough, the cops will stake out your store. One time they did it for me. They arrived in a van that practically screamed "police department property" and parked out front of our store at Eighty-fifth and Madison for eight hours. During the stakeout, the store was robbed, and the cops didn't catch any of the perpetrators. It sounds unbelievable, but it is true. The cops were on break, they were sleeping, I don't know what they were doing.

NEW YORK'S FINEST

The city tries to help. Larry Kieves, who was head of economic development, is an intelligent guy who I could get to listen to me. At the time, I owned thirty cookie stores in Manhattan, and they were getting robbed twenty-five times a week. That didn't just cost me money; it cost me customers and employees, because people didn't want to work in stores that were getting robbed all the time. The cops weren't doing anything. They said they had more important things like rapes and murders to attend to. Which is true, but if somebody is bleeding out of three arteries, you can't just sew up two of them and expect him to live.

So Larry arranged a meeting for me with two big-shot police officials. Well, I showed up for the meeting at 9 A.M.; there was this commander or something with so many medals on his chest that he could barely stand up, and he was stone cold drunk. His assistant was there, and he was just as drunk. They took out a thick set of computer print-outs, and they said, "We don't understand why you have a problem because citywide, crime is down 9 percent." That's the kind of help you get from the city.

If New York isn't able to come to grips with quality-of-life issues, more people are going to leave. Even the hard-working Koreans who run all those successful fruit markets are beginning to leave.

NUISANCE TAXES

The one time the city doesn't ignore you is when it comes to nuisance taxes. They have regulations for nearly every piece of equipment in my stores and restaurant and plenty of inspectors to come around and find fictitious violations. I had a one-story building that was being repossessed for back taxes because I hadn't paid my elevator tax. I tried for six months, but I couldn't get a city official to come see that I didn't have an elevator in a building with no second floor.

Then the Consumer Affairs Department wanted to arrest me for running an illegal sale. I advertised that I was selling cookies for $5.95 a pound in a special decorated box at a saving of $2.50. They claimed that since the cookies usually sell for $6.95, it was only a $1 saving. I screamed till I was blue in the face that the sale included the special box that cost me $1.50. Then there was the time they wanted to padlock my yogurt machine because I didn't have a yogurt-machine license. Give me a break.

The way you fight the city is by sending the media after them. The squeaky wheel really does get the grease. I have to give the city some credit for at least identifying what the issues are. They know the nuisance taxes are a burden. I would rather pay the city a lump sum every month than deal with the constant tickets. It is not only the money; it is time. If you are a small-business owner, you don't have time to go downtown to all these hearings on nuisance issues.

Japan is way ahead of us on most of this stuff. Now that I'm in business over there, I know. They take better care of their small businesses because their infrastructure is better developed. And they just don't have the same problems. Our employee manual is broken up into three sections: how you run the store, how you motivate the employees, and how you prevent crime. The Japanese are dumbfounded because they don't have the last two problems. Their workers work hard, and there is virtually no crime.

CONCLUSION

There is a psychological cost to doing business in New York that just doesn't exist anywhere else. If I had to do it over again, I'd probably start up in Nashville or Kansas City or someplace where the rents are reasonable, the people hard-working, the crime rate low, and the bureaucracy manageable. Would I miss New York? Probably. Which is one reason why I haven't left yet. For me, it is the ultimate love-hate relationship.

26
GETTING OUT

Getting out of a business is really contrary to an entrepreneur's way of thinking. Most of the time he is scheming about how to expand his business and make it grow to be a bigger thing next year than it was last year. But getting out is one of the things you should think about from the moment it appears your business can stand on its own legs.

A business is more confining than a marriage. With a marriage, you can go to a divorce court and say you want out. But with a business, you have to keep running it, sell it to somebody, or fold it. It is a legal entity with a life of its own, and it won't be easy to kill when you get tired of it without some very serious financial repercussions. People should think long and hard about whatever business they go into to see if they can be comfortable with it for the long haul. Basically, you cannot develop a business with an eye toward selling that business and walking away. When you start a business, you are probably going to be in it for a long time.

LIFE CYCLES

Businesses go through different levels and growth periods. The people who start businesses are usually less interested in running them. Maybe Fred Smith of Federal Express is going to be happy shipping millions of packages from one city to another; I don't know. Most people who get their jollies creating things want to go on to something new rather than stay with the same old thing.

For me, it was a big kick to take a failing restaurant that I had started, Manhattan Market, and convert it into Chez Louis, which is a very successful restaurant. I felt in my gut that people would rather eat roasted and grilled food than nouvelle cuisine. Getting into the supermarket refrigerated dough business and making no-cholesterol muffins is fun, too.

KEEPING THE ADRENALINE PUMPING

If I started in the cookie business, does that mean I have to keep selling cookies for the rest of my life? The answer is clearly no. Diversification is something that can get you going in other directions to keep your mind fresh, to help you keep on regenerating the creative process. For me, selling cookies is not one of my long-term goals. But I've decided, for good or for bad, that I like the food business. I like all aspects of it. So nobody out there is going to say to me one day, "You are forbidden to sell hamburgers." If I decided to sell hamburgers one day, I'd have the freedom to do that.

Still, you have to be careful. Just because you started one business successfully doesn't mean that you will be equally successful with the next one. Look at Fred Smith of Federal Express again. Everything was going great for him moving those packages all over the world, so he came up with this idea called Zap Mail. Now, Zap Mail was a very expensive and cumbersome facsimile service. Smith wanted to pick up your document by messenger, take it to his fax machine,

send the document to another of his fax machines someplace else, and then deliver it to your addressee. He lost
hundreds of millions dollars at it before he folded it. Didn't
he know that within two years, fax machines were going to
cost practically nothing and everybody would have them in
their office so that there would be no need for this cumbersome service? If he didn't, somebody should have told him.

TIES THAT BIND

One of the things that happens to entrepreneurs is that they
become emotionally involved with their business. That is a
very dangerous trap and can hurt you in two basic ways.
Number one, at least early on, you become so identified with
that business, both in the public's eye and your own, that if
you want to get out, you can't, because the business won't
work without you. Number two, the decisions you make are
sometimes based on the emotional passions of the business,
rather than on detached analytical thinking, the way that
they should be. The reason Larry Tisch is richer than all
the rest of us is that he is not emotionally attached to his
business. He sold Loews theater operations, which was the
core of the family enterprises, for a good price, and he has
felt no qualms whatsoever about selling CBS records and
magazines.

DISENGAGING

One smart thing an entrepreneur can do after his business
is up and running and he gets bored is to try to push it in a
direction where he has less of the responsibility and less of
the ongoing aggravation. You can hire people to take on
more of the aggravation as well as the day-to-day details.

There is a fine line between my deciding if it is worth my
time to figure something out and letting somebody else do
it. Take the case of Steve Stein. Steve was a partner in the
law firm that represented me, until I hired him as president
in January 1984. The week that he started work, I was in

Japan opening up our first cookie store there. I was in awful shape. I'd had a horrendous flight, and the Japanese had taken me out drinking until four in the morning. Then I get this panicked telephone call from Stein, who had been on the job for exactly one hour when he got the following inquiry. A doctor called him from Providence, Rhode Island, saying that somebody had just eaten a David's cookie and was in intensive care and could die any minute. Would he, Stein, please tell the doctor all the ingredients in the cookie so that the doctor could find out if the victim was allergic to any of them.

You may be surprised to learn that we get calls like this all the time. What better way to find out the ingredients in our cookie dough, which are still secret after all these years. Stein asked me what he should do. I told him, "I'm tired, my head hurts, you figure it out."

What he did was call the guy back to confirm he was a doctor—which didn't prove anything because there are plenty of doctors around who would like to own cookie stores. He told the doctor, "If the patient goes on life support, you call me, and we'll tell you some of the ingredients." Well, the doctor went away and wasn't heard from again, so we assumed it all came out all right. In any event, Stein learned real fast how to make decisions.

It is nice to delegate because that way you can get rid of some of these aggravations. You don't have to worry about every conceivable little thing that comes up. And if your subordinates want authority and the money that goes with it, they have to take some of the crap, too. That's part of the game.

LOOKING FOR A WAY OUT

I know endless sons of developers who say the only way to learn about real estate development is to be raised by a father in the business. Nearly all of the big-name developers in New York City came from families whose fathers were in the business. But I don't think that is going to work for me.

My daughters are still young—eight and five—but I don't think they have the vaguest interest in going into this business.

What's going to happen to David's? I think we are going to have a couple of more scrambling years defining our market share in supermarkets. Our brand name is really getting more valuable every day. Then, when everything is clicking, we will either do a big joint venture, sell the business, or keep it going—I really don't know.

TAKE THE MONEY AND RUN

Some people think they can go into a business that competes with a big company so that the big company will come along and buy them out. That doesn't work. In the case of my business, people think that as soon as I get tired of it I can just go to Pillsbury and sell it for millions of dollars. Wrong. The cases of corporate America coming to a small entrepreneur and saying, "Here are millions of dollars. Now go away," are less than one-half of one percent.

GOING PUBLIC

If you sell your stock to the public, you may have an easy way to get out. Anybody who goes public can basically sell his stock and walk away. The Saatchis of Saatchi and Saatchi advertising own only 3 percent of their own company. The trouble is that most investors are not going to want to buy into a company called David's unless David says he is going to stick around.

The fact of the matter is that few people are going public this week or maybe for the rest of this decade. Since the crash of 1987, knocked the stock market on its tush, the prices haven't been high enough to make it worthwhile. I can do better looking for private investors.

Regardless of how you dispose of your stock, as soon as your holdings drop below that 50 percent line, you are in a totally different environment. If you own more than 50 percent, you are saying, "This is my business." If you own less than 50 percent, you have the opportunity to walk away.

STAYING PRIVATE

If you decide to keep your company private rather than public but would like to get out of running the business, you have to find somebody you can trust to run it for you. The best way to do that is to make him a partner, because then he has a stake in the operation. That's what I'm doing—giving stock to key employees. And that's fine, because I am happy to make money for people who make me money.

FINDING A BUYER

If you have a quick-lube franchise in Toledo you are not going to take it to Bear Stearns to sell it. But if you have a track record and it is known, you can take your business to an investment banking firm to sell it. Tell the bank you want them to do an offering memorandum. They will ask you for $100,000 up front. You say, "Oh, no. This is a win-win situation. If we sell it, you get your brokerage fee; if we don't, that's your risk." You have to be really firm about that because there are investment bankers out there who make a living by taking $100,000 up front and not moving the business.

So they do an offering memorandum; then you and they will sit down and identify prospects, and you will see whether there is any interest, at what price, and what that means. If the business does sell—and there is no guarantee that it will—they will likely charge you 5 percent of the first $1 million selling price, 4 percent of the second million dollars, 3 percent of the third million dollars, 2 percent of the fourth million dollars, 1 percent of the fifth million, and the rest is negotiable.

EVERYTHING IS NEGOTIABLE

When we tried to do a deal with the Bank of New England

in 1987, we didn't want to sell the whole company—only enough to raise $4 million. The deal we arranged was that they were going to get 2 percent of the $4 million, or $80,000. That deal fell apart for a number of reasons, including our allegedly not having the right marketing guy. In fact, we don't have *any* marketing guy, and it is working out fine. But they put a low valuation on the company: only $12 million. And by the time the buyer got around to offering us $12 million, they wanted close to 33 percent of the stock. We thought that was too much.

The Japanese gave us a different and better deal. We did a convertible preferred stock deal with them that put a $20 million valuation on the company. In exchange for their putting up the money, we gave them preferred stock in the company. Even though we have to pay interest on the money that we received from them, the $20 million valuation we got in the deal will be important. The next time we try to raise money, we will be able to say, "Look, here is a $50 billion Japanese company that after hiring Arthur Young and endless accountants, and running back and forth to Tokyo, decided that David's is worth $20 million." That is better than any kind of internal analysis about how much you are worth, because somebody actually paid that much. After all, something is worth only what somebody will pay for it.

If you are looking for a money partner, it is incredibly helpful if that partner brings something else to the table. In our case, we looked for a gigantic supermarket chain to invest in David's, because then we could have access to 1,500 supermarket outlets overnight. We didn't have any luck, regrettably.

DO NOT BE AFRAID TO MARKET YOUR COMPANY YOURSELF

If the investment banker route fails, try putting an ad in the back of the *Wall Street Journal*.

HANGING ON TOO LONG

One of the classic mistakes entrepreneurs make is trying to stay with their companies after they are sold. They sign contracts saying they will stay on as chairman of the board or a consultant for five years and live happily ever after. It never happens. I've never known an entrepreneur who has lasted more than eighteen months with the company after he sold it. They are made to believe that the new owner wants them around, but the new owner really doesn't. Even if he did initially, he quickly finds out that he wants to run things his way, and the founder has to go.

RUNNING A FRANCHISE MAKES GETTING OUT EASIER

It is easier for a franchisee to get out of a franchise store because he is dealing with a known commodity with a well-understood worth. When he goes to sell his store, he will be able to operate in a market that is defined. The turnover at Dunkin' Donuts franchises is astronomical because everybody is always selling those stores.

Otherwise, running a franchise is the same as starting your own business. You are always on the hook. You can't wake up one day and say, "You know what? I've had fun being a cookie maven for five years but I'm not anymore, so I'm going to leave." It doesn't work that way. You are in.

You can always walk away from a job—you quit. You can't quit your own business. For one thing, it usually supports you; for another, there is usually some debt involved that you are personally on the hook for or have pledged some assets against.

NIRVANA

What it comes down to is this: if you can maneuver yourself into a position where you have total freedom to put your business up for sale, know you are going to get a decent bid and walk away, you are in a situation in which very few entrepreneurs ever find themselves. People sometimes have a very good business, but they are so identified with it individually that they can't get out. If the businesses are not that identified with an individual, they may not be such good businesses in the first place.

Then you have the problem of postpartum depression. Assuming you sell the business, what do you do? Many people, although they complain and moan all day about the aggravation, may not be able to live without it.

STAY FLEXIBLE

It is important to keep your options open. I have no preconceived notions. Pillsbury could walk in here today to buy me, and I could say yes or no. We are actually talking to some very interesting companies that have the kind of distribution that we need; we could do something for each other. They are in the supermarket dairy case business, though they don't sell any dough. They have the brokers and distributors out there that could be really helpful for us.

The bottom line is that I am twitching today as much as I twitched nine years ago when the business started. It hasn't gotten any better, it hasn't gotten any worse. I have maintained that same level of hysteria that everything is all going to go wrong and it is all going to blow up in five seconds. That, of course, is a function of being in business for yourself. When you begin each day with an I-believe-that-everything-is-going-right philosophy, you are going to be in deep trouble. You will be too complacent.

WAITING FOR A WINDFALL

Don't. You'll die waiting.

We've been waiting three years for Dunkin' Donuts to make up its mind about whether or not they want to sell our cookies in their stores. We are probably going to get the deal, but we are a captive of Dunkin Donuts's decision-making process: whether or not they are interested in the cookies, whether they can cut back their own research and development to make the numbers, how much they are going to spend on promotion and rolling out the product. But you just can't sit around and wait for them to make up their minds. There is nothing definite in this world.

THE FUTURE

If I didn't have the business, would I miss it? I don't know. I'm living with it. But I also know it is going to kill me. I think I'm ready to take a year off—a sabbatical—to see what happens.

You try to smooth out the highs and the lows. You can't survive any other way. You'd be on an emotional roller coaster otherwise. But I still get these painful twinges. You react to the good news and the bad news, and you learn about controlling your emotions. When we got the word that the deal to open cookie stores in France—which I dearly wanted to do—fell apart, I felt an instant twinge, like someone had turned on the electricity. Then it was back to, "Oh, well. We'll do something else." When we heard the good news about the Japanese deal, there was an instant glow like "That's nice," and then it was on to the next thing.

27
LOOKING AHEAD

So, you've read my book. If I'm so smart, how come I'm not richer? Well, perhaps by the time this book comes out, I will be. On the other hand, I may be in the soup.

IRONS IN THE FIRE

We are poised for our cookie business to explode—in supermarket refrigerator cases, in private-label cookie dough, in supermarket kiosks. But even with the Japanese multimillion dollar investment, we do not have enough capital to expand properly. That could cause us to get trampled.

If I start to go running around out there with my refrigerated cookie dough and Pillsbury decides to launch a big television advertising campaign with the Dough Boy, I could be in big trouble. Of course, things aren't running so smoothly at Pillsbury these days. Its core business has stagnated, and Burger King isn't going anywhere. There are signals the company might be broken up.

Quite honestly, I sometimes feel trapped by this business. One of the frustrating things that any entrepreneur faces as he sees his business grow is realizing he doesn't have enough money to do it right. The tendency is to sit back and say, "If only I could get hold of the product development money that Pillsbury has, I know I could do a better job than they do." You start going crazy about the fact that you are constantly beating your head against the wall looking for additional resources.

This is a very dangerous time for my business right now. The thing I am always worrying about is how to maintain our core business if everything goes wrong. On the one hand, we are trying to strengthen what we have; on the other, we are trying to grow. And clearly we have to grow or we are going to be in serious trouble. We might even go out of business because we can't grow fast enough. Yet I'm hesitant to spend the money to build a new plant or drastically increase our supermarket penetration.

WHAT KEEPS ME UP LATE AT NIGHTS

Sometimes my pessimistic nature gets the better of me. I'm not convinced there are any opportunities left in the food business. Everything has been made, everything has been eaten, we've seen every conceivable twist. The business is getting trendier and trendier. The hot thing now at the food shows is chocolate-dipped potato chips and pretzels. It's crazy.

Nobody is going to come out with a chocolate truffle that tastes that much better than anybody else's chocolate truffle. Nobody is going to come out with a cookie that tastes that much better than mine. What kind of novelty candy can you put in ice cream to make it taste different? We have Tootsie Roll ice cream, M&M's ice cream, we have every conceivable kind of novelty ice cream out there. It has all been invented.

I also believe there is about to be a backlash. There is so much press and media attention on the food business, on cookie and ice cream taste contests, that I think people are sick of it. This is a time for retrenching, reappraising. It is not going to be as hyped up as it was between 1979 and 1983.

Then I start thinking about taking known quantities like pizza or hot dogs, putting a twist on them, and making them into businesses. How do you make it, market it, and distribute it? Then I start feeling optimistic. In fact, the good news is that the specialty food business is growing fast; twenty percent a year and up. The world is going upscale; everybody wants better, better, better.

DISTRIBUTION

My other big worry is that we have almost no outlets left for selling our products the way we did five years ago. Individual specialty stores are an evolving concept, and I can't figure out where they are going. They are too expensive to operate one by one, and you can't get good people to stay with them—they get bored.

As I sit here, the whole supermarket business is being redefined. Every day, shelves are being bought up by big national marketers like Coke and Pepsi to the detriment of small operations like me. They can afford to pay the hefty slotting fees that supermarkets charge to get their stuff on their shelves, and the small guys can't. If there is no new force in there, Coke and Pepsi are going to win. What that is going to do to how America buys food, I really don't know yet.

I'm convinced the next wave will be twenty-five specialty stores under one roof. That concept interests me. You have a bigger critical mass so you can attract more people. And you can cut down on your rent and labor costs because you can spread the overhead out over more operations. Instead of having all the stores run independently, you group them together under one roof and get one person to manage them. It is a bigger challenge for the manager. He gets $25,000, with the ability to double his salary based on performance, which is exactly what we have to pay somebody to run a high-volume cookie store of 300 square feet in New York City.

TAKING IT DAY BY DAY

I have never really set any goals for myself. After I opened my first store, I didn't have any conscious desire to expand. In fact, I told people that I didn't want to franchise. But after people came to me, I decided to start franchising. I got my lawyer, who didn't know anything about franchising either, drew up a disclosure document, and we were in the franchise business. I just fell into it.

To this day, I still don't have any goals. I don't think it makes any difference. I can say I'd like to make $100 million and have a private jet, but I wouldn't be doing things any differently. I'd like to be as rich as Donald Trump so I can have his toys—the helicopter, the yacht—but I wouldn't want his aggravation. My goal right now is to keep my weight down and get my cholesterol down. My doctor says I have to or I'm a dead man. But it could be anything. Maybe I'll decide to get into shape so I can beat up Mike Tyson, the heavyweight boxing champ. I could become the Jewish White Hope. OK, I can dream.

I'm trying to build my company so that it has real value if I decide to sell it. Multiple-outlet fast-food stores have become a drag on the market. Nobody cares if you have one store or 5,000 stores because of the problems inherent in running them. So when you go to sell them, you can't get what they are worth. Orange Julius, the orange drink franchise, had 818 locations, and the company was bought for less than $17 million—and that wasn't even cash. Fannie Farmer, the candy store, has about 400 locations, and you could pick up that company for $4 million over the debt.

On the other hand, shelf space in supermarkets is worth a lot. People will pay real money for it. That's why Henry Lambert got $57 million when he sold his Pasta and Cheese brand of pasta. He wasn't making any money, but he had market share—the number-one-selling fresh pasta—and he had shelf space in supermarkets.

Supermarket shelf space is a game only the big guys can play. Money talks. I would not be surprised if some supermarket owner didn't figure out soon that he's not in the food business; he's really in the real estate business. His business is making a return on his shelf space. So he puts up a for-rent sign and co-ops his supermarket within categories. If you are selling potato chips, for instance, you would pay a certain amount of money and be allocated a certain amount of space in the snack-food section.

What's interesting about the co-op idea is that it is a self-policing system. If the stuff doesn't sell, a guy can't afford to hold on to his shelf space, so he has to give it up or sell it to someone else.

I want a product I can sell through normal distribution channels. That's why we're putting all our effort into getting shelf space for our cookie dough, because if you have shelf space, you have something to sell to a buyer. As I've said, I would much rather be in twenty supermarket cases with my cookie dough than open another David's Cookies in Manhattan.

Long term, what I am dealing with is not whether David's cookies taste good (they do) or whether they are made with the best ingredients (they are) or even whether they taste better than Debbi Fields's cookies (unquestionably!). The challenge is how to build equity with my brand name. Because in the long run, that is what really is going to make this company worth something. Whatever I can do to promote that name will be to my and my company's eventual benefit.

ACQUISITIONS

Who says that David's Specialty Foods can't tomorrow make a tender offer for Texaco? We can do whatever we want to do. We are not locked into any one line of business—that's an important lesson to remember.

If I *do* decide to buy something, it seems to me that the right idea is to find businesses that are for sale cheap but have a cachet of quality, like Zabar's. That is the Wal-Mart phenomenon: sell the same stuff for less. If I was ever going to start another food business, I would go after brand name products, like Cuisinarts, and sell them cheaply to get people into the store. Then I would run most of the stuff through at fair but not great prices. So people would say, "I just bought a pound of salmon at Dabar's (or whatever I call it) for $25. Isn't that a great price?" when it is the same price everybody else charges.

SEARCHING FOR UNIQUE PROPERTIES IN UNIQUE NICHES

At this moment, I'm looking for companies in the specialty-food business that have significant market share in an esoteric category that has been sleepy for a long time. I don't care if the company is making money or not, so long as it has a lock on its special market and great upside potential.

Look at this company called Jovah, which makes halvah. Halvah, which is a flaky confection of crushed sesame seeds in a base of syruplike honey, is mostly eaten by Middle Easterners. Jovah is owned by two brothers. One is seventy-nine, the other is seventy-seven, and they have no heirs. They can't make enough halvah to meet demand. Everybody I talk to says they can't get enough halvah. These guys go to a food show and instead of having to look for new orders, they have customers come up to them and complain about not getting as much as they ordered. The brothers don't care; they just tell the customers not to bother them. They are in an ideal business: a niche market that won't go away and that has no competition. Unfortunately, they haven't put the company up for sale. But I'm waiting.

Another example of a company I'd like to buy is Fox's U-Bet Syrup. It makes the chocolate syrup used in egg creams, a very ethnic product. For those of you who didn't grow up in New York City, an egg cream has neither egg nor cream in it. It consists of chocolate syrup, milk, and carbonated water. Once again, there is an established niche market and no competition. The only problem is that Fox's does only $800,000 a year in sales, so the company isn't big enough.

I tried to buy Carvel. It has a lock on the soft ice cream market in the northwest, where Dairy Queen isn't very strong, and it has hundreds of franchise outlets. But by the time Tom Carvel, the founder and principal owner, takes his money out, there isn't much left in the company. Carvel isn't doing great now. What I would do is upgrade the whole product line. Make it upscale soft ice cream with no chemicals, only real ingredients. Then I think it would really take off.

There are not a lot of companies that have the kind of niches we are looking for. I'd love to buy Godiva chocolates, but Campbell Soup is asking $100 million for it. That's way too much for a company that made $2 million last year and whose sales have been flat for five years.

The danger in that is you can get enormously hurt going after the top of the market in any business. I would much rather have a Zabar's operation than one like Bildner's supermarket, the ultrachic chain whose New York outlets are now shuttered. There are more people who are interested in cheap than there are those who want the most expensive.

PERSONAL CHALLENGES

I talk about getting out, but I'm not ready yet. Sometimes I step back and look at what I do every day, the aggravation, the yelling and screaming. Then I realize that all I started out to do is sell five or six different kinds of cookies. How did it get so complicated? It is not as if I'm making nuclear weapons or trying to win the Iran-Iraq war.

If I were to disassociate myself from David's and go back to the restaurant and spend all day perfecting the perfect cassoulet, it might be interesting or tasty, but it would not be challenging. Besides, I don't want to be too near food right now anyway—I eat too much of it.

Here's an example of the kind of challenge I look for now: solving the shortage of macadamia nuts by buying a macadamia nut farm. Macadamia nuts take seven years to grow, from the time you plant the tree. You can grow good ones in only a few areas around the world. And there seems to be an unlimited demand for them. Eight percent of our cookies take them.

Maybe macadamia nuts are a rare commodity. But that gets my suspicious nature going. I say to myself, "Wait a minute, I hear about cocoa bean shortages causing a run on chocolate every year, and it never happens. There is never a shortage of anything."

THE FUN PART

Being in business is endlessly fascinating. Customers write me the most wonderful letters. Here's one I got recently:

"Dear David. We are a happily married couple with one great common interest: peanut butter. For our Valentine's Day celebration this year, we plan to spend the weekend in the bathtub covered with peanut butter ice cream, a rare treat since we both have to travel quite a lot and we really want it to be special. We've redecorated the bathroom and installed a wacky little heart-shaped lighting fixture, but there is one thing that is really putting a damper on the whole frolic: your peanut butter ice cream. Now David, what happened to the peanuts that should be making it the ultimate experience? There is really not a sniff of nut in it, just chunks of cookie that cannot really contribute any heights of sexual awareness, a real no-no for steamy sessions in our new Valentine's Day bathroom. But David, don't take this news too harshly, we've had some pretty interesting times snatching your nibbles of cookies in between kisses. We still miss the peanuts though, and only you have the power to make this day an all-out peanut butter success. Perhaps a few sharp words from you would make these mischievous little nuts hop in to your ice cream vat instead of someone else's. David, we implore you to shape up and rescue our romance."

I love it.
So I am forging ahead. I worry a lot about the future of

the specialty-food business, what Pillsbury is up to, how to expand without putting the business on the line. My fatal flaw is I am always looking for the next deal. At the same time, as long as I have people behind to pick up the pieces, it can be an exciting way of doing business. I just have to keep doing what I do best: fighting with landlords, trying to find good people, scheming how to get more cookie dough into supermarkets, searching for new opportunities, and running through walls.

126524